Knowledge Graphs RAG

A Practical Guide to Designing and Implementing Graph-Based Systems

©

Written By

Maxime Lane

Knowledge Graphs RAG: A Practical Guide to Designing and Implementing Graph-Based Systems

Published by:
Maxime Lane

First Edition: February 2025

Table of Content

Preface

In today's data-driven world, understanding how to design and implement graph-based systems is more important than ever. ***Knowledge Graphs RAG: A Practical Guide to Designing and Implementing Graph-Based Systems*** is born out of the need to bridge theoretical concepts with practical applications. This book is designed to serve as both a comprehensive resource and a hands-on guide for anyone interested in the transformative potential of knowledge graphs and Retrieval-Augmented Generation.

What You Will Learn

- **Fundamental Concepts:** You will start with the basics of graph theory and the unique structure of knowledge graphs.
- **Design Principles:** Learn how to design robust, scalable, and efficient graph-based systems.
- **Practical Implementation:** Detailed examples, code samples, and step-by-step instructions will guide you through building and querying your own knowledge graphs.
- **Advanced Topics:** Dive into the integration of RAG, explore advanced algorithms, and understand how graph-based systems can enhance AI and data-driven decision-making.
- **Real-World Applications:** Through case studies and practical projects, you will see how these systems are used in various industries.

Whether you are a student, a developer, or a data science professional, this book is structured to enhance your understanding and equip you with practical skills.

Why This Book?

- **Hands-On Approach:** We emphasize practical, real-world applications over abstract theory. You will learn by doing, with code examples and projects designed to build your confidence.
- **Step-by-Step Guidance:** Each section is carefully structured to build on the previous one, ensuring a smooth progression from basic concepts to advanced techniques.
- **Clear and Accessible Language:** We use simple, clear language to explain complex ideas, making the book accessible to readers with various technical backgrounds.

We invite you to dive in, experiment with the examples, and apply these techniques to your own projects. Let this book be your companion on your journey to mastering knowledge graphs and graph-based systems.

How to Use This Book

This book is designed to be both a reference guide and a practical manual. Here's how you can make the most of it:

Structure and Navigation

1. **Progressive Learning:**
   - **Start with Part I:** The introductory sections lay the foundation with key concepts and theoretical background.
   - **Move to Part II:** Deepen your understanding with detailed discussions on graph theory, data modeling, and system architecture.
   - **Explore Part III:** Engage with step-by-step implementation guides, complete with practical code examples and real-world case studies.
   - **Advanced Topics in Part IV:** For readers looking to push the boundaries, this section delves into advanced algorithms and emerging trends.
2. **Practical Examples and Projects:**
   - Each chapter includes hands-on exercises and code samples. We recommend that you work through these examples using your own development environment.
   - Sample projects are provided at the end of several chapters, allowing you to consolidate your learning through real-world applications.
3. **Supplementary Materials:**
   - **Appendices:** Use the appendices for additional resources, including a glossary of terms, reference code repositories, and further readings.
   - **Online Resources:** Links to online repositories and additional tutorials are provided throughout the book to enhance your learning experience.

Learning Tips

- **Work at Your Own Pace:**
  Feel free to skip ahead or revisit sections as needed. The modular structure allows you to focus on topics most relevant to your needs.
- **Practice Actively:**
  Implement the code examples and experiment with modifications. Practical application is key to mastering these concepts.
- **Participate in the Community:**
  Engage with fellow readers and experts via online forums or the companion website. Sharing insights and challenges will enrich your understanding and foster a collaborative learning environment.

By following these guidelines, you'll be well-prepared to dive deep into the world of knowledge graphs and RAG, gaining both theoretical insights and practical skills.

Conventions and Notation

To ensure clarity and consistency throughout this book, we have adopted the following conventions and notational guidelines:

Terminology

- **Nodes and Vertices:**
  Used interchangeably to refer to the individual entities in a graph.
- **Edges and Links:**
  Represent the relationships between nodes.
- **Graph:**
  Refers to the entire network of nodes and edges.
- **RAG:**
  Abbreviation for Retrieval-Augmented Generation. We will consistently use "RAG" to refer to this concept throughout the book.

Formatting Conventions

- **Code Blocks:**
  All code examples are presented in dedicated code blocks. Each example includes comments to explain its functionality. For instance:

```python
# This is a sample code block.
# It demonstrates how to create a simple graph using
networkx.

import networkx as nx

# Create an empty graph
G = nx.Graph()

# Add nodes and an edge between them
G.add_node("Node1")
G.add_node("Node2")
G.add_edge("Node1", "Node2")

print("Graph nodes:", G.nodes())
print("Graph edges:", G.edges())
```

- **Tables and Diagrams:**
  Tables and diagrams are used to summarize information. Each table includes a clear title and headers. All diagrams are labeled and referenced in the text for ease of understanding.
- **Key Terms:**
  Key terms are defined when they first appear. For quick reference, a glossary is included in the appendices.

Mathematical Notation

- **Symbols and Equations:**
  When mathematical symbols or equations are used, they are explained in detail. For example, in a section on graph algorithms, the degree of a node $d(v)d(v)d(v)$ is defined as the number of edges connected to node vvv.

Reference Style

- **Citations:**
  Academic references and industry sources are cited in the text and listed in the bibliography. This ensures that readers can trace the origins of the ideas and explore them further.
- **Consistency:**
  We maintain consistent terminology and formatting throughout the book to help you follow along easily.

Chapter 1: Introduction to Knowledge Graphs and RAG

In this chapter, we lay the groundwork by exploring two interrelated concepts: Knowledge Graphs and Retrieval-Augmented Generation (RAG). We begin by defining what knowledge graphs are, then move to an explanation of RAG, and finally, we discuss how these two areas converge to create robust, intelligent systems. Throughout, we use straightforward language, real-world examples, tables, and code snippets to help you understand these concepts in practical terms.

1.1 What Are Knowledge Graphs?

A **knowledge graph** is a data structure that represents information in a graph format. In this format, entities (also known as nodes) are connected by relationships (also known as edges). This approach mirrors the way humans naturally think about and organize knowledge, making it an excellent tool for representing complex and interconnected information.

Key Concepts

- **Nodes (Entities):**
  These represent distinct items such as people, organizations, products, or concepts. For example, in a knowledge graph about movies, nodes might include *Actors*, *Directors*, and *Films*.
- **Edges (Relationships):**
  These define the relationships between nodes. For instance, an edge might indicate that "Leonardo DiCaprio *acted in* Inception" or "Christopher Nolan *directed* Inception".
- **Properties (Attributes):**
  Both nodes and edges can have properties—additional details that provide more context. For example, an actor node might have properties like *birthdate*, *nationality*, and *awards won*.
- **Schema/Ontology:**
  This is the underlying structure or set of rules that define what types of nodes and relationships exist in the graph, similar to a blueprint.

Comparison Table

The table below summarizes the differences between a traditional relational database and a knowledge graph:

Aspect	Relational Database	Knowledge Graph
Data Structure	Tables with rows and columns	Nodes and edges
Relationships	Implicit via foreign keys	Explicit, directly defined as edges
Schema Flexibility	Rigid, predefined schema	Flexible, can evolve as new data emerges
Query Complexity	Efficient for structured data and join operations	Superior for exploring complex relationships
Use Case	Transactional systems, record-keeping	Knowledge representation, recommendation engines

Practical Example Using Python

Below is a simple Python example using the `networkx` library to demonstrate how to create a basic knowledge graph:

```python
# Import necessary libraries
import networkx as nx
import matplotlib.pyplot as plt

# Create an empty graph
G = nx.Graph()

# Adding nodes with attributes
G.add_node("Leonardo DiCaprio", type="Actor",
birth_year=1974)
G.add_node("Inception", type="Film", release_year=2010)
G.add_node("Christopher Nolan", type="Director",
birth_year=1970)

# Adding edges to define relationships
G.add_edge("Leonardo DiCaprio", "Inception",
relationship="acted in")
G.add_edge("Christopher Nolan", "Inception",
relationship="directed")
```

```
# Displaying nodes with attributes
print("Nodes in the knowledge graph:")
for node, attributes in G.nodes(data=True):
    print(f"{node}: {attributes}")

# Displaying edges with relationship labels
print("\nEdges in the knowledge graph:")
for source, target, attributes in G.edges(data=True):
    print(f"{source} - {target}: {attributes}")

# Visualizing the graph
plt.figure(figsize=(8, 6))
pos = nx.spring_layout(G)
nx.draw(G, pos, with_labels=True, node_color='lightgreen',
edge_color='gray', node_size=2000, font_size=10)
edge_labels = nx.get_edge_attributes(G, 'relationship')
nx.draw_networkx_edge_labels(G, pos, edge_labels=edge_labels,
font_color='red')
plt.title("Example Knowledge Graph")
plt.show()
```

Explanation of the Code:

- **Library Imports:**
  We use `networkx` for creating and managing the graph and `matplotlib.pyplot` for visualization.
- **Graph Creation:**
  An empty undirected graph `G` is created.
- **Adding Nodes and Attributes:**
  Nodes are added for an actor, a film, and a director, with relevant attributes.
- **Adding Edges:**
  Relationships (edges) are added to indicate that Leonardo DiCaprio acted in *Inception* and Christopher Nolan directed it.
- **Displaying and Visualizing:**
  The script prints out the nodes and edges and visualizes the graph, with edge labels showing the relationships.

This example serves as an introduction to how knowledge graphs function and how they can be implemented in code.

1.2 Understanding RAG (Retrieval-Augmented Generation)

Retrieval-Augmented Generation (RAG) is an innovative approach that combines traditional retrieval methods with advanced generative models. This technique enhances the capabilities of AI systems by retrieving relevant information from a knowledge base and using it to generate more informed and contextually accurate responses.

What is RAG?

At its core, RAG is designed to improve the output of generative models (such as language models) by providing them with external, up-to-date information. Here's how it works:

1. **Retrieval Component:**
   The system searches through a large corpus of data (e.g., documents, knowledge graphs) to find the most relevant pieces of information related to a given query.
2. **Generation Component:**
   The retrieved information is then fed into a generative model that produces a coherent, contextually enhanced response. This model can generate natural language text that incorporates the factual data retrieved earlier.

Key Benefits of RAG

- **Enhanced Accuracy:**
  By grounding responses in verified data, RAG improves the factual accuracy of generated content.
- **Dynamic Knowledge:**
  RAG systems can access and incorporate the latest information, making them more adaptable to changing contexts.
- **Contextual Relevance:**
  The combination of retrieval and generation ensures that responses are both contextually rich and relevant to the query.

Practical Example of RAG Workflow

Imagine you have a chatbot designed to answer questions about movies. When asked, "Who directed Inception?" a RAG system would:

1. **Retrieve** relevant data from a knowledge graph or database (e.g., the fact that "Christopher Nolan directed Inception").
2. **Generate** a complete response that integrates the retrieved data, such as "Christopher Nolan directed the film Inception, which was released in 2010."

While a full code implementation of RAG is beyond the scope of this introductory section, the following pseudocode outlines the process:

```python
# Pseudocode for a basic RAG system

def retrieve_information(query):
    # Search the knowledge base for relevant data
    relevant_data = search_knowledge_base(query)
    return relevant_data

def generate_response(query, retrieved_data):
    # Generate a response using a language model,
incorporating retrieved data
    response = language_model.generate(query,
context=retrieved_data)
    return response

# Example usage:
query = "Who directed Inception?"
data = retrieve_information(query)  # Returns: "Christopher
Nolan"
final_response = generate_response(query, data)
print(final_response)  # Expected output: "Christopher Nolan
directed the film Inception."
```

In practice, this process would involve integrating powerful retrieval systems (e.g., Elasticsearch) with advanced language models (e.g., GPT-based models).

1.3 The Convergence of Graph-Based Systems and RAG

The integration of knowledge graphs and RAG represents a convergence of two powerful paradigms in data representation and AI. This convergence leverages the strengths of both approaches to create systems that are not only capable of complex data representation but also adept at generating insightful, data-driven responses.

Why Convergence Matters

- **Enhanced Information Retrieval:**
  Knowledge graphs provide a rich, structured source of interconnected data. When combined with RAG, systems can retrieve highly relevant data points and use them to generate precise and accurate responses.
- **Improved Contextual Understanding:**
  The semantic relationships captured in knowledge graphs help RAG systems understand context better. For example, knowing the relationships between directors, actors, and films improves the system's ability to generate comprehensive answers to movie-related queries.
- **Dynamic and Adaptable Systems:**
  As new data is added to the knowledge graph, the retrieval component of a RAG system automatically benefits, ensuring that the generated responses remain current and contextually appropriate.

Real-World Applications

The convergence of these systems has significant implications in various domains:

- **Customer Support:**
  Chatbots powered by RAG integrated with knowledge graphs can provide accurate and context-aware responses to customer queries, drawing from extensive product or service databases.
- **Healthcare:**
  Medical information systems can retrieve patient data and research findings from structured knowledge graphs to generate informed recommendations.
- **Education:**
  Intelligent tutoring systems can use knowledge graphs to represent subject matter and apply RAG to generate personalized learning content.

Diagram: Convergence Workflow

Below is a simplified diagram illustrating the convergence of knowledge graphs and RAG:

```sql
sql
```

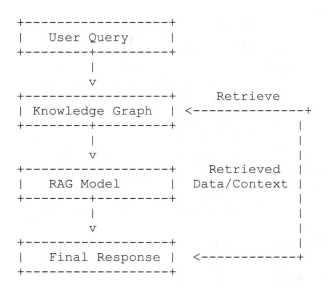

```
+------------------+
|   User Query     |
+--------+---------+
         |
         v
+------------------+      Retrieve
| Knowledge Graph  | <--------------+
+--------+---------+                |
         |                          |
         v                          |
+------------------+     Retrieved  |
|   RAG Model      |   Data/Context |
+--------+---------+                |
         |                          |
         v                          |
+------------------+                |
|  Final Response  | <------------+
+------------------+
```

Explanation of the Diagram:

1. **User Query:**
   The process starts with the user's query.
2. **Knowledge Graph Retrieval:**
   The system queries the knowledge graph to retrieve relevant data.
3. **RAG Model Processing:**
   The retrieved data is provided as context to the RAG model, which then generates a coherent and contextually enriched response.
4. **Final Response:**
   The final response is returned to the user, integrating both structured data and generative capabilities.

- **Knowledge graphs** represent data as interconnected nodes and edges, offering a flexible and natural way to model complex information.
- **RAG** enhances generative models by integrating external, retrieved data, leading to more accurate and context-aware outputs.
- **The convergence** of these technologies enables systems that combine rich data representation with powerful, dynamic content generation, opening new possibilities in various industries.

1.4 Motivation and Applications Across Industries

Understanding the motivation behind knowledge graphs and Retrieval-Augmented Generation (RAG) is essential for appreciating their growing adoption. This section explains why these technologies are important and highlights a variety of real-world applications across different industries.

Why Knowledge Graphs and RAG Matter

The modern data landscape is characterized by:

- **Volume:** Massive amounts of data are generated every day.
- **Variety:** Data comes in many forms, such as text, images, and structured records.
- **Complexity:** Data often has complex interrelationships that traditional databases can struggle to represent effectively.

Knowledge graphs offer a solution by:

- **Modeling Relationships Explicitly:** They capture the rich, interconnected nature of data, which is ideal for representing real-world relationships.
- **Enhancing Data Discovery:** By providing a natural way to explore data, knowledge graphs help users uncover hidden patterns and insights.
- **Supporting Flexible Schemas:** They adapt easily to changes in data, allowing organizations to evolve their models as needed.

Retrieval-Augmented Generation (RAG) complements knowledge graphs by:

- **Bringing Freshness to AI Responses:** RAG models retrieve up-to-date, relevant information before generating a response, ensuring higher accuracy.
- **Combining Strengths:** They leverage the power of large language models while grounding responses in factual, retrievable data.
- **Improving User Interaction:** This approach enhances user queries in applications like chatbots, search engines, and recommendation systems.

Applications Across Industries

Knowledge graphs and RAG are making significant impacts in several industries. The table below summarizes key industries and their applications:

Industry	Applications	Benefits
Healthcare	Patient records, medical research, drug discovery	Improved diagnostics, personalized treatment, and better data integration.
Finance	Fraud detection, risk management, customer segmentation	Enhanced fraud prevention, efficient compliance, and targeted services.
Retail & E-commerce	Product recommendation, inventory management, customer insights	Increased sales through personalized experiences and improved inventory tracking.
Education	Intelligent tutoring systems, curriculum design, research support	Adaptive learning, enhanced content delivery, and personalized study paths.
Manufacturing	Supply chain management, predictive maintenance, quality control	Optimized operations, reduced downtime, and better resource planning.
Media & Entertainment	Content recommendation, sentiment analysis, trend detection	Improved user engagement and more relevant content suggestions.
Government & Public Sector	Citizen services, policy analysis, data transparency	More efficient public services and better decision-making processes.

Real-World Examples

1. **Healthcare Example:**
   Imagine a healthcare system where patient data, research articles, and treatment protocols are connected in a knowledge graph. When a doctor enters symptoms into a system enhanced with RAG, the

system retrieves relevant patient history and recent studies, generating a comprehensive treatment recommendation.

2. **Retail Example:**
   In an e-commerce setting, a knowledge graph links products, customer reviews, and purchase histories. A RAG-based recommendation engine can generate personalized suggestions for shoppers, incorporating real-time trends and stock information to improve the customer experience.

3. **Education Example:**
   Educational platforms use knowledge graphs to map out courses, prerequisites, and learning outcomes. RAG systems can then generate tailored study guides or answer complex student queries by referencing the interconnected course content and academic resources.

By integrating these technologies, organizations can unlock the true potential of their data, leading to more intelligent systems and better outcomes.

1.5 Book Structure and How to Navigate

This book is organized to provide both theoretical foundations and practical applications, ensuring that readers of all levels can find value in the content. Here's a comprehensive guide on how the book is structured and how to navigate it effectively.

Overall Structure

The book is divided into several parts, each designed to build upon the previous one. Below is an overview of the main parts and what you can expect in each:

Part	Content Focus
Part I: Introduction and Overview	Lays the foundation with basic concepts, motivation, and the scope of knowledge graphs and RAG.
Part II: Foundations of Graph Theory and Knowledge Graphs	Covers essential theories, definitions, and the technical underpinnings of graph-based systems.

Part	Content Focus
Part III: Designing Graph-Based Systems	Provides step-by-step guidance on requirements analysis, data modeling, and system architecture for knowledge graphs.
Part IV: Implementing Graph-Based Systems	Focuses on practical implementation, complete with code examples, case studies, and troubleshooting tips.
Part V: Advanced Topics and Emerging Trends	Explores cutting-edge applications, advanced algorithms, and future directions in the field.
Part VI: Case Studies and Practical Applications	Presents real-world examples and detailed case studies across different industries to illustrate practical use cases.
Part VII: Appendices and Additional Resources	Offers supplementary materials, including glossaries, sample projects, and further readings.

How to Navigate This Book

To make the most out of this guide, consider the following strategies:

1. **Progressive Learning:**
   o **Start with Part I:** Begin with the introductory sections if you are new to the subject. They provide the context and motivation behind the book.
   o **Move Sequentially:** If you prefer a structured learning experience, follow the parts in order. The earlier sections lay the foundation that the later, more advanced topics build upon.
   o **Selective Reading:** If you have specific needs or are already familiar with the basics, feel free to skip ahead to the parts that match your interests (e.g., Part III for design, Part IV for implementation).
2. **Hands-On Exercises:**
   o **Code Examples:** Each implementation section includes complete, well-commented code examples. It is recommended that you run these examples in your own development environment to deepen your understanding.
   o **Case Studies and Projects:** Practical exercises and real-world case studies are provided to help you apply what you

have learned. Try to work through these examples and consider how they relate to your own projects.

3. **Supplementary Materials:**
   - o **Appendices:** Utilize the appendices for additional resources, such as a glossary of terms, further reading lists, and detailed explanations of key concepts.
   - o **Online Resources:** Where applicable, links to online repositories and additional tutorials are provided throughout the book. These resources offer extra support and updated content.

4. **Reference and Review:**
   - o **Key Tables and Diagrams:** The book includes tables and diagrams summarizing important concepts. Use these visual aids as quick references to reinforce your learning.
   - o **Consistent Notation:** The conventions and notations introduced in the Front Matter are maintained throughout the book. Familiarize yourself with these early on, as they will help you follow along with more technical sections.

Example Navigation Tips

- **If You're a Beginner:**
  Start with Chapters 1 and 2 to build your foundational knowledge. Make sure to work through the simple code examples and review the glossary if any terms are unfamiliar.
- **If You're a Practitioner:**
  Focus on Parts III and IV, where practical system design and implementation are discussed in depth. The step-by-step guides and case studies will be especially useful for applying these concepts in your projects.
- **If You're Interested in Cutting-Edge Developments:**
  Read Part V to learn about advanced algorithms, RAG integration, and future trends. This part is designed for those who want to explore the latest research and emerging technologies in graph-based systems.

1.4 Motivation and Applications Across Industries

Understanding the motivation behind knowledge graphs and Retrieval-Augmented Generation (RAG) is essential for appreciating their growing adoption. This section explains why these technologies are important and highlights a variety of real-world applications across different industries.

Why Knowledge Graphs and RAG Matter

The modern data landscape is characterized by:

- **Volume:** Massive amounts of data are generated every day.
- **Variety:** Data comes in many forms, such as text, images, and structured records.
- **Complexity:** Data often has complex interrelationships that traditional databases can struggle to represent effectively.

Knowledge graphs offer a solution by:

- **Modeling Relationships Explicitly:** They capture the rich, interconnected nature of data, which is ideal for representing real-world relationships.
- **Enhancing Data Discovery:** By providing a natural way to explore data, knowledge graphs help users uncover hidden patterns and insights.
- **Supporting Flexible Schemas:** They adapt easily to changes in data, allowing organizations to evolve their models as needed.

Retrieval-Augmented Generation (RAG) complements knowledge graphs by:

- **Bringing Freshness to AI Responses:** RAG models retrieve up-to-date, relevant information before generating a response, ensuring higher accuracy.
- **Combining Strengths:** They leverage the power of large language models while grounding responses in factual, retrievable data.
- **Improving User Interaction:** This approach enhances user queries in applications like chatbots, search engines, and recommendation systems.

Applications Across Industries

Knowledge graphs and RAG are making significant impacts in several industries. The table below summarizes key industries and their applications:

Industry	Applications	Benefits
Healthcare	Patient records, medical research, drug discovery	Improved diagnostics, personalized treatment, and better data integration.
Finance	Fraud detection, risk management, customer segmentation	Enhanced fraud prevention, efficient compliance, and targeted services.
Retail & E-commerce	Product recommendation, inventory management, customer insights	Increased sales through personalized experiences and improved inventory tracking.
Education	Intelligent tutoring systems, curriculum design, research support	Adaptive learning, enhanced content delivery, and personalized study paths.
Manufacturing	Supply chain management, predictive maintenance, quality control	Optimized operations, reduced downtime, and better resource planning.
Media & Entertainment	Content recommendation, sentiment analysis, trend detection	Improved user engagement and more relevant content suggestions.
Government & Public Sector	Citizen services, policy analysis, data transparency	More efficient public services and better decision-making processes.

Real-World Examples

1. **Healthcare Example:**
   Imagine a healthcare system where patient data, research articles, and treatment protocols are connected in a knowledge graph. When a doctor enters symptoms into a system enhanced with RAG, the system retrieves relevant patient history and recent studies, generating a comprehensive treatment recommendation.
2. **Retail Example:**
   In an e-commerce setting, a knowledge graph links products, customer reviews, and purchase histories. A RAG-based recommendation engine can generate personalized suggestions for

shoppers, incorporating real-time trends and stock information to improve the customer experience.

3. **Education Example:**
   Educational platforms use knowledge graphs to map out courses, prerequisites, and learning outcomes. RAG systems can then generate tailored study guides or answer complex student queries by referencing the interconnected course content and academic resources.

By integrating these technologies, organizations can unlock the true potential of their data, leading to more intelligent systems and better outcomes.

1.5 Book Structure and How to Navigate

This book is organized to provide both theoretical foundations and practical applications, ensuring that readers of all levels can find value in the content. Here's a comprehensive guide on how the book is structured and how to navigate it effectively.

Overall Structure

The book is divided into several parts, each designed to build upon the previous one. Below is an overview of the main parts and what you can expect in each:

Part	Content Focus
Part I: Introduction and Overview	Lays the foundation with basic concepts, motivation, and the scope of knowledge graphs and RAG.
Part II: Foundations of Graph Theory and Knowledge Graphs	Covers essential theories, definitions, and the technical underpinnings of graph-based systems.
Part III: Designing Graph-Based Systems	Provides step-by-step guidance on requirements analysis, data modeling, and system architecture for knowledge graphs.
Part IV: Implementing Graph-Based Systems	Focuses on practical implementation, complete with code examples, case studies, and troubleshooting tips.

Part	Content Focus
Part V: Advanced Topics and Emerging Trends	Explores cutting-edge applications, advanced algorithms, and future directions in the field.
Part VI: Case Studies and Practical Applications	Presents real-world examples and detailed case studies across different industries to illustrate practical use cases.
Part VII: Appendices and Additional Resources	Offers supplementary materials, including glossaries, sample projects, and further readings.

How to Navigate This Book

To make the most out of this guide, consider the following strategies:

1. **Progressive Learning:**
   - **Start with Part I:** Begin with the introductory sections if you are new to the subject. They provide the context and motivation behind the book.
   - **Move Sequentially:** If you prefer a structured learning experience, follow the parts in order. The earlier sections lay the foundation that the later, more advanced topics build upon.
   - **Selective Reading:** If you have specific needs or are already familiar with the basics, feel free to skip ahead to the parts that match your interests (e.g., Part III for design, Part IV for implementation).
2. **Hands-On Exercises:**
   - **Code Examples:** Each implementation section includes complete, well-commented code examples. It is recommended that you run these examples in your own development environment to deepen your understanding.
   - **Case Studies and Projects:** Practical exercises and real-world case studies are provided to help you apply what you have learned. Try to work through these examples and consider how they relate to your own projects.
3. **Supplementary Materials:**
   - **Appendices:** Utilize the appendices for additional resources, such as a glossary of terms, further reading lists, and detailed explanations of key concepts.

- o **Online Resources:** Where applicable, links to online repositories and additional tutorials are provided throughout the book. These resources offer extra support and updated content.
4. **Reference and Review:**
   - o **Key Tables and Diagrams:** The book includes tables and diagrams summarizing important concepts. Use these visual aids as quick references to reinforce your learning.
   - o **Consistent Notation:** The conventions and notations introduced in the Front Matter are maintained throughout the book. Familiarize yourself with these early on, as they will help you follow along with more technical sections.

Example Navigation Tips

- **If You're a Beginner:**
  Start with Chapters 1 and 2 to build your foundational knowledge. Make sure to work through the simple code examples and review the glossary if any terms are unfamiliar.
- **If You're a Practitioner:**
  Focus on Parts III and IV, where practical system design and implementation are discussed in depth. The step-by-step guides and case studies will be especially useful for applying these concepts in your projects.
- **If You're Interested in Cutting-Edge Developments:**
  Read Part V to learn about advanced algorithms, RAG integration, and future trends. This part is designed for those who want to explore the latest research and emerging technologies in graph-based systems.

By understanding the structure of the book and following these navigation tips, you can tailor your reading experience to best suit your learning style and professional needs.

Chapter 2: Historical Evolution and Future Outlook

In this chapter, we explore the rich history that has led to today's advanced graph-based systems. We begin by examining the evolution of graph theory and databases, followed by a discussion of significant milestones in the development of knowledge graphs. Understanding this historical context provides valuable insight into the motivations behind current technologies and hints at future trends.

2.1 The Evolution of Graph Theory and Databases

Early Foundations of Graph Theory

Graph theory has its roots in mathematics, with its formal beginnings often traced back to the work of Swiss mathematician Leonhard Euler in the 18th century. Euler's solution to the Seven Bridges of Königsberg problem is considered one of the first applications of graph theory. In this problem, Euler abstracted the layout of the city into a network of nodes (land masses) and edges (bridges), establishing the basic principles of connectivity and traversal.

Key Developments in Graph Theory:

- **18th Century – Euler's Bridges of Königsberg:**
  Euler introduced the idea of representing complex problems as a collection of nodes and edges.
- **19th Century – Emergence of Mathematical Graphs:**
  Mathematicians such as Gustav Kirchhoff used graphs to analyze electrical circuits, establishing the foundation for network analysis.
- **20th Century – Formalization and Expansion:**
  The formal study of graph theory expanded dramatically. Concepts like trees, cycles, and connectivity became standard topics in mathematics and computer science.

Evolution of Databases

The evolution of databases parallels the progress in graph theory, adapting new models to handle increasingly complex data requirements.

Early Data Storage:

- **File Systems:**
  Early computer systems stored data in simple file structures without relational connections.

Relational Databases:

- **1970s – Introduction of the Relational Model:**
  Edgar F. Codd's relational model revolutionized data storage by organizing data into tables with rows and columns. This model, based on set theory and logic, allowed for more efficient querying and data integrity.

  Table 2.1: Key Characteristics of Relational Databases

Characteristic	Description
Structure	Data is stored in tables (relations) with rows (records) and columns (attributes).
Schema	Predefined, rigid schema ensures data consistency and integrity.
Query Language	SQL (Structured Query Language) provides a standardized way to query and manipulate data.
Relationships	Managed through foreign keys, which link tables based on common attributes.

- **Limitations:**
  While relational databases work well for structured data, they often struggle with representing complex, interrelated data, particularly when relationships are deeply nested or evolve over time.

Emergence of Graph Databases:

- **Late 2000s – Rise of Graph Databases:**
  As data became more interconnected, the limitations of relational

databases became apparent. Graph databases emerged to address these challenges by directly representing relationships as first-class citizens.

- o **Nodes and Edges:**
  Graph databases store data as nodes (entities) and edges (relationships), making it natural to model complex networks.
- o **Schema Flexibility:**
  Unlike relational databases, graph databases allow for a dynamic schema that can evolve as new data and relationships are discovered.

Table 2.2: Comparison of Relational and Graph Databases

Feature	Relational Databases	Graph Databases
Data Model	Tables, rows, columns	Nodes and edges
Schema	Rigid and predefined	Flexible and dynamic
Relationships	Indirect, through foreign keys	Direct and explicit
Query Complexity	Efficient for structured queries but complex for joins	Efficient for queries involving multi-level relationships

Impact on Today's Data Systems

The evolution from file systems to relational and graph databases has paved the way for today's advanced knowledge graphs and RAG systems. The development of graph databases has particularly influenced how we model and retrieve complex relationships, making them ideal for applications like recommendation systems, social networks, and semantic search.

2.2 Milestones in the Development of Knowledge Graphs

Knowledge graphs represent a significant advancement in data representation, built on the theoretical foundations and practical experiences of past decades. This section highlights key milestones that have shaped the development of knowledge graphs.

Early Concepts and Semantic Networks

- **1960s – The Birth of Semantic Networks:**
  Early work in artificial intelligence introduced semantic networks—graph structures that represented knowledge in a way that mimicked human understanding. These networks were used to model concepts and the relationships between them, forming the precursor to modern knowledge graphs.
- **1980s – Expert Systems:**
  Expert systems incorporated semantic networks to simulate the decision-making abilities of human experts. These systems demonstrated the value of interconnected data in solving complex problems.

The Modern Knowledge Graph Era

- **2001 – Introduction of RDF (Resource Description Framework):**
  The World Wide Web Consortium (W3C) introduced RDF as a standard model for data interchange on the web. RDF provided a way to describe relationships using subject-predicate-object triples, which laid the groundwork for building knowledge graphs.
- **2006 – Google's Knowledge Graph:**
  One of the most influential milestones occurred when Google introduced its Knowledge Graph. This system leveraged the principles of graph theory to improve search results by understanding the relationships between entities. The Knowledge Graph enabled Google to provide more relevant search results by offering context and connections that traditional keyword-based searches could not achieve.

  Figure 2.1: Simplified View of Google's Knowledge Graph

```csharp
        [Entity: Leonardo DiCaprio]
                  |
        [acted in]
                  |
        [Entity: Inception]
                  |
        [directed by]
                  |
    [Entity: Christopher Nolan]
```

- **2010s – Expansion and Adoption:**
  The success of Google's Knowledge Graph spurred widespread interest in knowledge graphs across various industries. Academic research and industry adoption accelerated, leading to the development of specialized graph databases (e.g., Neo4j, GraphDB) and integration of graph-based approaches in diverse applications.

Milestone Timeline:

Year	Milestone	Impact
1960s	Emergence of semantic networks	Early modeling of human-like knowledge representation
1980s	Expert systems incorporating semantic networks	Demonstrated practical applications in problem-solving
2001	Introduction of RDF	Established a standard for data interchange in graph form
2006	Google's Knowledge Graph	Revolutionized search with context-aware, interconnected data
2010s	Proliferation of graph databases and research in knowledge graphs	Widespread adoption in various industries, enhancing data analysis

Future Outlook

As we look ahead, several trends suggest that knowledge graphs and related technologies will continue to evolve:

- **Integration with Machine Learning:**
  Future systems will increasingly combine graph data with machine learning models. Techniques like Graph Neural Networks (GNNs) are already emerging, promising even more powerful data representations and insights.
- **Real-Time and Dynamic Graphs:**
  The need for real-time analytics is driving the development of systems that can update and query knowledge graphs dynamically as new data is ingested.
- **Expansion Across Industries:**
  From healthcare to finance and beyond, knowledge graphs are

expected to play a pivotal role in driving innovation by enabling more sophisticated data integration, personalized services, and advanced decision-making.

- **Standardization and Interoperability:**
  As more organizations adopt knowledge graphs, efforts toward standardizing data formats and protocols will be critical. This will ensure that different systems can interoperate, leading to a more connected digital ecosystem.

2.3 Emergence and Growth of RAG Techniques

Retrieval-Augmented Generation (RAG) represents a significant innovation in the field of natural language processing and information retrieval. RAG techniques emerged as a way to address the limitations of traditional generative models, which sometimes produce responses that are outdated, factually incorrect, or lacking in context. By incorporating an external retrieval mechanism, RAG models enhance the quality and relevance of generated responses.

Historical Background

Prior to RAG, two primary approaches dominated the field of AI-generated text:

- **Pure Generative Models:**
  Models like early versions of GPT and other language models generated text solely based on patterns learned during training. While powerful, these models sometimes struggled with factual consistency, as they did not have a direct mechanism to access updated or domain-specific information.
- **Retrieval-Based Systems:**
  These systems focused on retrieving relevant documents or passages from a large corpus. Although they excelled at providing factual accuracy by returning existing information, they lacked the flexibility to generate new, context-aware responses.

The Birth of RAG

RAG emerged by combining the strengths of both approaches. The technique involves two main components:

1. **Retrieval Component:**
   The system first searches a large knowledge base or document corpus to retrieve relevant pieces of information based on the user's query. This step ensures that the response is grounded in real, up-to-date data.
2. **Generation Component:**
   A generative model (such as a transformer-based language model) then takes the retrieved information and produces a coherent, contextually rich answer. This component has the flexibility to generate natural language text that weaves together retrieved facts with its own learned patterns.

Example Workflow for a RAG System

Below is a simplified pseudocode that outlines the RAG process:

```python
def retrieve_information(query, knowledge_base):
    # Search the knowledge base for documents relevant to the
query
    relevant_docs = search_index(query, knowledge_base)
    return relevant_docs

def generate_response(query, context):
    # Generate a response using a language model,
incorporating the retrieved context
    response = language_model.generate(query,
additional_context=context)
    return response

# Main RAG process
def rag_system(query, knowledge_base):
    # Step 1: Retrieve relevant documents
    context = retrieve_information(query, knowledge_base)

    # Step 2: Generate a response using the retrieved context
    final_response = generate_response(query, context)

    return final_response

# Example usage:
query = "What are the benefits of knowledge graphs in
healthcare?"
knowledge_base = load_knowledge_base("healthcare_articles")
response = rag_system(query, knowledge_base)
print(response)
```

Explanation:

- **retrieve_information:**
  This function searches a knowledge base to find documents that are relevant to the user's query.
- **generate_response:**
  It then uses a language model to generate a response that incorporates the retrieved context.
- **rag_system:**
  This function integrates both steps to provide a final, enriched answer.

Growth and Adoption

The integration of RAG techniques has accelerated in recent years due to several factors:

- **Advancements in Language Models:**
  The development of powerful transformer-based models has provided a robust generative component that can produce high-quality text.
- **Improved Retrieval Technologies:**
  Modern retrieval systems (using technologies like Elasticsearch or dense vector search with embedding models) ensure that the context provided to generative models is highly relevant and up-to-date.
- **Real-World Applications:**
  Industries ranging from customer support to research and education have adopted RAG systems to improve the accuracy and utility of automated responses. Companies like OpenAI and Google are continuously refining these techniques, further driving their adoption.

2.4 Current Trends and Future Prospects

As the field of artificial intelligence continues to evolve, several trends are shaping the current landscape and future prospects of RAG techniques.

Current Trends

1. **Hybrid Models:**
   Modern AI systems increasingly combine retrieval and generation in

a seamless workflow. Hybrid models ensure that the generated content is both creative and factually grounded, leading to more reliable applications in areas like customer service, automated content creation, and technical support.

2. **Real-Time Data Integration:**
   One of the key trends is the integration of real-time data into RAG systems. By continuously updating the underlying knowledge base, these systems can provide the most current information. This is particularly important in rapidly changing fields such as finance and news.

3. **Domain-Specific RAG:**
   Organizations are developing RAG models tailored to specific industries or applications. For example, a RAG system for healthcare might be optimized to retrieve the latest medical research, while one for legal services could focus on retrieving current case law and regulations.

4. **Improved User Interaction:**
   Enhanced user interfaces and interactive features are being developed to allow users to refine queries or provide feedback, which can then be used to further improve the retrieval process. This iterative approach leads to better and more personalized responses.

Future Prospects

The future of RAG techniques looks promising, with several exciting developments on the horizon:

1. **Enhanced Integration with Graph Databases:**
   As knowledge graphs become more sophisticated, integrating them directly with RAG systems will allow for even richer context. Graph databases can provide structured, interconnected data that enhances both the retrieval and generation processes.

2. **Adaptive Learning and Fine-Tuning:**
   Future RAG systems are likely to incorporate adaptive learning techniques that fine-tune both the retrieval and generation components based on user interactions and feedback. This continuous improvement loop will result in increasingly accurate and personalized responses.

3. **Cross-Domain Applications:**
   As RAG techniques mature, we can expect to see their application across a broader range of fields, including education, entertainment, and government. The ability to generate factually correct and context-

aware responses will make these systems indispensable in many sectors.

4. **Ethical and Responsible AI:**
   With the growing impact of AI on society, there will be an increased focus on ensuring that RAG systems are developed and deployed responsibly. This includes addressing issues related to data privacy, bias in retrieval and generation, and ensuring transparency in how responses are generated.

Table: Key Trends and Future Prospects of RAG Techniques

Trend/Prospect	Description	Impact
Hybrid Models	Seamless integration of retrieval and generative models.	More reliable and contextually accurate responses.
Real-Time Data Integration	Continuous updating of knowledge bases with the latest data.	Enhanced accuracy and timeliness of responses.
Domain-Specific Systems	Tailored RAG models for specific industries.	Improved relevance and effectiveness in specialized applications.
Graph Database Integration	Direct use of knowledge graphs in the RAG workflow.	Richer context and deeper insights.
Adaptive Learning	Fine-tuning based on user interactions and feedback.	Continual improvement in system performance and personalization.
Ethical AI Focus	Emphasis on responsible and transparent AI practices.	Increased trust and adoption in sensitive applications.

2.5 Impact on AI, Data Science, and Beyond

The advancements in RAG techniques are not only revolutionizing natural language processing but are also having a profound impact on the broader fields of AI and data science.

Transforming AI and Machine Learning

- **Improved Natural Language Understanding:**
  RAG techniques enhance the ability of AI systems to understand and generate human-like text by providing them with accurate, real-time context. This results in more effective conversational agents, virtual assistants, and customer support systems.
- **Bridging the Gap Between Data Retrieval and Generation:**
  By combining retrieval with generation, RAG systems mitigate the limitations of standalone generative models. This bridge enables AI systems to offer more reliable insights, answer complex queries, and even generate creative content based on factual data.
- **Enhanced Model Interpretability:**
  The explicit retrieval step in RAG systems provides a transparent mechanism for understanding the source of the generated content. This interpretability is critical in applications where trust and accountability are paramount, such as healthcare and finance.

Advancing Data Science Practices

- **Rich Data Integration:**
  RAG systems are built on robust retrieval mechanisms that can tap into diverse datasets, including structured databases, unstructured text, and knowledge graphs. This capability allows data scientists to work with richer, more interconnected data, leading to deeper insights and more informed decision-making.
- **Automation of Knowledge Discovery:**
  With the ability to generate context-aware responses, RAG systems automate parts of the knowledge discovery process. Data scientists can use these systems to quickly extract relevant information from massive datasets, speeding up research and innovation.
- **Support for Complex Analytical Tasks:**
  RAG techniques can be integrated into advanced analytical workflows, supporting tasks such as predictive analytics, anomaly detection, and trend forecasting. The combination of retrieval and generation makes it easier to interpret complex data patterns and generate actionable insights.

Broader Implications and Applications

The impact of RAG techniques extends beyond AI and data science into various other sectors:

- **Healthcare:**
  RAG systems can assist clinicians by providing real-time access to the latest research, patient histories, and treatment protocols. This integration can lead to better diagnostics and more personalized patient care.
- **Education:**
  In educational settings, RAG-powered tutoring systems can offer students customized learning experiences by retrieving relevant educational content and generating tailored explanations.
- **Finance:**
  Financial analysts can leverage RAG systems to quickly access up-to-date market data, regulatory information, and financial news, improving decision-making and risk assessment.
- **Legal and Government:**
  RAG techniques can help legal professionals and policymakers by retrieving pertinent legal precedents, regulatory updates, and case-specific data, ensuring that decisions are well-informed and contextually relevant.

Summary

In this section of Chapter 2, we explored the emergence and growth of RAG techniques, current trends and future prospects, and the broader impact of these technologies on AI, data science, and beyond. We learned that:

- **RAG Techniques** emerged as a hybrid solution, integrating retrieval methods with generative models to produce factually accurate and contextually enriched outputs.
- **Current Trends** in RAG include hybrid models, real-time data integration, domain-specific systems, and ethical AI practices, while future prospects point toward even deeper integration with graph databases, adaptive learning, and cross-domain applications.
- **Impact on AI and Data Science** is profound, as RAG techniques enhance natural language understanding, improve model

interpretability, and enable richer data integration. Beyond these fields, applications span healthcare, education, finance, and legal sectors.

By combining detailed technical explanations with real-world examples and tables, this chapter provides a comprehensive overview of how RAG techniques are shaping the future of intelligent systems and data-driven decision-making.

Chapter 3: Fundamentals of Graph Theory

Graph theory is a branch of mathematics and computer science that studies graphs—structures used to model pairwise relations between objects. In this chapter, we will introduce the foundational terminology and definitions used in graph theory, discuss the various types of graphs (such as directed, undirected, and weighted), and explain the common representations and data structures for working with graphs in practical applications.

3.1 Basic Terminology and Definitions

Before diving into the different types of graphs and their representations, it is essential to understand the basic terminology and definitions that form the building blocks of graph theory.

Key Terms

- **Graph:**
  A graph GGG is an ordered pair $G=(V,E)G = (V, E)G=(V,E)$, where:
  - VVV is a set of vertices (or nodes).
  - EEE is a set of edges (or links) that connect pairs of vertices.
- **Vertex (Node):**
  A vertex represents an entity or object in a graph. For example, in a social network graph, each person is represented as a vertex.
- **Edge (Link):**
  An edge represents the connection or relationship between two vertices. For instance, a friendship between two people in a social network graph.
- **Adjacent Vertices:**
  Two vertices are considered adjacent (or neighbors) if they are connected directly by an edge.
- **Degree:**
  The degree of a vertex is the number of edges connected to it. In a directed graph, we distinguish between:
  - **In-degree:** The number of edges coming into a vertex.
  - **Out-degree:** The number of edges going out from a vertex.
- **Path:**
  A path in a graph is a sequence of vertices where each consecutive

pair is connected by an edge. Paths can be used to measure the distance between nodes.

- **Cycle:**
  A cycle is a path that starts and ends at the same vertex without repeating any edges (and, in many cases, without repeating vertices, except for the starting/ending vertex).
- **Connected Graph:**
  A graph is said to be connected if there is a path between every pair of vertices.

Table: Summary of Basic Graph Terminology

Term	Definition
Graph (G)	An ordered pair $G=(V,E)$ $G = (V, E)$ $G=(V,E)$, where VVV is a set of vertices and EEE is a set of edges.
Vertex (Node)	An individual element or object in the graph (e.g., a person in a social network).
Edge (Link)	A connection between two vertices (e.g., a friendship between two people).
Degree	The number of edges connected to a vertex (includes in-degree and out-degree in directed graphs).
Path	A sequence of vertices where each pair is connected by an edge.
Cycle	A path that begins and ends at the same vertex.
Connected Graph	A graph in which every pair of vertices is connected by a path.

Code Example: Basic Graph Creation

Below is a simple Python code example using the `networkx` library to illustrate the creation of a basic graph and the computation of degrees for each node.

```python
# Importing the necessary library
import networkx as nx

# Create an empty graph
G = nx.Graph()
```

```
# Add vertices (nodes)
G.add_node("A")
G.add_node("B")
G.add_node("C")
G.add_node("D")

# Add edges (links) between nodes
G.add_edge("A", "B")
G.add_edge("A", "C")
G.add_edge("B", "C")
G.add_edge("C", "D")

# Display nodes and their degrees
print("Nodes and their degrees:")
for node in G.nodes():
    print(f"Node {node} has degree {G.degree(node)}")
```

Explanation:

- **Graph Creation:**
  We create an empty graph G and add four nodes: A, B, C, and D.
- **Adding Edges:**
  Edges are added to connect the nodes (e.g., A is connected to B and C).
- **Computing Degrees:**
  The code iterates over each node and prints its degree (i.e., the number of edges connected to it).

3.2 Types of Graphs (Directed, Undirected, Weighted, etc.)

Graphs can vary based on the nature of the relationships they model. The most common types include directed graphs, undirected graphs, and weighted graphs. Below, we explain each type with examples.

Undirected Graphs

- **Definition:**
  In an undirected graph, edges have no direction. The edge (u,v)(u, v)(u,v) is identical to the edge (v,u)(v, u)(v,u). These graphs are used

when the relationship between vertices is bidirectional (e.g., mutual friendships).

- **Example:**
Consider a simple social network where two people are friends. The friendship is mutual, so the graph is undirected.

Directed Graphs (Digraphs)

- **Definition:**
In a directed graph, edges have a specific direction, indicated by an arrow. The edge $(u,v)(u, v)(u,v)$ goes from vertex uuu to vertex vvv and is not necessarily the same as $(v,u)(v, u)(v,u)$. These graphs are useful when the relationship is asymmetric (e.g., Twitter follow relationships).
- **Example:**
In a Twitter network, if user A follows user B, it does not imply that B follows A.

Weighted Graphs

- **Definition:**
In a weighted graph, each edge is assigned a weight (or cost) that represents the strength, distance, or capacity of the connection between vertices. These weights are often numerical values.
- **Example:**
In a transportation network, weights might represent the distance between cities or the travel time.

Mixed Graphs

- **Definition:**
Some graphs are both directed and weighted, meaning that they have directional edges and each edge has an associated weight.
- **Table: Comparison of Graph Types**

Graph Type	Edge Direction	Edge Weight	Typical Use Case
Undirected	No	Optional	Social networks, undirected relationships

Graph Type	Edge Direction	Edge Weight	Typical Use Case
Directed	Yes	Optional	Web links, Twitter following relationships
Weighted	Optional	Yes	Road networks, network flows
Directed & Weighted	Yes	Yes	Transportation, citation networks

Code Example: Creating Different Graph Types

Below is a Python code example using `networkx` to create an undirected graph, a directed graph, and a weighted graph.

```python
import networkx as nx
import matplotlib.pyplot as plt

# Undirected Graph Example
undirected_graph = nx.Graph()
undirected_graph.add_edge("Alice", "Bob")
undirected_graph.add_edge("Alice", "Carol")
undirected_graph.add_edge("Bob", "Carol")

# Directed Graph Example
directed_graph = nx.DiGraph()
directed_graph.add_edge("Alice", "Bob")
directed_graph.add_edge("Bob", "Carol")
directed_graph.add_edge("Carol", "Alice")

# Weighted Graph Example (Undirected Weighted Graph)
weighted_graph = nx.Graph()
weighted_graph.add_edge("A", "B", weight=5)
weighted_graph.add_edge("A", "C", weight=3)
weighted_graph.add_edge("B", "C", weight=2)

# Displaying the weighted edges with their weights
print("Weighted Graph Edges and Weights:")
for u, v, data in weighted_graph.edges(data=True):
    print(f"Edge {u}-{v} has weight {data['weight']}")

# Visualizing the weighted graph
plt.figure(figsize=(6, 4))
pos = nx.spring_layout(weighted_graph)
```

```
nx.draw(weighted_graph, pos, with_labels=True,
node_color='skyblue', edge_color='gray', node_size=1500,
font_size=12)
edge_labels = nx.get_edge_attributes(weighted_graph,
'weight')
nx.draw_networkx_edge_labels(weighted_graph, pos,
edge_labels=edge_labels)
plt.title("Undirected Weighted Graph Example")
plt.show()
```

Explanation:

- **Undirected Graph:**
  We create an undirected graph representing relationships between Alice, Bob, and Carol.
- **Directed Graph:**
  A directed graph is created where relationships have direction. For example, Alice follows Bob, Bob follows Carol, and Carol follows Alice.
- **Weighted Graph:**
  A weighted undirected graph is created where each edge has a weight attribute (e.g., representing distance or cost). The code prints each edge's weight and visualizes the graph using Matplotlib.

3.3 Graph Representations and Data Structures

Graphs can be represented in various ways in computer memory. The choice of data structure often depends on the operations that need to be performed and the properties of the graph. The two most common representations are the adjacency list and the adjacency matrix.

Adjacency List

- **Definition:**
  An adjacency list represents a graph as a collection of lists or dictionaries. Each vertex stores a list of its adjacent vertices. This representation is efficient in terms of space, especially for sparse graphs.
- **Example Representation:**

  ```
  css
  ```

```
Graph: {
    "A": ["B", "C"],
    "B": ["A", "C"],
    "C": ["A", "B", "D"],
    "D": ["C"]
}
```

- **Advantages:**
  - o Space-efficient for sparse graphs.
  - o Easy to iterate over neighbors of a vertex.
- **Code Example:**

```python
# Representing a graph using an adjacency list in
Python
adjacency_list = {
    "A": ["B", "C"],
    "B": ["A", "C"],
    "C": ["A", "B", "D"],
    "D": ["C"]
}

# Print the adjacency list
print("Adjacency List Representation:")
for vertex, neighbors in adjacency_list.items():
    print(f"{vertex}: {neighbors}")
```

Adjacency Matrix

- **Definition:**
  An adjacency matrix is a 2D array (or list of lists) where each cell [i][j][i][j][i][j] indicates whether there is an edge between vertex iii and vertex jjj. In weighted graphs, this cell can store the weight of the edge instead of a simple boolean.
- **Example Representation:**

For vertices A,B,C,DA, B, C, DA,B,C,D, an unweighted graph may be represented as:

	A	B	C	D
A	0	1	1	0
B	1	0	1	0
C	1	1	0	1

A B C D

D 0 0 1 0

- **Advantages:**
  - o Provides constant-time access to check if an edge exists between any two vertices.
  - o Useful for dense graphs.
- **Code Example:**

```python
import numpy as np

# Define an adjacency matrix for a simple undirected
graph with vertices A, B, C, D
# Using the order A, B, C, D
adjacency_matrix = np.array([
    [0, 1, 1, 0],   # A
    [1, 0, 1, 0],   # B
    [1, 1, 0, 1],   # C
    [0, 0, 1, 0]    # D
])

print("Adjacency Matrix Representation:")
print(adjacency_matrix)
```

Explanation:

- **Adjacency List:**
  The graph is stored as a dictionary where keys are vertices and values are lists of neighbors. This is straightforward and efficient for iterating over neighbors.
- **Adjacency Matrix:**
  The graph is stored in a 2D NumPy array, where each element indicates whether an edge exists between two vertices. This format is useful when you need to quickly check for the existence of an edge.

3.4 Core Algorithms in Graph Theory

Graph algorithms are the backbone of many applications in computer science and data analysis. In this section, we introduce several fundamental algorithms that are used to traverse, search, and find optimal paths in graphs. We will cover:

- **Breadth-First Search (BFS)**
- **Depth-First Search (DFS)**
- **Dijkstra's Algorithm for Shortest Paths**
- **Other Notable Algorithms** (brief overview)

Each algorithm will be explained along with its purpose, a high-level description, and a complete code example using Python.

Breadth-First Search (BFS)

Purpose:
Breadth-First Search is used to explore a graph layer by layer, starting from a source node. It is especially useful for finding the shortest path in unweighted graphs.

Algorithm Overview:

1. Start at the source vertex.
2. Visit all the neighbors of the source.
3. Move to the next level: visit the neighbors of all the nodes at the current level.
4. Continue until all nodes are visited.

Complexity:
Time complexity is $O(V+E)O(V + E)O(V+E)$, where VVV is the number of vertices and EEE is the number of edges.

Code Example:

```python
import networkx as nx
from collections import deque

def bfs(graph, start):
    """
    Perform Breadth-First Search (BFS) on a graph from a
starting node.

    Parameters:
        graph (nx.Graph): The graph to search.
```

```
        start (any): The starting vertex.

    Returns:
        visited (list): List of nodes in the order they were
visited.
    """
    visited = []
    queue = deque([start])

    while queue:
        vertex = queue.popleft()
        if vertex not in visited:
            visited.append(vertex)
            # Enqueue all unvisited neighbors
            queue.extend([neighbor for neighbor in
graph.neighbors(vertex) if neighbor not in visited])
    return visited

# Example usage:
G = nx.Graph()
G.add_edges_from([("A", "B"), ("A", "C"), ("B", "D"), ("C",
"D"), ("C", "E")])
print("BFS starting from A:", bfs(G, "A"))
```

Explanation:

- We use a **deque** (double-ended queue) to efficiently pop nodes from the front.
- The algorithm visits each node, adding its unvisited neighbors to the queue.
- The order in which nodes are visited is printed, demonstrating layer-by-layer traversal.

Depth-First Search (DFS)

Purpose:
Depth-First Search explores as far along a branch as possible before backtracking. It is useful for tasks such as detecting cycles and performing topological sorting.

Algorithm Overview:

1. Start at the source vertex.
2. Recursively visit an unvisited neighbor.

3. Backtrack when no unvisited neighbors remain.
4. Continue until all nodes are visited.

Complexity:
Time complexity is also O(V+E)O(V + E)O(V+E).

Code Example:

python

```
def dfs(graph, start, visited=None):
    """
    Perform Depth-First Search (DFS) on a graph starting from
a given node.

    Parameters:
        graph (nx.Graph): The graph to search.
        start (any): The starting vertex.
        visited (list): List to keep track of visited nodes.

    Returns:
        visited (list): List of nodes in the order they were
visited.
    """
    if visited is None:
        visited = []
    visited.append(start)

    for neighbor in graph.neighbors(start):
        if neighbor not in visited:
            dfs(graph, neighbor, visited)
    return visited

# Example usage:
print("DFS starting from A:", dfs(G, "A"))
```

Explanation:

- This recursive function marks a node as visited and then recursively visits all unvisited neighbors.
- The order of node visitation shows deep traversal into one branch before backtracking.

Dijkstra's Algorithm for Shortest Paths

Purpose:
Dijkstra's algorithm is designed to find the shortest path from a source vertex to all other vertices in a weighted graph with non-negative weights.

Algorithm Overview:

1. Initialize distances from the source to all nodes as infinite, except the source which is zero.
2. Use a priority queue to select the vertex with the smallest known distance.
3. Update the distances for all adjacent vertices.
4. Repeat until all vertices are processed.

Complexity:
Using a priority queue, the complexity is $O((V+E)\log V)O((V + E) \log V)O((V+E)\log V)$.

Code Example:

```python
import heapq

def dijkstra(graph, start):
    """
    Compute the shortest paths from the start vertex to all
    other vertices in a weighted graph.

    Parameters:
        graph (dict): The graph represented as an adjacency
    list where each edge has a weight.
                Example: {"A": {"B": 1, "C": 4}, "B":
    {"A": 1, "C": 2, "D": 5}, ... }
        start (str): The starting vertex.

    Returns:
        distances (dict): The shortest distances from the
    start to each vertex.
    """
    distances = {vertex: float('infinity') for vertex in
graph}
    distances[start] = 0
    priority_queue = [(0, start)]
```

```
    while priority_queue:
        current_distance, current_vertex =
heapq.heappop(priority_queue)

        # If the popped vertex distance is greater than the
current known, skip it.
        if current_distance > distances[current_vertex]:
            continue

        for neighbor, weight in
graph[current_vertex].items():
            distance = current_distance + weight
            # If a shorter path to neighbor is found
            if distance < distances[neighbor]:
                distances[neighbor] = distance
                heapq.heappush(priority_queue, (distance,
neighbor))
    return distances

# Example weighted graph represented as an adjacency list
weighted_graph = {
    "A": {"B": 1, "C": 4},
    "B": {"A": 1, "C": 2, "D": 5},
    "C": {"A": 4, "B": 2, "D": 1},
    "D": {"B": 5, "C": 1}
}

print("Shortest paths from A:", dijkstra(weighted_graph,
"A"))
```

Explanation:

- The graph is represented as a dictionary of dictionaries, where keys are vertices and values are dictionaries of neighbor: weight pairs.
- A **priority queue** (using `heapq`) ensures that the vertex with the smallest current distance is processed first.
- The algorithm updates the shortest known distances and returns the final distances from the start vertex.

Other Notable Algorithms

While BFS, DFS, and Dijkstra's algorithm are among the most commonly used, other algorithms such as the **A*** search algorithm (for heuristic-based shortest path finding) and **Bellman-Ford algorithm** (for graphs with negative edge weights) are also important. These are often studied in more advanced courses or specialized applications.

3.5 Case Examples Illustrating Graph Concepts

Real-world applications of graph theory can help solidify the understanding of the theoretical concepts introduced in this chapter. In this section, we explore two case examples that demonstrate the practical use of graph algorithms.

Case Example 1: Social Network Analysis

Scenario:
Consider a social network where each user is represented as a node and friendships are represented as edges. We want to:

- Explore the network using BFS to find the level of connection between users.
- Use DFS to discover clusters or communities within the network.

Graph Construction:

```python
# Create a social network graph
social_graph = nx.Graph()
social_graph.add_edges_from([
    ("Alice", "Bob"),
    ("Alice", "Carol"),
    ("Bob", "David"),
    ("Carol", "Emily"),
    ("David", "Frank"),
    ("Emily", "Frank"),
    ("Frank", "Grace")
])

# BFS from 'Alice'
bfs_result = bfs(social_graph, "Alice")
print("BFS traversal in social network starting from Alice:",
bfs_result)

# DFS from 'Alice'
dfs_result = dfs(social_graph, "Alice")
```

```
print("DFS traversal in social network starting from Alice:",
dfs_result)
```

Explanation:

- **BFS Traversal:**
  This helps determine the degree of separation (i.e., the minimum number of connections) between Alice and other users.
- **DFS Traversal:**
  This can reveal clusters or communities within the network. For instance, nodes visited consecutively in DFS might indicate closely connected subgroups.

Case Example 2: Transportation Network

Scenario:
Imagine a transportation network where cities are nodes, and roads connecting them are weighted edges representing distances. The goal is to compute the shortest route between a starting city and all other cities using Dijkstra's algorithm.

Graph Construction:

python

```
# Define a transportation network as a weighted graph
transportation_graph = {
    "CityA": {"CityB": 50, "CityC": 100},
    "CityB": {"CityA": 50, "CityC": 40, "CityD": 70},
    "CityC": {"CityA": 100, "CityB": 40, "CityD": 60,
"CityE": 80},
    "CityD": {"CityB": 70, "CityC": 60, "CityE": 30},
    "CityE": {"CityC": 80, "CityD": 30}
}

# Compute shortest paths from 'CityA'
shortest_paths = dijkstra(transportation_graph, "CityA")
print("Shortest paths from CityA:", shortest_paths)
```

Explanation:

- **Weighted Graph:**
  The transportation network is modeled with cities as nodes and roads as edges with distances as weights.

- **Dijkstra's Algorithm:**
  The algorithm computes the shortest distance from CityA to all other cities, providing practical insights into route planning and network optimization.

Summary

- **Core Algorithms in Graph Theory:**
  Introduced BFS, DFS, and Dijkstra's algorithm, each accompanied by clear explanations, complexity considerations, and complete Python code examples.
- **Case Examples Illustrating Graph Concepts:**
  Demonstrated how these algorithms are applied in real-world scenarios such as social network analysis and transportation networks, helping to translate theoretical concepts into practical applications.

By understanding and applying these core algorithms and case examples, you gain the foundational skills required to analyze, design, and implement graph-based systems. This knowledge is crucial as you progress into more advanced topics and real-world applications in later chapters.

Chapter 4: Introduction to Knowledge Graphs

Knowledge graphs have emerged as a powerful paradigm for representing and interlinking information. They offer a flexible, intuitive, and efficient way to model complex relationships in a form that is easy for both humans and machines to understand. In this chapter, we will cover three key areas:

1. **Defining Knowledge Graphs:** What they are and why they matter.
2. **Components and Architecture of Knowledge Graphs:** An in-depth look at their building blocks.
3. **Graph Models vs. Relational Models:** A comparison highlighting the strengths and limitations of each approach.

4.1 Defining Knowledge Graphs

A **knowledge graph** is a structured representation of information where entities (nodes) and their relationships (edges) are modeled in a graph format. This representation allows complex interconnections among data elements to be stored, queried, and visualized in a natural and intuitive manner.

Key Characteristics

- **Interconnected Entities:**
  Entities such as people, places, or concepts are connected by relationships that describe how they are related. For example, in a knowledge graph about movies, an actor node might be connected to a film node by an edge labeled "acted in."
- **Semantic Enrichment:**
  Beyond simply storing data, knowledge graphs often include semantic information such as labels, types, and attributes that give context to the nodes and edges. This semantic layer makes it easier to perform meaningful queries and infer new relationships.
- **Flexibility:**
  Unlike rigid table structures in traditional databases, knowledge graphs are schema-flexible. They can evolve as new types of entities

and relationships are added, accommodating changes in the data landscape.

Table: Basic Definition of a Knowledge Graph

Aspect	Description
Nodes (Entities)	Represent distinct objects or concepts (e.g., a person, product, or idea).
Edges (Relationships)	Define how nodes are related (e.g., "friend of," "located in," "authored").
Attributes (Properties)	Additional details associated with nodes or edges (e.g., age, date of release, weight).
Semantic Layer	Enriches data with context through labels and types, enabling more complex queries and reasoning.

Practical Example

Imagine a small knowledge graph for a movie domain. The graph might include nodes for actors, movies, and directors, with edges that describe relationships such as "acted in" and "directed."

4.2 Components and Architecture of Knowledge Graphs

Understanding the components and overall architecture of knowledge graphs is key to designing, implementing, and scaling these systems.

Core Components

1. **Entities (Nodes):**
   - o **Definition:** Individual items or objects represented in the graph.
   - o **Example:** "Inception" (a film), "Leonardo DiCaprio" (an actor).
2. **Relationships (Edges):**
   - o **Definition:** The connections or interactions between entities.
   - o **Example:** "Leonardo DiCaprio acted in Inception."

3. **Attributes (Properties):**
   - **Definition:** Key-value pairs associated with nodes or edges that provide additional information.
   - **Example:** An actor node might have properties such as "birth_year: 1974" or "nationality: American."
4. **Ontology or Schema:**
   - **Definition:** A formal representation that defines the types of nodes, edges, and the permissible properties. It establishes the rules and constraints of the knowledge graph.
   - **Example:** An ontology for a movie knowledge graph might define node types like "Actor," "Movie," and "Director," and specify that an "Actor" can have an "acted in" relationship with a "Movie."
5. **Data Ingestion and Integration Layer:**
   - **Definition:** Processes and tools that extract data from various sources, transform it, and load it into the graph.
   - **Example:** ETL (Extract, Transform, Load) pipelines that integrate data from databases, APIs, and CSV files.
6. **Query and Analysis Engine:**
   - **Definition:** Tools and languages (such as SPARQL or Cypher) used to retrieve and analyze data stored in the graph.
   - **Example:** Querying the graph to find all movies where a particular actor has performed.

Architecture Diagram

Below is a simplified diagram of a typical knowledge graph architecture:

pgsql

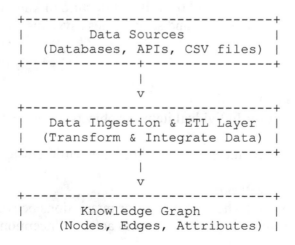

```
+-------------------------------+
|          Data Sources         |
|   (Databases, APIs, CSV files)|
+--------------+----------------+
               |
               v
+-------------------------------+
|    Data Ingestion & ETL Layer |
|   (Transform & Integrate Data)|
+--------------+----------------+
               |
               v
+-------------------------------+
|         Knowledge Graph       |
|    (Nodes, Edges, Attributes) |
```

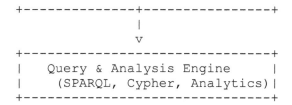

```
+--------------+---------------+
               |
               v
+-----------------------------+
|   Query & Analysis Engine   |
|    (SPARQL, Cypher, Analytics)|
+-----------------------------+
```

Explanation

- **Data Sources:**
  Various data sources feed into the knowledge graph system.
- **ETL Layer:**
  This layer is responsible for cleaning, transforming, and integrating the data before it is added to the graph.
- **Knowledge Graph:**
  The central repository where interconnected entities, relationships, and attributes are stored.
- **Query Engine:**
  Tools and languages enable users to interact with the graph, extracting meaningful insights and answering complex queries.

Code Example: Building a Simple Knowledge Graph with Python

Below is a Python example using the `networkx` library to create a basic knowledge graph for a movie domain.

```python
python

import networkx as nx
import matplotlib.pyplot as plt

# Create an empty graph to represent the knowledge graph
KG = nx.Graph()

# Add nodes with attributes
KG.add_node("Inception", type="Movie", release_year=2010)
KG.add_node("Leonardo DiCaprio", type="Actor",
birth_year=1974)
KG.add_node("Christopher Nolan", type="Director",
birth_year=1970)

# Add edges with relationship labels
KG.add_edge("Leonardo DiCaprio", "Inception",
relationship="acted in")
```

```
KG.add_edge("Christopher Nolan", "Inception",
relationship="directed")

# Display nodes with their attributes
print("Knowledge Graph Nodes:")
for node, attributes in KG.nodes(data=True):
    print(f"{node}: {attributes}")

# Visualizing the Knowledge Graph
plt.figure(figsize=(8, 6))
pos = nx.spring_layout(KG)
nx.draw(KG, pos, with_labels=True, node_color='lightblue',
edge_color='gray', node_size=2000, font_size=10)
edge_labels = nx.get_edge_attributes(KG, 'relationship')
nx.draw_networkx_edge_labels(KG, pos,
edge_labels=edge_labels, font_color='red')
plt.title("Simple Movie Knowledge Graph")
plt.show()
```

Explanation:

- **Graph Creation:**
  We start by creating an empty graph to serve as the knowledge graph.
- **Adding Nodes and Attributes:**
  Nodes for the movie *Inception*, actor *Leonardo DiCaprio*, and director *Christopher Nolan* are added along with relevant attributes.
- **Adding Edges:**
  Relationships between the nodes are added, labeled as "acted in" and "directed."
- **Visualization:**
  The graph is visualized using Matplotlib, with node labels and edge relationship labels to make the connections clear.

4.3 Graph Models vs. Relational Models

Both graph models and relational models are used for data storage and retrieval, but they differ significantly in structure, flexibility, and application suitability.

Relational Models

- **Structure:**
  Data is stored in tables with rows and columns. Each table represents a specific entity type, and relationships are maintained through foreign keys.
- **Schema:**
  Relational databases have a rigid, predefined schema. Changes to the schema often require extensive modifications to the database structure.
- **Query Language:**
  SQL (Structured Query Language) is used to perform queries and join operations across multiple tables.
- **Use Cases:**
  Ideal for transactional systems, financial records, and scenarios where data is highly structured and relationships are relatively simple.

Graph Models

- **Structure:**
  Data is stored as nodes (entities) and edges (relationships). Relationships are first-class citizens and are explicitly represented.
- **Schema:**
  Graph models are schema-flexible, meaning they can easily evolve as new types of entities and relationships are introduced.
- **Query Language:**
  Graph-specific query languages such as SPARQL and Cypher are used to explore complex relationships and patterns.
- **Use Cases:**
  Best suited for applications that require modeling of complex, interconnected data—such as social networks, recommendation systems, and semantic search.

Comparison Table

Feature	Relational Models	Graph Models
Data Structure	Tables (rows and columns)	Nodes and edges
Schema	Rigid, predefined	Flexible, schema-less

Feature	Relational Models	Graph Models
Relationships	Implicit, managed via foreign keys	Explicit, directly represented as edges
Query Language	SQL	SPARQL, Cypher
Best Suited For	Structured, tabular data; transactional systems	Complex, interconnected data; dynamic, evolving data

Code Example: Simple Comparison Using Data Representations

Below is a conceptual example in Python illustrating how one might represent the same dataset in both a relational style (using a list of dictionaries) and a graph model (using `networkx`).

Relational Model Representation

```python
# Representing data in a relational style using a list of
dictionaries
movies = [
    {"id": 1, "title": "Inception", "release_year": 2010},
]
actors = [
    {"id": 1, "name": "Leonardo DiCaprio", "birth_year":
1974},
]
# Representing relationships via foreign keys
roles = [
    {"actor_id": 1, "movie_id": 1, "role": "Lead"}
]

print("Relational Model Data:")
print("Movies:", movies)
print("Actors:", actors)
print("Roles:", roles)
```

Graph Model Representation

```python
# Using networkx to represent the same dataset as a graph
KG = nx.Graph()

# Adding nodes with attributes
```

```
KG.add_node("Inception", type="Movie", release_year=2010)
KG.add_node("Leonardo DiCaprio", type="Actor",
birth_year=1974)

# Adding an edge to represent the relationship
KG.add_edge("Leonardo DiCaprio", "Inception",
relationship="acted in")

print("\nGraph Model Data (Nodes and Edges):")
for node, attr in KG.nodes(data=True):
    print(f"{node}: {attr}")
for u, v, attr in KG.edges(data=True):
    print(f"{u} - {v}: {attr}")
```

Explanation:

- **Relational Model:**
  Data is stored in separate lists for movies, actors, and roles.
  Relationships are inferred via matching IDs.
- **Graph Model:**
  The same entities and relationships are stored as nodes and edges,
  with the relationship explicitly defined in the graph structure.

4.4 Semantic Enrichment and Linking Data

Semantic enrichment is the process of enhancing raw data by adding
metadata that provides context and meaning. In the realm of knowledge
graphs, this process plays a critical role by transforming isolated data points
into interconnected, semantically rich representations. Linking data refers to
connecting disparate datasets through shared concepts and relationships,
thereby creating a network of knowledge that is both machine-interpretable
and human-understandable.

Key Objectives of Semantic Enrichment

1. **Disambiguation:**
   Enriching data helps distinguish between entities with similar names
   or characteristics. For example, the term "Apple" might refer to a
   fruit or a technology company. Adding contextual metadata clarifies
   the intended meaning.
2. **Contextualization:**
   Metadata provides context by linking data elements to standardized

vocabularies, taxonomies, or ontologies. This ensures that data is understood uniformly across different systems and applications.

3. **Enhanced Discoverability:**
   By semantically linking data, systems can perform more advanced queries and reasoning. This enables better data discovery, integration, and analysis.

4. **Interoperability:**
   Semantic enrichment facilitates the integration of heterogeneous datasets. When data is annotated with shared ontologies or standards (such as RDF or OWL), it can be more easily shared and merged across platforms and domains.

Techniques for Semantic Enrichment

- **Annotation with Ontologies:**
  Use established ontologies (e.g., FOAF, schema.org, or domain-specific vocabularies) to tag data elements. This not only standardizes the data but also makes it easier to link similar data across different sources.
- **Entity Recognition and Disambiguation:**
  Natural Language Processing (NLP) techniques can identify entities in unstructured text and link them to canonical representations in a knowledge graph.
- **Relationship Extraction:**
  Algorithms can extract relationships from textual data and formalize them as edges in the knowledge graph. For example, extracting that "Leonardo DiCaprio starred in Inception" links the actor to the movie with a clear relationship.

Table: Semantic Enrichment Process

Step	Description	Example
Data Collection	Gather raw data from various sources (e.g., text, databases, APIs).	News articles, product catalogs, research papers.
Entity Recognition	Identify and extract key entities (e.g., names, locations, dates) from the data.	Recognizing "Apple Inc." as a company versus "apple" as a fruit.

Step	Description	Example
Ontology Mapping	Map the extracted entities to a structured ontology or vocabulary.	Tagging "Apple Inc." with schema.org/Organization.
Relationship Extraction	Identify relationships between entities and formalize them as graph edges.	Linking "Steve Jobs" to "Apple Inc." with the relation "founded".
Data Linking	Connect enriched data with other datasets using common identifiers or semantic tags.	Linking company data with financial records through unique IDs.

Code Example: Enriching Data with RDF

Below is a simplified example using Python's `rdflib` library to create a small RDF graph that semantically enriches data about a company and its founder.

```python
frcm rdflib import Graph, Literal, RDF, URIRef, Namespace

# Create a new RDF graph
g = Graph()

# Define Namespaces for schema.org and our custom namespace
SCHEMA = Namespace("http://schema.org/")
EX = Namespace("http://example.org/")

# Bind namespaces to prefixes for clarity
g.bind("schema", SCHEMA)
g.bind("ex", EX)

# Create URIs for entities
company = URIRef("http://example.org/AppleInc")
founder = URIRef("http://example.org/SteveJobs")

# Add triples to the graph (subject, predicate, object)
# Define the company as an Organization with a name
g.add((company, RDF.type, SCHEMA.Organization))
g.add((company, SCHEMA.name, Literal("Apple Inc.")))

# Define the founder as a Person with a name
g.add((founder, RDF.type, SCHEMA.Person))
```

```
g.add((founder, SCHEMA.name, Literal("Steve Jobs")))

# Link the founder to the company with a "founder"
relationship
g.add((company, SCHEMA.founder, founder))

# Print out all triples in the graph
for subj, pred, obj in g:
    print(f"{subj} -- {pred} --> {obj}")

# The resulting RDF graph now semantically enriches the data:
# - Apple Inc. is identified as an Organization.
# - Steve Jobs is identified as a Person.
# - The relationship "founder" links Steve Jobs to Apple Inc.
```

Explanation:

- **Namespaces and Binding:**
  We define standard (schema.org) and custom (example.org)
  namespaces to structure our data.
- **Triple Creation:**
  Each triple represents a fact. For example, the triple linking the
  company to its type (Organization) and the one connecting the
  founder to the company via the "founder" relationship.
- **Output:**
  Printing all triples demonstrates how semantic enrichment transforms
  raw data into a connected, machine-readable format.

4.5 Industry Use Cases and Success Stories

Knowledge graphs and semantic enrichment are being successfully applied
across various industries. Their ability to represent complex relationships
and integrate heterogeneous data sources has led to improved decision-
making, enhanced user experiences, and innovative business solutions.

Industry Use Cases

1. **Healthcare**
   - **Use Case:**
     Knowledge graphs are used to integrate patient records,
     clinical trial data, and medical research. This enables

personalized treatment recommendations and supports advanced diagnostic tools.

- o **Success Story:**
  A leading healthcare provider integrated a knowledge graph to consolidate disparate data sources. This enabled doctors to access a patient's complete medical history along with the latest research on treatments, resulting in more accurate diagnoses and improved patient outcomes.

2. **Finance**
   - o **Use Case:**
     In finance, knowledge graphs help in fraud detection, risk management, and customer segmentation. By linking transaction data with customer profiles and external financial news, institutions can better detect anomalies and predict market trends.
   - o **Success Story:**
     A major bank implemented a knowledge graph to monitor financial transactions. The system detected unusual patterns and linked them with external data on fraudulent activities, leading to the early prevention of potential fraud cases.

3. **Retail & E-commerce**
   - o **Use Case:**
     Knowledge graphs power recommendation engines by linking products, customer reviews, and purchase histories. This results in more personalized shopping experiences and increased sales.
   - o **Success Story:**
     An e-commerce giant used a knowledge graph to enhance its recommendation system. By semantically linking products with user behavior and external trends, the platform achieved a significant increase in conversion rates and customer satisfaction.

4. **Education**
   - o **Use Case:**
     Educational platforms use knowledge graphs to map curriculum content, track student progress, and provide personalized learning pathways. This helps in creating adaptive learning systems that cater to individual student needs.
   - o **Success Story:**
     A prominent online learning platform developed a knowledge graph to connect courses, topics, and learner profiles. This

enabled the system to recommend tailored learning resources, improving course completion rates and learner engagement.

Table: Summary of Industry Use Cases

Industry	Application	Key Benefits
Healthcare	Patient records, treatment recommendations	Improved diagnostics, personalized care
Finance	Fraud detection, risk management	Early fraud prevention, better market predictions
Retail	Product recommendations, customer insights	Enhanced personalization, increased sales
Education	Curriculum mapping, personalized learning	Adaptive learning, improved engagement and completion

Real-World Success Stories

- **Case Study: Integrating Healthcare Data**
  A multi-hospital network deployed a knowledge graph to unify patient data from different sources, including electronic health records (EHRs) and research databases. The resulting system enabled healthcare professionals to quickly retrieve patient histories and relevant research articles, ultimately leading to more effective treatment plans.
- **Case Study: Financial Fraud Detection**
  By employing a knowledge graph, a financial institution was able to link customer transaction data with external fraud databases. The enriched data allowed for real-time monitoring and detection of suspicious patterns, reducing the incidence of fraud by a substantial margin.
- **Case Study: Personalized Retail Recommendations**
  An international retail brand used a knowledge graph to integrate product information, customer reviews, and social media trends. This integration powered a recommendation engine that boosted cross-selling opportunities and enhanced the overall shopping experience.

Visualization Example: Knowledge Graph in E-commerce

Imagine a simplified knowledge graph for an e-commerce platform:

```
less

              [Customer: John Doe]
                  /        \
                 /          \
    [Purchased: Smartphone]--[Reviewed: Smartphone]
              |                     |
         [Category: Electronics]--[Mentioned: Trendy]
```

Explanation:

- **Nodes:**
  Represent customers, products, and categories.
- **Edges:**
  Indicate relationships such as purchases, reviews, and product categories.
- **Semantic Linking:**
  The graph connects customer actions with product attributes and external trends, enabling personalized recommendations.

Summary

- **Semantic Enrichment and Linking Data:**
  We defined semantic enrichment as the process of adding meaningful metadata to data and discussed techniques such as ontology mapping, entity recognition, and relationship extraction. A detailed code example using RDF demonstrated how to semantically enrich data for a knowledge graph.
- **Industry Use Cases and Success Stories:**
  We reviewed how knowledge graphs are being applied in various industries—healthcare, finance, retail, and education—highlighting the tangible benefits and providing real-world case studies. A summary table and visualization example further illustrated the power of semantically enriched data in solving complex business challenges.

This comprehensive treatment of semantic enrichment and its industry applications underscores the transformative impact of knowledge graphs. By linking and enriching data semantically, organizations can unlock deeper insights, improve operational efficiency, and drive innovation across a wide range of sectors.

Chapter 5: Standards, Protocols, and Technologies

In the world of knowledge graphs, adherence to common standards and protocols is essential for data interoperability, sharing, and semantic consistency. In this chapter, we will explore three critical areas:

1. **Resource Description Framework (RDF)**
2. **Ontologies and the Web Ontology Language (OWL)**
3. **Query Languages: SPARQL and Beyond**

Each section provides an in-depth discussion, practical examples, and tables where appropriate to illustrate how these technologies work and why they are important.

5.1 Resource Description Framework (RDF)

Overview

The Resource Description Framework (RDF) is a foundational standard for representing information on the Web. RDF provides a framework for describing resources (entities) and their relationships in a structured, machine-readable format. It uses a triple-based model to represent data in the form of subject–predicate–object statements.

Key Concepts

- **Triple:**
  An RDF triple is a statement composed of three parts:
    - **Subject:** The resource being described.
    - **Predicate:** The property or relationship.
    - **Object:** The value or another resource linked to the subject.
- **URI (Uniform Resource Identifier):**
  RDF uses URIs to uniquely identify subjects, predicates, and sometimes objects, ensuring global uniqueness and interoperability.

- **Serialization Formats:**
  RDF data can be represented in several serialization formats, including:
  - **RDF/XML:** An XML-based syntax.
  - **Turtle:** A compact and readable text format.
  - **JSON-LD:** A JSON-based format that is easy to integrate with web applications.

Table: RDF Triple Example

Component	Description	Example
Subject	The resource being described.	`<http://example.org/AppleInc>`
Predicate	The property or relationship.	`<http://schema.org/name>`
Object	The value or related resource.	`"Apple Inc."` (a literal) or `<http://example.org/SteveJobs>`

Practical Example: Creating an RDF Graph Using Python

Below is a complete code example using Python's `rdflib` library to create and serialize an RDF graph that describes a company and its founder.

```python
from rdflib import Graph, Literal, RDF, URIRef, Namespace

# Create a new RDF graph
g = Graph()

# Define namespaces for schema.org and our custom namespace
SCHEMA = Namespace("http://schema.org/")
EX = Namespace("http://example.org/")

# Bind the namespaces to prefixes for clarity
g.bind("schema", SCHEMA)
g.bind("ex", EX)

# Define URIs for our resources
company_uri = EX.AppleInc
founder_uri = EX.SteveJobs

# Add triples to the graph
# Triple: Apple Inc. is an Organization
```

```
g.add((company_uri, RDF.type, SCHEMA.Organization))
g.add((company_uri, SCHEMA.name, Literal("Apple Inc.")))

# Triple: Steve Jobs is a Person
g.add((founder_uri, RDF.type, SCHEMA.Person))
g.add((founder_uri, SCHEMA.name, Literal("Steve Jobs")))

# Triple: Apple Inc. has a founder Steve Jobs
g.add((company_uri, SCHEMA.founder, founder_uri))

# Serialize the graph to Turtle format and print
print(g.serialize(format="turtle").decode("utf-8"))
```

Explanation:

- **Graph Creation:**
  We create an RDF graph and define two namespaces—one for the common vocabulary (schema.org) and another custom namespace.
- **Adding Triples:**
  Each call to `g.add()` creates a triple. For instance, the triple stating that *Apple Inc.* is an organization is represented using RDF type and the corresponding URI.
- **Serialization:**
  The graph is serialized in Turtle format, which is human-readable and widely used.

5.2 Ontologies and the Web Ontology Language (OWL)

Overview

Ontologies are formal representations of knowledge that define the types, properties, and interrelationships of entities within a particular domain. The Web Ontology Language (OWL) is a semantic web language designed to create and share ontologies. OWL builds upon RDF and RDF Schema (RDFS) by adding more vocabulary for describing properties and classes, along with richer semantics for reasoning.

Key Concepts

- **Classes:**
  Represent groups or categories of things (e.g., Person, Organization).
- **Properties:**
  Define relationships between classes or attributes of classes. There are two main types:
    - **Object Properties:** Relate two individuals (e.g., "founder").
    - **Datatype Properties:** Relate an individual to a data value (e.g., "name" or "birthYear").
- **Individuals:**
  The actual instances of classes (e.g., *Apple Inc.*, *Steve Jobs*).
- **Restrictions and Axioms:**
  OWL allows the definition of restrictions on properties (e.g., cardinality constraints) and axioms that enable automated reasoning over the ontology.

Table: Key Elements in OWL

Element	Description	Example
Class	A category or group of things.	`Person`, `Organization`
Object Property	A property that links two individuals.	`founder` (links a person to an organization)
Datatype Property	A property that links an individual to a literal value.	`name`, `birthYear`
Individual	A specific instance of a class.	`Steve Jobs` (an instance of `Person`)
Restriction	Constraints on how properties can be used.	A person must have at least one `name` property

Practical Example: Defining an Ontology with OWL Using Protégé

While a full coding example with OWL often involves specialized editors like Protégé, here's a conceptual example of how you might define a simple ontology in OWL using Turtle syntax:

```
turtle
```

```
@prefix owl: <http://www.w3.org/2002/07/owl#> .
@prefix rdf: <http://www.w3.org/1999/02/22-rdf-syntax-ns#> .
@prefix rdfs: <http://www.w3.org/2000/01/rdf-schema#> .
@prefix ex: <http://example.org/> .
@prefix schema: <http://schema.org/> .

# Define the ontology
ex:CompanyOntology a owl:Ontology .

# Define Classes
ex:Organization a owl:Class ;
    rdfs:label "Organization" .

ex:Person a owl:Class ;
    rdfs:label "Person" .

# Define Object Property: founder
ex:founder a owl:ObjectProperty ;
    rdfs:domain ex:Organization ;
    rdfs:range ex:Person ;
    rdfs:label "founder" .

# Define Datatype Property: name
ex:name a owl:DatatypeProperty ;
    rdfs:domain owl:Thing ;
    rdfs:range rdfs:Literal ;
    rdfs:label "name" .
```

Explanation:

- **Prefixes:**
  We define several namespaces for OWL, RDF, RDFS, and our custom vocabulary.
- **Ontology Declaration:**
  We declare an ontology called `CompanyOntology`.
- **Class Definitions:**
  Classes for `Organization` and `Person` are defined with labels.
- **Property Definitions:**
  An object property `founder` is defined with its domain and range, meaning that it links an organization to a person. A datatype property `name` is also defined.

This simple ontology can be expanded and refined in tools like Protégé, which provide a graphical interface for managing OWL ontologies.

5.3 Query Languages: SPARQL and Beyond

Overview

Query languages are essential for retrieving and manipulating data in knowledge graphs. SPARQL (SPARQL Protocol and RDF Query Language) is the standard query language for RDF data, enabling users to perform complex queries across diverse datasets. In addition to SPARQL, other query languages and extensions have emerged to address specific use cases and improve usability.

SPARQL Basics

- **Triple Patterns:**
  SPARQL queries consist of triple patterns that match the structure of RDF triples.
- **Query Forms:**
  Common SPARQL query forms include SELECT (for retrieving variables), ASK (for boolean queries), CONSTRUCT (for building new RDF graphs), and DESCRIBE (for getting information about a resource).

Sample SPARQL Query

Below is a simple SPARQL query that retrieves the names of organizations and their founders from an RDF dataset:

```sparql
PREFIX schema: <http://schema.org/>
PREFIX ex: <http://example.org/>

SELECT ?organization ?orgName ?founder ?founderName
WHERE {
    ?organization a schema:Organization ;
                  schema:name ?orgName ;
                  schema:founder ?founder .
    ?founder a schema:Person ;
          schema:name ?founderName .
}
```

Explanation:

- **PREFIX:**
  The query defines prefixes for schema.org and the custom namespace.
- **SELECT Clause:**
  Specifies the variables to be returned: the organization URI, its name, the founder URI, and the founder's name.
- **WHERE Clause:**
  Matches triple patterns where an organization has a name and a founder, and the founder has a name.

Beyond SPARQL

While SPARQL is the de facto standard for querying RDF data, other query languages and extensions exist:

- **GraphQL:**
  Although not designed specifically for RDF, GraphQL is used in many modern applications to query graph-like data structures with a flexible, JSON-based syntax.
- **Cypher:**
  Primarily used with property graph databases like Neo4j, Cypher offers an expressive and easy-to-read syntax for querying graph data. Example Cypher Query:

```cypher
MATCH (p:Person)-[:FOUNDED]->(o:Organization)
RETURN p.name AS Founder, o.name AS Organization
```

- **SPARQL Extensions:**
  Several extensions to SPARQL have been developed to support advanced functionalities like federated queries (querying across multiple endpoints) and spatial queries.

Table: Comparison of Query Languages

Query Language	Primary Use Case	Key Features
SPARQL	Querying RDF data	Triple pattern matching, standard for RDF

Query Language	Primary Use Case	Key Features
GraphQL	Querying modern web APIs	JSON-based, flexible and strongly typed
Cypher	Querying property graphs (e.g., Neo4j)	Readable syntax, pattern matching in graph data
SPARQL Extensions	Advanced querying over RDF data	Federated queries, spatial queries, etc.

Practical Example: Querying an RDF Graph with SPARQL Using Python

Below is a Python example that demonstrates how to execute a SPARQL query using the `rdflib` library.

```python
from rdflib import Graph, Namespace

# Create a new RDF graph and load data (using the same graph
from earlier examples)
g = Graph()
g.parse(data='''
    @prefix schema: <http://schema.org/> .
    @prefix ex: <http://example.org/> .

    ex:AppleInc a schema:Organization ;
                schema:name "Apple Inc." ;
                schema:founder ex:SteveJobs .

    ex:SteveJobs a schema:Person ;
                schema:name "Steve Jobs" .
''', format="turtle")

# Define namespaces
SCHEMA = Namespace("http://schema.org/")
EX = Namespace("http://example.org/")

# SPARQL query to retrieve organization and founder names
query = """
PREFIX schema: <http://schema.org/>
PREFIX ex: <http://example.org/>

SELECT ?organization ?orgName ?founder ?founderName
WHERE {
    ?organization a schema:Organization ;
```

```
            schema:name ?orgName ;
            schema:founder ?founder .
    ?founder a schema:Person ;
            schema:name ?founderName .
}
"""

# Execute the SPARQL query
results = g.query(query)

# Print results
print("Query Results:")
for row in results:
    print(f"Organization: {row.orgName}, Founder:
{row.founderName}")
```

Explanation:

- **Graph Loading:**
  An RDF graph is created and populated with example data using Turtle syntax.
- **SPARQL Query:**
  The query defined retrieves organizations and their founders by matching triple patterns.
- **Execution and Output:**
  The query is executed against the graph, and the results are printed to the console.

Summary

- **Resource Description Framework (RDF):**
  We explained the triple-based model of RDF, discussed serialization formats, and provided a practical Python example using `rdflib` to create and serialize an RDF graph.
- **Ontologies and the Web Ontology Language (OWL):**
  We defined ontologies, described the key elements of OWL (classes, properties, individuals, restrictions), and provided an example of how an ontology might be defined in Turtle syntax.
- **Query Languages: SPARQL and Beyond:**
  We introduced SPARQL as the standard language for querying RDF data, provided a sample SPARQL query, and compared SPARQL with other query languages such as GraphQL and Cypher. A practical

Python example demonstrated how to execute a SPARQL query against an RDF graph.

5.4 Data Interchange Formats (JSON-LD, Turtle, etc.)

Overview

Data interchange formats are crucial for sharing, storing, and transmitting structured data across different systems. In the context of knowledge graphs and the semantic web, several serialization formats have been developed to represent RDF data. The most common formats include:

- **Turtle (Terse RDF Triple Language):**
  A compact, human-readable syntax for expressing RDF data.
- **JSON-LD (JSON for Linked Data):**
  A JSON-based format that is easy to integrate with web applications and APIs.
- **RDF/XML:**
  An XML-based syntax that was one of the first standard formats for RDF data.

Each format has its own advantages and is suited for different scenarios.

Turtle

Description:
Turtle is widely used because of its concise and readable syntax. It represents RDF triples in a plain text format that is easy for humans to understand.

Example in Turtle:

```turtle
@prefix schema: <http://schema.org/> .
@prefix ex: <http://example.org/> .

ex:AppleInc a schema:Organization ;
        schema:name "Apple Inc." ;
        schema:founder ex:SteveJobs .

ex:SteveJobs a schema:Person ;
```

```
schema:name "Steve Jobs" .
```

Explanation:

- **Prefixes:**
  The @prefix declarations define shorthand notations for longer URIs.
- **Triples:**
  Each statement is terminated by a semicolon (;) or a period (.). The example shows two resources (Apple Inc. and Steve Jobs) with their types and properties.

JSON-LD

Description:
JSON-LD is a JSON-based format that provides a simple way to represent Linked Data in a familiar JSON structure. It is particularly useful for web developers as it integrates easily with JavaScript and modern web APIs.

Example in JSON-LD:

```json
{
  "@context": {
    "schema": "http://schema.org/",
    "ex": "http://example.org/"
  },
  "@graph": [
    {
      "@id": "ex:AppleInc",
      "@type": "schema:Organization",
      "schema:name": "Apple Inc.",
      "schema:founder": {
        "@id": "ex:SteveJobs"
      }
    },
    {
      "@id": "ex:SteveJobs",
      "@type": "schema:Person",
      "schema:name": "Steve Jobs"
    }
  ]
}
```

Explanation:

- **@context:**
  Maps short prefixes to full URIs, similar to Turtle prefixes.
- **@graph:**
  Contains an array of nodes (resources). Each node uses `@id` to identify the resource and `@type` to declare its class.
- **Nested Objects:**
  Relationships (e.g., `schema:founder`) can reference other resources using their `@id`.

RDF/XML

Description:
RDF/XML was one of the earliest formats for serializing RDF. While it is more verbose than Turtle and JSON-LD, it is still used in many legacy systems.

Example in RDF/XML:

xml

```
<?xml version="1.0"?>
<rdf:RDF xmlns:rdf="http://www.w3.org/1999/02/22-rdf-syntax-ns#"
         xmlns:schema="http://schema.org/"
         xmlns:ex="http://example.org/">
  <rdf:Description rdf:about="http://example.org/AppleInc">
    <rdf:type rdf:resource="http://schema.org/Organization"/>
    <schema:name>Apple Inc.</schema:name>
    <schema:founder
rdf:resource="http://example.org/SteveJobs"/>
  </rdf:Description>
  <rdf:Description rdf:about="http://example.org/SteveJobs">
    <rdf:type rdf:resource="http://schema.org/Person"/>
    <schema:name>Steve Jobs</schema:name>
  </rdf:Description>
</rdf:RDF>
```

Explanation:

- **Namespaces:**
  XML namespaces are defined using the `xmlns` attribute.
- **rdf:Description:**
  Each resource is described within an `<rdf:Description>` element, with properties nested inside.

Table: Comparison of RDF Serialization Formats

Format	Syntax	Advantages	Common Use Cases
Turtle	Text-based	Human-readable, compact, easy to write and read	Development, data sharing
JSON-LD	JSON-based	Integrates with web APIs, easy for developers	Web applications, JavaScript integration
RDF/XML	XML-based	Well-supported by legacy systems, formal structure	Interoperability with XML systems

5.5 Integration with Linked Data and Semantic Web

Overview

The Semantic Web is an extension of the current web, where information is given well-defined meaning through linked data. Integration with linked data involves adhering to principles that allow disparate data sources to be connected in a standardized, machine-readable way. This integration is achieved by:

- Using dereferenceable URIs.
- Adhering to Linked Data principles.
- Leveraging vocabularies and ontologies.

Linked Data Principles

Tim Berners-Lee defined four key principles for Linked Data:

1. **Use URIs as Names for Things:**
   Every resource (entity) should have a unique URI.
2. **Use HTTP URIs:**
   HTTP URIs enable people and machines to look up those names.
3. **Provide Useful Information:**
   When a URI is dereferenced, useful information should be provided using standard formats (e.g., RDF, JSON-LD).

4. **Include Links to Other URIs:**
   Links to related resources should be included to improve
   discoverability and connectivity.

Integration with the Semantic Web

Integration with linked data and the semantic web involves publishing,
sharing, and consuming RDF data on the web. This is achieved through:

- **Linked Data Platforms:**
  Systems that store and serve RDF data, such as Apache Jena or
  Virtuoso.
- **SPARQL Endpoints:**
  Web services that allow users to query datasets using SPARQL.
- **Interlinking Datasets:**
  Connecting data from different sources by reusing common
  vocabularies and linking resources via their URIs.

Practical Example: Publishing and Linking Data

Consider an example where an organization publishes its data on a public
SPARQL endpoint. By using common vocabularies like schema.org and
linking its data with external datasets (e.g., DBpedia), the organization
enables richer queries and cross-domain integrations.

Example Scenario:

- **Step 1:**
  The organization publishes its knowledge graph using a platform like
  Apache Jena Fuseki.
- **Step 2:**
  The published data includes links to external resources. For example,
  a company node might include a link to its DBpedia resource.
- **Step 3:**
  Users can query the SPARQL endpoint to retrieve both internal data
  and linked external data.

Code Example: Interlinking Data with External URIs

Below is an example in Turtle where a local resource is linked to an external
dataset (e.g., DBpedia):

```turtle
@prefix schema: <http://schema.org/> .
@prefix ex: <http://example.org/> .
@prefix dbpedia: <http://dbpedia.org/resource/> .

ex:AppleInc a schema:Organization ;
        schema:name "Apple Inc." ;
        schema:founder ex:SteveJobs ;
        schema:sameAs dbpedia:Apple_Inc .

ex:SteveJobs a schema:Person ;
        schema:name "Steve Jobs" ;
        schema:sameAs dbpedia:Steve_Jobs .
```

Explanation:

- **schema:sameAs:**
  The `schema:sameAs` property is used to indicate that the local resource is equivalent to an external resource. In this example, *Apple Inc.* and *Steve Jobs* are linked to their respective DBpedia URIs.
- **Interlinking:**
  This linkage enables users to traverse from the local dataset to the broader web of linked data, accessing additional information available in external sources.

Table: Benefits of Integration with Linked Data and the Semantic Web

Benefit	Description	Example
Enhanced Discoverability	Linking data allows for richer, cross-domain queries and data discovery.	A query retrieves local data and related information from DBpedia.
Data Interoperability	Standardized formats and shared vocabularies enable different systems to work together seamlessly.	Multiple datasets using RDF and common ontologies can be merged.
Improved Data Quality	Cross-referencing with external datasets helps verify and enrich local data.	Linking a product to external reviews or ratings.

Benefit	Description	Example
Scalability	Distributed data on the semantic web can be integrated and queried without central control.	Federated SPARQL queries spanning several endpoints.

Real-World Use Case: Government Open Data

Many governments are publishing open data as linked data to promote transparency and innovation. For instance:

- **Example:**
  A government might publish data about public services, transportation, and health facilities using RDF. By linking this data to external datasets (e.g., geographical information systems), citizens and developers can create applications that offer comprehensive insights into public services.
- **Benefits:**
  Enhanced data interoperability, improved public service analytics, and fostered innovation through data reuse.

Summary

- **Data Interchange Formats:**
  We discussed the most common RDF serialization formats—Turtle, JSON-LD, and RDF/XML—highlighting their syntax, advantages, and use cases. Detailed examples and a comparison table illustrate how these formats support the sharing and consumption of knowledge graph data.
- **Integration with Linked Data and the Semantic Web:**
  We reviewed the principles of linked data, such as using dereferenceable URIs and linking to external datasets. Practical examples, including a Turtle snippet, demonstrated how to interlink local data with external resources (e.g., DBpedia). Additionally, we highlighted the benefits of such integration for discoverability, interoperability, and data quality.

This comprehensive treatment of data interchange formats and integration strategies equips you with the necessary tools to work effectively within the semantic web and leverage the power of linked data. By adhering to these standards and protocols, you can ensure that your knowledge graphs are both interoperable and scalable across diverse systems and domains.

Chapter 6: Requirements Analysis and Domain Modeling

In this chapter, we focus on the early phases of designing a graph-based system. A successful graph-based system begins with a thorough understanding of both the business and technical requirements. We then move on to identifying the key entities and relationships that will form the backbone of the system and finally discuss how domain-driven design (DDD) principles can be applied to structure the graph effectively.

6.1 Understanding Business and Technical Requirements

Overview

Before building any system, it is crucial to gather and analyze the requirements. In the context of graph-based systems, both business and technical requirements provide guidance on how the data is interconnected, how it will be used, and what performance and scalability constraints must be met.

Business Requirements

Business requirements answer the questions:

- **What problems are we trying to solve?**
- **Who are the stakeholders and end-users?**
- **What insights or capabilities must the system provide?**

Key Aspects:

1. **Use Cases and Scenarios:**
   Identify the scenarios in which the graph system will be used. For example, if designing a recommendation system for e-commerce, common use cases might include product recommendations based on user behavior or collaborative filtering among similar users.

2. **Stakeholder Needs:**
   Engage with stakeholders to understand their goals. This might include executives seeking high-level insights, analysts needing detailed query capabilities, and developers concerned with system integration.
3. **Data Sources and Quality:**
   Determine what data sources will feed into the graph, their formats, and the quality of the data. Assess whether data cleaning, normalization, or enrichment is needed.

Technical Requirements

Technical requirements outline the system's architecture and performance expectations:

- **Scalability:**
  What volume of data and query load is expected? Graph systems often need to handle complex, interconnected datasets and support real-time querying.
- **Integration:**
  How will the system integrate with existing data sources, APIs, or other enterprise systems? This could include compatibility with data interchange formats (such as JSON-LD, Turtle) or integration with linked data.
- **Performance and Latency:**
  What are the performance benchmarks for query response times? This influences decisions about indexing, caching, and hardware.
- **Security and Compliance:**
  What security protocols, data privacy measures, or regulatory requirements must be followed?

Table: Sample Requirements for an E-commerce Graph System

Requirement Type	Description	Example
Business	Product recommendation, customer segmentation, enhanced search capabilities	Provide personalized recommendations based on purchase history
Data Source	Multiple data sources including transactional databases,	Integrate data from SQL databases and public review APIs

Requirement Type	Description	Example
	customer reviews, and social media feeds	
Scalability	Must support high query load during peak shopping periods	Handle 10,000 concurrent users with real-time recommendations
Integration	Interoperability with existing ERP and CRM systems	Use REST APIs and RDF-based formats for data interchange
Performance	Query response time of under 200 ms for most queries	Optimize indexes and caching strategies
Security	Compliance with data privacy regulations (e.g., GDPR)	Encrypt sensitive user data and anonymize personal identifiers

Summary

Understanding both the business and technical requirements lays a solid foundation for designing a robust graph-based system. It ensures that the system not only meets stakeholder needs but is also scalable, performant, and secure.

6.2 Identifying Key Entities and Relationships

Overview

Once requirements are defined, the next step is to determine what entities (nodes) and relationships (edges) are critical to the domain. This process involves:

- **Entity Identification:** Listing the key objects or concepts in the domain.
- **Relationship Mapping:** Determining how these entities are interrelated.

Steps for Identification

1. **Review Requirements and Use Cases:**
   Revisit the requirements documentation to extract common themes, such as frequent interactions or key data points.
2. **Domain Expertise:**
   Collaborate with domain experts to verify that the identified entities and relationships reflect real-world processes.
3. **Entity-Relationship (ER) Diagrams:**
   Create visual diagrams to map out entities and their relationships. This is a valuable tool for both planning and communicating the design.

Example: E-commerce Domain

In an e-commerce context, consider the following entities and relationships:

Key Entities:

- **Customer:** Represents users who shop on the platform.
- **Product:** Represents items available for purchase.
- **Order:** Represents a transaction or purchase event.
- **Review:** Represents feedback from customers on products.
- **Category:** Represents product classifications.

Key Relationships:

- **Customer–Order:** A customer places one or more orders.
- **Order–Product:** An order includes one or more products.
- **Customer–Review:** A customer writes reviews for products.
- **Product–Category:** Products belong to one or more categories.

Table: Entities and Relationships in an E-commerce Graph

Entity	Attributes	Relationships
Customer	Name, Email, Address, Loyalty Status	Places Order, Writes Review
Product	Name, Price, Description, Stock Level	Included in Order, Belongs to Category, Reviewed by Customer

Entity	Attributes	Relationships
Order	Order ID, Date, Total Amount	Contains Products, Linked to Customer
Review	Rating, Comment, Date	Written by Customer, Associated with Product
Category	Category Name, Description	Contains Products

Code Example: Representing Entities and Relationships in Python

Below is a Python code example using the `networkx` library to model a simplified e-commerce graph:

python

```python
import networkx as nx
import matplotlib.pyplot as plt

# Create a directed graph to capture the flow of transactions
G = nx.DiGraph()

# Adding key entities as nodes with attributes
G.add_node("Customer: John Doe", type="Customer",
email="john@example.com")
G.add_node("Product: Smartphone", type="Product", price=699)
G.add_node("Product: Headphones", type="Product", price=199)
G.add_node("Order: 1001", type="Order", date="2025-01-15",
total=898)
G.add_node("Review: R1", type="Review", rating=5,
comment="Excellent!")

# Adding relationships as directed edges
G.add_edge("Customer: John Doe", "Order: 1001",
relationship="places")
G.add_edge("Order: 1001", "Product: Smartphone",
relationship="contains")
G.add_edge("Order: 1001", "Product: Headphones",
relationship="contains")
G.add_edge("Customer: John Doe", "Review: R1",
relationship="writes")
G.add_edge("Review: R1", "Product: Smartphone",
relationship="reviews")

# Visualizing the graph
plt.figure(figsize=(10, 7))
```

```
pos = nx.spring_layout(G)
nx.draw(G, pos, with_labels=True, node_color='lightgreen',
edge_color='gray', node_size=2500, font_size=10)
edge_labels = nx.get_edge_attributes(G, 'relationship')
nx.draw_networkx_edge_labels(G, pos, edge_labels=edge_labels,
font_color='blue')
plt.title("Simplified E-commerce Graph")
plt.show()
```

Explanation:

- **Node Creation:**
  Each node represents an entity (e.g., a customer, product, order, review) with its attributes.
- **Edge Creation:**
  Directed edges represent relationships, such as a customer placing an order or writing a review.
- **Visualization:**
  The graph is visualized with node labels and edge labels to clearly display the relationships.

Summary

Identifying key entities and relationships is a critical step in domain modeling. By mapping out the entities, their attributes, and how they interconnect, you form a clear picture of the domain that the graph-based system will represent. This process ensures that all necessary data elements are captured and that their interrelationships are well understood.

6.3 Domain-Driven Design for Graph Systems

Overview

Domain-Driven Design (DDD) is an approach to software development that emphasizes collaboration between technical experts and domain experts. In the context of graph systems, DDD helps align the data model with the real-world domain, ensuring that the graph accurately reflects the business processes and rules.

Key Principles of Domain-Driven Design

1. **Ubiquitous Language:**
   Establish a common language that both developers and domain experts use when discussing the system. This language should be reflected in the naming of entities, relationships, and attributes in the graph.
2. **Bounded Contexts:**
   Divide the domain into distinct bounded contexts—subdomains where specific models apply. Each bounded context can be represented as a subgraph, ensuring that different parts of the system are modular and maintainable.
3. **Entities and Value Objects:**
   Differentiate between entities (which have a unique identity) and value objects (which represent attributes and do not have a unique identity). In graph systems, entities are modeled as nodes with distinct URIs, while value objects may be stored as node properties.
4. **Aggregates:**
   An aggregate is a cluster of domain objects that can be treated as a single unit. In a graph, aggregates can be represented as tightly connected subgraphs that encapsulate domain logic and consistency rules.

Applying DDD to Graph Systems

Steps:

1. **Collaborative Modeling:**
   Work with domain experts to build a conceptual model of the domain. Use diagrams and sketches to outline entities, relationships, and bounded contexts.
2. **Identify Aggregates:**
   Determine which entities naturally group together. For instance, in an e-commerce domain, an order and its related products, reviews, and payment details might form an aggregate.
3. **Define Interfaces:**
   Establish clear interfaces between different bounded contexts. In graph systems, these interfaces may be represented by specific relationship types or connecting nodes that allow communication between subgraphs.
4. **Iterative Refinement:**
   As the domain evolves, continuously refine the model. The schema-

less nature of graph databases makes it easier to evolve the data model over time.

Example: Applying DDD in an E-commerce Graph

Scenario:
In our e-commerce domain, we might define the following bounded contexts:

- **Customer Management:**
  Focuses on customer profiles, preferences, and loyalty programs.
- **Order Processing:**
  Handles orders, payments, and shipping details.
- **Product Catalog:**
  Manages products, categories, and reviews.

Aggregate Example:
An order aggregate might include:

- **Order (Entity):**
  Unique order details.
- **Products (Entities):**
  Items included in the order.
- **Payment (Value Object):**
  Payment method details stored as attributes.
- **Shipping (Value Object):**
  Shipping address and method.

Table: Example of Bounded Contexts in E-commerce

Bounded Context	Key Entities	Primary Responsibilities
Customer Management	Customer, Loyalty Program	Managing customer profiles, preferences, rewards
Order Processing	Order, Payment, Shipping	Processing orders, handling payments, managing shipments
Product Catalog	Product, Category, Review	Managing product information, categorization, feedback

Code Example: Representing Bounded Contexts in a Graph

Below is a simplified Python example that shows how you might label nodes to indicate their bounded context within an e-commerce graph:

python

```
import networkx as nx
import matplotlib.pyplot as plt

# Create a graph
G = nx.Graph()

# Add nodes with bounded context as an attribute
G.add_node("Customer: Jane Doe", type="Customer",
context="Customer Management")
G.add_node("Order: 2001", type="Order", context="Order
Processing")
G.add_node("Product: Laptop", type="Product",
context="Product Catalog")
G.add_node("Review: R2", type="Review", context="Product
Catalog")

# Add edges to represent relationships across bounded
contexts
G.add_edge("Customer: Jane Doe", "Order: 2001",
relationship="places")
G.add_edge("Order: 2001", "Product: Laptop",
relationship="contains")
G.add_edge("Customer: Jane Doe", "Review: R2",
relationship="writes")
G.add_edge("Review: R2", "Product: Laptop",
relationship="reviews")

# Visualize the graph with context information
plt.figure(figsize=(10, 7))
pos = nx.spring_layout(G)
nx.draw(G, pos, with_labels=True, node_color='lightyellow',
edge_color='black', node_size=2500, font_size=10)
edge_labels = nx.get_edge_attributes(G, 'relationship')
nx.draw_networkx_edge_labels(G, pos, edge_labels=edge_labels,
font_color='red')
plt.title("E-commerce Graph with Bounded Contexts")
plt.show()
```

Explanation:

- **Node Attributes:**
  Each node includes a `context` attribute indicating its bounded context (e.g., "Customer Management" or "Order Processing").
- **Inter-Context Relationships:**
  Edges connect nodes from different contexts (e.g., a customer placing an order), showing how the system integrates across bounded contexts.
- **Visualization:**
  The visualization helps illustrate the modular structure of the domain as represented in the graph.

Summary

Domain-Driven Design for graph systems ensures that the data model aligns closely with the real-world domain. By collaborating with domain experts, identifying aggregates and bounded contexts, and iteratively refining the model, you can design a graph-based system that is both flexible and maintainable. DDD not only improves communication among stakeholders but also guides the technical implementation of the system.

6.4 Developing Use Cases and User Stories

Overview

Use cases and user stories are essential tools in requirements analysis that help bridge the gap between abstract requirements and practical system functionality. They describe how different types of users (or "actors") will interact with the system to achieve specific goals. In the context of a graph-based system, these narratives assist in clarifying how data entities and relationships should be modeled and queried.

Use Cases

Definition:
A use case is a description of a specific interaction between a user and the system that results in a useful outcome. Use cases are usually documented in a structured format and focus on the steps involved in accomplishing a task.

Key Elements of a Use Case:

- **Title:** A brief name for the use case.

- **Actor(s):** Who is involved (e.g., end-users, system administrators).
- **Preconditions:** What must be true or completed before the use case begins.
- **Basic Flow:** The normal sequence of steps taken to achieve the goal.
- **Alternate Flows:** Variations or exceptions to the normal sequence.
- **Postconditions:** The state of the system after the use case is completed.

Example: E-commerce Product Recommendation Use Case

- **Title:** Generate Personalized Product Recommendations
- **Actor:** Customer
- **Preconditions:**
  - The customer is logged in.
  - The system has access to the customer's purchase history and browsing data.
- **Basic Flow:**

  0. The customer accesses the recommendations page.
  1. The system queries the knowledge graph to retrieve products linked to the customer's interests and previous purchases.
  2. The system displays a list of recommended products.

- **Alternate Flow:**
  - If no recommendations are found, the system displays popular products or prompts the customer to explore categories.
- **Postconditions:**
  - The customer sees a personalized set of product recommendations, which may lead to further interactions (e.g., product clicks, purchases).

User Stories

Definition:
User stories are short, simple descriptions written from the perspective of the end-user. They focus on the value delivered by the system rather than the technical details.

Format:
A common template for a user story is:
"As a [type of user], I want [an action] so that [a benefit/a value]."

Example: E-commerce Recommendation User Story

- **User Story:**
  "As a frequent shopper, I want to receive personalized product recommendations based on my browsing and purchase history so that I can quickly find items I am interested in."

Table: Comparison of Use Cases and User Stories

Aspect	Use Cases	User Stories
Detail Level	Detailed step-by-step interactions	Brief, high-level narrative
Focus	Specific system interactions and flows	User goals and the value of the functionality
Audience	Developers, testers, business analysts	End-users and product owners
Documentation Format	Structured (title, actor, preconditions, flows, postconditions)	Simple, conversational (template-based)

Practical Approach

1. **Workshops and Interviews:**
   Engage stakeholders through workshops and interviews to gather detailed requirements and identify key interactions.
2. **Story Mapping:**
   Use story mapping techniques to visualize the user journey. This helps in organizing and prioritizing use cases and user stories.
3. **Iterative Refinement:**
   Regularly review and refine both use cases and user stories as new requirements emerge or business processes evolve.

Summary of 6.4

Developing detailed use cases and concise user stories is essential to capturing how the system will be used in real-world scenarios. These narratives serve as a guide for modeling data entities and their interactions within a graph-based system, ensuring that technical designs align with business objectives and user needs.

6.5 Mapping Requirements to Graph Structures

Overview

Mapping requirements to graph structures involves translating the functional and non-functional requirements, use cases, and user stories into a data model that accurately represents the domain. In a graph-based system, this means determining which entities become nodes, how relationships are represented as edges, and what attributes need to be captured as properties.

Steps to Map Requirements to Graph Structures

1. **Extract Entities and Relationships:**
   o Review use cases and user stories to identify the key entities (e.g., Customer, Product, Order) and the relationships (e.g., places, contains, writes).
   o Create an initial list or diagram that shows these entities and relationships.
2. **Define Node and Edge Properties:**
   o For each entity, determine what attributes are essential. For instance, a Customer node may have properties like name, email, and loyalty status.
   o For each relationship, define any necessary properties. For example, an Order might have a date or a total amount on the edge that links it to a Customer.
3. **Determine Bounded Contexts and Aggregates:**
   o Use the Domain-Driven Design principles outlined earlier to identify bounded contexts. This helps in grouping related entities and relationships into aggregates.
   o Each aggregate can then be modeled as a subgraph, ensuring that the relationships within are tightly coupled.
4. **Visualize the Graph Structure:**
   o Create visual representations, such as Entity-Relationship Diagrams (ERDs) or graph sketches, to illustrate how the data will be interconnected.
   o Refine these diagrams based on stakeholder feedback.

5. **Validate Against Use Cases:**
   - Walk through the use cases and user stories using the visualized graph. Ensure that the model supports all required interactions and can answer the necessary queries.
   - Adjust the graph model as needed to close any gaps.

Example: Mapping an E-commerce Domain to a Graph Structure

Requirement Recap from Use Cases and User Stories:

- **Entities:** Customer, Product, Order, Review, Category
- **Relationships:**
  - A Customer places an Order.
  - An Order contains one or more Products.
  - A Customer writes a Review.
  - A Review is associated with a Product.
  - A Product belongs to a Category.

Graph Representation:

- **Nodes:**
  - Customer nodes with properties: name, email, loyalty status.
  - Product nodes with properties: name, price, description.
  - Order nodes with properties: order ID, date, total amount.
  - Review nodes with properties: rating, comment, date.
  - Category nodes with properties: category name, description.
- **Edges:**
  - "places" edge between Customer and Order.
  - "contains" edge between Order and Product.
  - "writes" edge between Customer and Review.
  - "reviews" edge between Review and Product.
  - "belongs to" edge between Product and Category.

Table: Mapping E-commerce Requirements to Graph Structures

Requirement	Graph Element	Properties/Attributes	Example
Customer details	Node	Name, Email, Loyalty Status	`"Customer: John Doe"`

Requirement	Graph Element	Properties/Attributes	Example
Product information	Node	Name, Price, Description	`"Product: Smartphone"`
Order information	Node	Order ID, Date, Total Amount	`"Order: 1001"`
Review information	Node	Rating, Comment, Date	`"Review: R1"`
Category information	Node	Category Name, Description	`"Category: Electronics"`
Customer places an Order	Edge (relationship)	(May include order-specific metadata)	Edge from `"Customer: John Doe"` to `"Order: 1001"`
Order contains a Product	Edge (relationship)	(Quantity, if needed)	Edge from `"Order: 1001"` to `"Product: Smartphone"`
Customer writes a Review	Edge (relationship)	(Date of review, if not part of node properties)	Edge from `"Customer: John Doe"` to `"Review: R1"`
Review is associated with a Product	Edge (relationship)		Edge from `"Review: R1"` to `"Product: Smartphone"`
Product belongs to a Category	Edge (relationship)		Edge from `"Product: Smartphone"` to `"Category: Electronics"`

Code Example: Implementing the E-commerce Graph in Python

Below is a complete Python code snippet using the `networkx` library that maps the e-commerce requirements to a graph structure.

```python
python

import networkx as nx
import matplotlib.pyplot as plt
```

```python
# Create a directed graph to capture relationships clearly
ecommerce_graph = nx.DiGraph()

# Add nodes with attributes for each key entity
ecommerce_graph.add_node("Customer: John Doe",
type="Customer", email="john@example.com", loyalty="Gold")
ecommerce_graph.add_node("Product: Smartphone",
type="Product", price=699, description="Latest model
smartphone")
ecommerce_graph.add_node("Product: Headphones",
type="Product", price=199, description="Noise-cancelling
headphones")
ecommerce_graph.add_node("Order: 1001", type="Order",
date="2025-01-15", total=898)
ecommerce_graph.add_node("Review: R1", type="Review",
rating=5, comment="Excellent product!")
ecommerce_graph.add_node("Category: Electronics",
type="Category", description="Electronic devices and
accessories")

# Add edges to represent relationships
ecommerce_graph.add_edge("Customer: John Doe", "Order: 1001",
relationship="places")
ecommerce_graph.add_edge("Order: 1001", "Product:
Smartphone", relationship="contains")
ecommerce_graph.add_edge("Order: 1001", "Product:
Headphones", relationship="contains")
ecommerce_graph.add_edge("Customer: John Doe", "Review: R1",
relationship="writes")
ecommerce_graph.add_edge("Review: R1", "Product: Smartphone",
relationship="reviews")
ecommerce_graph.add_edge("Product: Smartphone", "Category:
Electronics", relationship="belongs to")
ecommerce_graph.add_edge("Product: Headphones", "Category:
Electronics", relationship="belongs to")

# Visualize the graph
plt.figure(figsize=(12, 8))
pos = nx.spring_layout(ecommerce_graph)
nx.draw(ecommerce_graph, pos, with_labels=True,
node_color='lightblue', edge_color='gray', node_size=3000,
font_size=10)
edge_labels = nx.get_edge_attributes(ecommerce_graph,
'relationship')
nx.draw_networkx_edge_labels(ecommerce_graph, pos,
edge_labels=edge_labels, font_color='red')
plt.title("E-commerce Graph Structure Mapped from
Requirements")
plt.show()
```

Explanation:

- **Nodes and Attributes:**
  Each node represents an entity in the e-commerce domain. Attributes such as email, price, date, etc., capture essential details.
- **Edges and Relationships:**
  Directed edges show how entities are interconnected, reflecting the real-world flows like a customer placing an order or a product belonging to a category.
- **Visualization:**
  The graph is visualized using Matplotlib, with edge labels indicating the relationship types.

Summary of 6.5

Mapping requirements to graph structures is the process of transforming abstract business needs and user interactions into a concrete data model. By identifying entities, defining relationships, and determining the necessary attributes, you create a blueprint that guides the implementation of the graph-based system. This process ensures that every requirement is represented in the data model, enabling the system to support the desired use cases effectively.

.

Chapter 7: Data Modeling and Ontology Design

Designing effective knowledge graphs and graph-based systems begins with solid data modeling and well-structured ontologies. In this chapter, we cover the core principles of ontology design, the steps involved in building a conceptual model, and the importance of taxonomies, hierarchies, and semantic layers. This process is essential for creating data structures that are both semantically rich and easily navigable.

7.1 Principles of Ontology Design

Ontology design involves creating formal representations of knowledge within a domain. A well-designed ontology provides a shared vocabulary, captures the relationships between concepts, and enables reasoning over data. Here are some key principles to follow:

1. Clarity and Consistency

- **Definition:**
  The ontology should have clear definitions for all classes and properties. Each term must be defined unambiguously to avoid confusion.
- **Best Practices:**
  - Use concise and precise language.
  - Maintain consistent naming conventions across the ontology.

2. Modularity and Reusability

- **Definition:**
  Divide the ontology into manageable, modular components that can be reused or extended as the domain evolves.
- **Best Practices:**
  - Create separate modules for different subdomains or bounded contexts.
  - Reuse existing ontologies (e.g., schema.org, FOAF) where applicable.

3. Extensibility

- **Definition:**
  Design the ontology to be extensible so that it can accommodate future changes without major restructuring.
- **Best Practices:**
  - Use inheritance and subclassing to allow new classes to extend existing ones.
  - Define properties in a generic way that permits additional details later.

4. Minimal Commitment

- **Definition:**
  Include only the essential concepts and relationships needed for the domain. Avoid over-complicating the ontology with unnecessary details.
- **Best Practices:**
  - Start with a simple core and gradually add more complexity as required.
  - Ensure that every class and property has a clear purpose.

5. Separation of Concerns

- **Definition:**
  Separate different aspects of the domain into distinct layers or modules. This helps manage complexity and improves maintainability.
- **Best Practices:**
  - Divide the ontology into layers such as core classes, domain-specific extensions, and application-specific annotations.

Table: Key Principles of Ontology Design

Principle	Description	Best Practice
Clarity and Consistency	Ensure all terms are well-defined and consistently named.	Use clear definitions and adhere to naming conventions.

Principle	Description	Best Practice
Modularity and Reusability	Divide the ontology into modular components for reuse and extension.	Create separate modules and reuse established vocabularies.
Extensibility	Design to allow easy addition of new concepts without major changes.	Use inheritance and generic property definitions.
Minimal Commitment	Include only essential concepts and relationships.	Start with a core model and extend gradually.
Separation of Concerns	Organize the ontology into distinct layers or modules.	Use layered architecture to separate core, domain, and application data.

7.2 Building a Conceptual Model

A conceptual model is a high-level representation of the domain that identifies key entities, relationships, and constraints. It serves as the blueprint for the ontology and helps ensure that the final graph-based system aligns with business needs.

Steps to Build a Conceptual Model

1. **Domain Analysis**
   o **Objective:**
     Understand the domain by reviewing requirements, use cases, and user stories.
   o **Actions:**
     ▪ Conduct interviews and workshops with domain experts.
     ▪ Gather and analyze existing documentation and data sources.
2. **Identify Key Entities and Relationships**
   o **Objective:**
     Determine which concepts (entities) are fundamental to the domain and how they interrelate.
   o **Actions:**
     ▪ List all relevant entities (e.g., Customer, Product, Order).

- Map out relationships between entities (e.g., a Customer places an Order).
3. **Define Attributes and Constraints**
    o **Objective:**
      Specify the properties (attributes) of each entity and any constraints that apply.
    o **Actions:**
        - For each entity, determine the key attributes (e.g., for a Customer: name, email).
        - Identify any constraints or rules (e.g., a Customer must have a unique email).
4. **Visualize the Model**
    o **Objective:**
      Create diagrams that visually represent the entities, relationships, and constraints.
    o **Actions:**
        - Use Entity-Relationship Diagrams (ERDs) or UML diagrams.
        - Iterate on the diagrams with stakeholder feedback.
5. **Refine the Model**
    o **Objective:**
      Validate and adjust the model to ensure completeness and accuracy.
    o **Actions:**
        - Compare the model against use cases and user stories.
        - Make necessary revisions based on domain expert feedback.

Example: Conceptual Model for an E-commerce Domain

Key Entities:

- **Customer:** Attributes include name, email, and loyalty status.
- **Product:** Attributes include name, price, and description.
- **Order:** Attributes include order ID, date, and total amount.
- **Review:** Attributes include rating, comment, and date.
- **Category:** Attributes include category name and description.

Relationships:

- A Customer places an Order.
- An Order contains one or more Products.

- A Customer writes a Review for a Product.
- A Product belongs to a Category.

Diagram Representation (Conceptual)

```csharp
    [Customer]
        |
   (places)
        |
    [Order]
        |
   (contains)
        |
    [Product] <-- (belongs to) --> [Category]
        |
   (reviews)
        |
    [Review]
```

Summary of 7.2

Building a conceptual model is a critical step in designing an ontology. It involves analyzing the domain, identifying key entities and relationships, defining attributes, and visualizing the data structure. This model serves as the foundation for the detailed ontology and ensures that the final design meets the needs of the domain.

7.3 Taxonomies, Hierarchies, and Semantic Layers

Semantic organization of data often involves creating taxonomies and hierarchies that provide structure and meaning. These elements help in categorizing information and establishing relationships at multiple levels of granularity.

Taxonomies

Definition:
A taxonomy is a classification system that organizes entities into a hierarchy of categories or classes. It typically follows a parent-child structure.

Example:
In an e-commerce domain, a product taxonomy might classify items into categories such as Electronics, Clothing, and Home & Kitchen.

Table: Sample Product Taxonomy

Category	Subcategories
Electronics	Smartphones, Laptops, Televisions
Clothing	Men's, Women's, Children's
Home & Kitchen	Appliances, Furniture, Decor

Hierarchies

Definition:
Hierarchies are similar to taxonomies but can include more complex relationships. They define the levels of abstraction and organization within a domain.

Example:
An organizational hierarchy might include levels such as CEO, Manager, and Employee.

Semantic Layers

Definition:
Semantic layers refer to the different levels of abstraction and meaning that can be applied to data. In a knowledge graph, semantic layers can distinguish between:

- **Core Concepts:** Fundamental entities that are central to the domain.
- **Derived Concepts:** Concepts that are inferred or derived from core data.
- **Contextual Annotations:** Additional information that provides context but is not essential to the core model.

Use in Ontologies:

- **Core Layer:**
  Contains the essential classes and properties (e.g., Customer, Product).
- **Extended Layer:**
  Includes additional details and relationships (e.g., Customer loyalty programs, Product reviews).
- **Application-Specific Layer:**
  Contains annotations or metadata that are specific to a particular application or use case.

Benefits of Organizing Data with Taxonomies, Hierarchies, and Semantic Layers

- **Improved Query Performance:**
  A well-structured hierarchy makes it easier to perform targeted queries.
- **Enhanced Discoverability:**
  Users can navigate through categories and subcategories to find relevant information.
- **Scalability:**
  A modular semantic structure allows for the addition of new categories and relationships without disrupting existing models.

Practical Example: Representing a Taxonomy in Turtle

Below is an example of how to represent a simple product taxonomy using Turtle syntax in RDF.

```turtle

@prefix schema: <http://schema.org/> .
@prefix ex: <http://example.org/> .

# Define classes for product categories
ex:Electronics a schema:Category ;
    schema:name "Electronics" .

ex:Smartphones a schema:Category ;
    schema:name "Smartphones" ;
    schema:parentCategory ex:Electronics .

ex:Laptops a schema:Category ;
```

```
    schema:name "Laptops" ;
    schema:parentCategory ex:Electronics .

ex:Clothing a schema:Category ;
    schema:name "Clothing" .

ex:MensClothing a schema:Category ;
    schema:name "Men's Clothing" ;
    schema:parentCategory ex:Clothing .
```

Explanation:

- **Namespaces:**
  The prefixes define the namespaces for schema.org and our custom vocabulary.
- **Classes and Properties:**
  Categories such as Electronics, Smartphones, and Laptops are defined. The property `schema:parentCategory` is used to establish the hierarchical relationship.
- **Hierarchy:**
  The example shows that Smartphones and Laptops are subcategories of Electronics, and Men's Clothing is a subcategory of Clothing.

Summary of 7.3

Taxonomies, hierarchies, and semantic layers are essential components of effective data modeling and ontology design. They provide structure to the data by categorizing and organizing entities into meaningful groups and levels. This layered approach not only aids in data discovery and query performance but also ensures that the ontology remains flexible and scalable as the domain evolves.

7.4 Aligning Domain Models with Graph Structures

Overview

Aligning your domain model with graph structures is the process of translating a high-level conceptual model—comprising key entities, relationships, and attributes—into a concrete graph-based data representation. This step is crucial because it ensures that the logical model derived from business requirements is accurately reflected in the technical implementation. A well-aligned graph model enables efficient querying, data integration, and reasoning.

Key Considerations

1. **Mapping Entities to Nodes:**
   - **Definition:**
     Each key entity identified in the domain model (such as Customer, Product, Order, etc.) should be represented as a node in the graph.
   - **Attributes as Node Properties:**
     The properties and attributes of each entity (like a customer's name, email, or loyalty status) become node properties.
2. **Representing Relationships as Edges:**
   - **Definition:**
     Relationships between entities are captured as edges connecting the corresponding nodes.
   - **Edge Properties:**
     If a relationship carries additional information (such as the date an order was placed or the quantity of a product ordered), these should be modeled as properties on the edge.
3. **Incorporating Hierarchies and Taxonomies:**
   - **Class Hierarchies:**
     Use inheritance or sub-classing to reflect hierarchical relationships. For example, if "Electronics" is a superclass and "Smartphones" is a subclass, this can be modeled with a "subclassOf" relationship.
   - **Semantic Layers:**
     Different layers (core, extended, application-specific) can be maintained by grouping related nodes or using tagging strategies.
4. **Maintaining Bounded Contexts:**
   - **Definition:**
     In domain-driven design, bounded contexts define areas of the domain that are modeled independently. When mapping to a graph, nodes within the same bounded context should be closely connected, while inter-context relationships are modeled with well-defined interfaces (edges).
   - **Example:**
     In an e-commerce system, customer data might be in one context and order data in another. An edge between

"Customer" and "Order" can denote the relationship while maintaining the separation of concerns.

Process for Alignment

1. **Review the Conceptual Model:**
   - o Revisit your ER diagrams or UML sketches.
   - o List all entities, relationships, and attributes.
2. **Define Graph Schema:**
   - o Determine the node types (labels) and edge types.
   - o Establish property names and data types for nodes and edges.
3. **Create a Mapping Document:**
   - o Develop a table that maps each element of your domain model to the corresponding graph element.
4. **Prototype the Graph:**
   - o Use a graph database or a library (e.g., Neo4j, NetworkX) to create a small-scale version of the graph.
   - o Validate the mapping with sample data and use cases.

Table: Mapping Domain Model to Graph Structure (E-commerce Example)

Domain Model Element	Graph Representation	Properties / Attributes	Example
Customer	Node	name, email, loyalty status	"Customer: John Doe" with properties: name="John Doe", email="john@example.com", loyalty="Gold"
Product	Node	name, price, description	"Product: Smartphone" with properties: price=699, description="Latest model"
Order	Node	orderID, date, total amount	"Order: 1001" with properties: date="2025-01-15", total=898
Review	Node	rating, comment, date	"Review: R1" with properties: rating=5, comment="Excellent!"

Domain Model Element	Graph Representation	Properties / Attributes	Example
Relationship (e.g., places)	Edge	May include order-specific details (e.g., timestamp)	Edge from `Customer: John Doe` to `Order: 1001` labeled `places`
Relationship (e.g., contains)	Edge	Could include quantity or other details	Edge from `Order: 1001` to `Product: Smartphone` labeled `contains`

Code Example: Prototyping an Aligned E-commerce Graph Using Python

Below is a Python code snippet using the `networkx` library that demonstrates how to map an e-commerce domain model to a graph structure:

```python
python

import networkx as nx
import matplotlib.pyplot as plt

# Create a directed graph to reflect directional
relationships
ecommerce_graph = nx.DiGraph()

# Define nodes with properties (entities)
ecommerce_graph.add_node("Customer: John Doe",
type="Customer", email="john@example.com", loyalty="Gold")
ecommerce_graph.add_node("Product: Smartphone",
type="Product", price=699, description="Latest model
smartphone")
ecommerce_graph.add_node("Order: 1001", type="Order",
date="2025-01-15", total=898)
ecommerce_graph.add_node("Review: R1", type="Review",
rating=5, comment="Excellent!")
ecommerce_graph.add_node("Category: Electronics",
type="Category", description="Electronic devices and
accessories")
```

```
# Define edges with relationship labels and optional
properties
ecommerce_graph.add_edge("Customer: John Doe", "Order: 1001",
relationship="places")
ecommerce_graph.add_edge("Order: 1001", "Product:
Smartphone", relationship="contains")
ecommerce_graph.add_edge("Customer: John Doe", "Review: R1",
relationship="writes")
ecommerce_graph.add_edge("Review: R1", "Product: Smartphone",
relationship="reviews")
ecommerce_graph.add_edge("Product: Smartphone", "Category:
Electronics", relationship="belongs to")

# Visualize the graph with labels
plt.figure(figsize=(12, 8))
pos = nx.spring_layout(ecommerce_graph)
nx.draw(ecommerce_graph, pos, with_labels=True,
node_color='lightblue', edge_color='gray', node_size=3000,
font_size=10)
edge_labels = nx.get_edge_attributes(ecommerce_graph,
'relationship')
nx.draw_networkx_edge_labels(ecommerce_graph, pos,
edge_labels=edge_labels, font_color='red')
plt.title("Aligned E-commerce Graph Structure")
plt.show()
```

Explanation:

- **Nodes:**
  Each node is added with a label indicating the entity (e.g., Customer, Product) and associated properties.
- **Edges:**
  Edges represent relationships such as "places" (customer to order) and "contains" (order to product). The labels on the edges help clarify the nature of the relationship.
- **Visualization:**
  The resulting graph visualization shows the mapped domain model, enabling stakeholders to verify that the conceptual model aligns with the technical graph structure.

7.5 Tools and Best Practices for Modeling

Overview

Selecting the right tools and adhering to best practices is essential for effective data modeling and ontology design. The right tools can facilitate collaboration, simplify complex tasks, and ensure that the model remains accurate and maintainable as the domain evolves.

Tools for Data Modeling and Ontology Design

1. **Protégé:**
   - **Description:**
     An open-source ontology editor widely used for creating and managing OWL ontologies.
   - **Features:**
     - Graphical user interface.
     - Support for importing and exporting in various formats (e.g., RDF/XML, Turtle).
     - Reasoning tools to check consistency and infer relationships.
   - **Use Cases:**
     Ideal for designing complex ontologies and collaborating with domain experts.
2. **TopBraid Composer:**
   - **Description:**
     A commercial tool for semantic modeling and ontology management.
   - **Features:**
     - Comprehensive support for RDF, OWL, and SPARQL.
     - Advanced visualization and editing capabilities.
   - **Use Cases:**
     Suitable for enterprise-level ontology management and integration projects.
3. **Graph Databases (e.g., Neo4j, Amazon Neptune):**
   - **Description:**
     Graph databases provide platforms to model, store, and query graph data.
   - **Features:**
     - Support for property graphs and RDF.
     - Query languages like Cypher (Neo4j) and SPARQL.
   - **Use Cases:**
     Useful for prototyping and deploying graph-based systems in production.
4. **Modeling Libraries (e.g., NetworkX, RDFLib):**

- o **Description:**
  Python libraries that allow you to programmatically create, manipulate, and visualize graphs and ontologies.
- o **Features:**
  - ▪ Easy integration with Python projects.
  - ▪ Extensive documentation and community support.
- o **Use Cases:**
  Ideal for rapid prototyping and academic research.

Best Practices for Modeling

1. **Start with a Core Model:**
   - o **Practice:**
     Begin with a minimal set of entities and relationships that capture the essential aspects of the domain.
   - o **Benefit:**
     Avoid over-complicating the model early on; refine and extend as needed.
2. **Iterative Development and Validation:**
   - o **Practice:**
     Model iteratively with continuous feedback from domain experts and stakeholders.
   - o **Benefit:**
     Early detection of misalignments between the conceptual model and business requirements ensures a more robust final design.
3. **Use Standardized Vocabularies:**
   - o **Practice:**
     Where possible, reuse existing ontologies and vocabularies (e.g., schema.org, FOAF).
   - o **Benefit:**
     Enhances interoperability, reduces duplication of effort, and leverages community best practices.
4. **Document the Model:**
   - o **Practice:**
     Maintain clear documentation, including diagrams, mapping tables, and annotations.
   - o **Benefit:**
     Facilitates maintenance, collaboration, and future enhancements.
5. **Leverage Visualization Tools:**

- o **Practice:**
  Use graphical visualization tools to represent the model and its relationships.
- o **Benefit:**
  Improves understanding and communication of complex structures.

Table: Tools and Their Key Features

Tool	Type	Key Features	Ideal Use Case
Protégé	Ontology Editor	GUI-based, OWL support, reasoning tools	Creating and managing complex ontologies
TopBraid Composer	Semantic Modeling	Enterprise features, advanced visualization	Enterprise-level ontology management
Neo4j	Graph Database	Cypher query language, robust property graph support	Prototyping and deploying graph-based systems
NetworkX	Python Library	Programmatic graph creation, visualization tools	Rapid prototyping and academic research
RDFLib	Python Library	RDF parsing and serialization, SPARQL support	Working with RDF data and integrating with Python apps

Code Example: Using RDFLib for Ontology Modeling

Below is a simple example demonstrating how to create an RDF graph representing a part of an ontology using Python's RDFLib:

```python
from rdflib import Graph, Literal, RDF, URIRef, Namespace

# Create an RDF graph
g = Graph()

# Define namespaces
EX = Namespace("http://example.org/")
SCHEMA = Namespace("http://schema.org/")

# Bind the namespaces for readability
g.bind("ex", EX)
```

```
g.bind("schema", SCHEMA)

# Define classes using standard RDF/OWL conventions
# Define a basic ontology for a simple e-commerce domain
g.add((EX.Customer, RDF.type,
URIRef("http://www.w3.org/2002/07/owl#Class")))
g.add((EX.Product, RDF.type,
URIRef("http://www.w3.org/2002/07/owl#Class")))

# Add labels for clarity
g.add((EX.Customer, SCHEMA.name, Literal("Customer")))
g.add((EX.Product, SCHEMA.name, Literal("Product")))

# Serialize the ontology in Turtle format
print(g.serialize(format="turtle").decode("utf-8"))
```

Explanation:

- **Namespaces and Binding:**
  The namespaces EX and SCHEMA are defined and bound for clarity.
- **Class Definitions:**
  Classes for "Customer" and "Product" are added to the RDF graph
  using OWL's concept of a class.
- **Labels:**
  Labels are added to give human-readable names to the classes.
- **Serialization:**
  The RDF graph is serialized in Turtle format, which can be examined
  for accuracy and clarity.

Summary of 7.5

Aligning domain models with graph structures and employing the right tools
and best practices are critical for the successful implementation of graph-
based systems. By:

- **Mapping domain elements to nodes and edges,**
- **Using visualizations and prototyping tools to validate the model,**
  and
- **Following iterative, documented, and standardized approaches,**

you ensure that the final model is robust, flexible, and aligned with business
needs.

Chapter 8: System Architecture for Graph-Based Systems

Designing an effective graph-based system requires careful consideration of architecture, data integration strategies, and storage technologies. In this chapter, we explore three main areas:

1. **Architectural Patterns and Design Principles:**
   The fundamental building blocks and design strategies that ensure scalability, maintainability, and performance.
2. **Data Ingestion and Integration Strategies:**
   Methods to extract, transform, and load data from diverse sources into a unified graph structure.
3. **Storage Solutions: Native Graph Databases vs. Multi-Model Approaches:**
   A comparison of storage options and their suitability for different use cases.

8.1 Architectural Patterns and Design Principles

Overview

When designing a graph-based system, architectural patterns and design principles provide a blueprint for ensuring that the system is robust, scalable, and adaptable to changing requirements. These patterns guide how components interact, how data flows through the system, and how services are organized.

Key Architectural Patterns

1. **Layered Architecture:**
   - **Description:**
     The system is divided into layers (e.g., presentation, business logic, data access) where each layer has a specific responsibility.

- o **Benefits:**
  Promotes separation of concerns, easier maintenance, and scalability.
- o **Example:**
  A web application might have a user interface layer, a service layer that processes graph queries, and a data layer that interacts with the graph database.

2. **Microservices Architecture:**
   - o **Description:**
     The system is decomposed into small, independent services that communicate via APIs.
   - o **Benefits:**
     Enhances scalability, allows independent deployment and development, and improves fault isolation.
   - o **Example:**
     A graph-based recommendation system may consist of separate microservices for user management, recommendation generation, and analytics.

3. **Event-Driven Architecture:**
   - o **Description:**
     The system is designed around the production, detection, and reaction to events.
   - o **Benefits:**
     Facilitates real-time processing, decouples components, and improves responsiveness.
   - o **Example:**
     In a social network graph, events such as "user added a friend" trigger updates in recommendation and notification services.

4. **Polyglot Persistence:**
   - o **Description:**
     Employing different storage technologies to handle different data types and use cases within the same system.
   - o **Benefits:**
     Optimizes performance by leveraging the strengths of each database technology.
   - o **Example:**
     A system might use a native graph database for relationship data and a document store for unstructured content.

Design Principles

1. **Separation of Concerns:**
   - **Description:**
     Isolate different aspects of the system (e.g., query processing, data storage, presentation) to reduce complexity.
   - **Implementation:**
     Use modular components and well-defined interfaces.
2. **Scalability:**
   - **Description:**
     Design the system to handle growth in data volume and query load.
   - **Implementation:**
     Adopt distributed architectures, caching strategies, and load balancing.
3. **Maintainability:**
   - **Description:**
     Ensure that the system can be easily updated and maintained.
   - **Implementation:**
     Use clear abstractions, modular design, and comprehensive documentation.
4. **Resilience:**
   - **Description:**
     Build the system to withstand failures and recover gracefully.
   - **Implementation:**
     Incorporate redundancy, failover mechanisms, and monitoring.

Table: Summary of Architectural Patterns

Pattern	Description	Benefits	Example Use Case
Layered Architecture	Separation into distinct layers	Improved modularity and easier maintenance	Web applications with clear UI, service, and data layers
Microservices Architecture	Independent services communicating via APIs	Scalability, independent deployment, fault isolation	Large-scale distributed systems, recommendation engines

Pattern	Description	Benefits	Example Use Case
Event-Driven Architecture	Reactive, asynchronous processing of events	Real-time processing, decoupling, responsiveness	Social networks, notification systems
Polyglot Persistence	Use of multiple databases for different needs	Optimized performance, data-specific storage	Systems requiring both graph and document storage

Summary of 8.1

Architectural patterns and design principles are critical for creating graph-based systems that are robust, scalable, and maintainable. By adopting a layered approach, leveraging microservices and event-driven designs, and ensuring separation of concerns and resilience, you lay the foundation for a system that can evolve with changing requirements and data volumes.

8.2 Data Ingestion and Integration Strategies

Overview

Data ingestion and integration are vital processes for populating a graph-based system with high-quality, interconnected data. These strategies involve extracting data from various sources, transforming it to fit the graph model, and loading it into the system.

Key Strategies

1. **Extract, Transform, Load (ETL):**
   - **Extract:**
     Gather data from multiple sources (e.g., relational databases, CSV files, APIs).
   - **Transform:**
     Clean, normalize, and map the data to the graph's schema.
   - **Load:**
     Insert the transformed data into the graph database.

- o **Example:**
  An e-commerce system may extract customer and order data from an SQL database, transform it into nodes and edges, and load it into a graph database.
2. **Change Data Capture (CDC):**
   - o **Description:**
     Monitor data sources for changes and incrementally update the graph.
   - o **Benefits:**
     Ensures that the graph remains current with minimal latency.
   - o **Example:**
     A CDC mechanism can detect new transactions in a financial database and update the corresponding relationships in the graph.
3. **Streaming Data Integration:**
   - o **Description:**
     Use real-time streaming platforms (e.g., Apache Kafka) to ingest data continuously.
   - o **Benefits:**
     Supports real-time analytics and dynamic graph updates.
   - o **Example:**
     Social media feeds or sensor data can be streamed into a graph system to update user interactions or IoT networks in near real-time.
4. **API-Driven Ingestion:**
   - o **Description:**
     Utilize REST or GraphQL APIs to retrieve and integrate data from external sources.
   - o **Benefits:**
     Facilitates integration with cloud services and third-party applications.
   - o **Example:**
     Pulling product reviews from an external API and linking them to product nodes in the graph.

Data Integration Techniques

- **Data Mapping:**
  Define how source data fields map to graph entities and relationships.
- **Data Cleansing:**
  Remove duplicates, resolve inconsistencies, and ensure data quality.

- **Batch vs. Real-Time Processing:**
  Choose batch processing for historical data loads and real-time processing for streaming or continuously updating data.

Table: Comparison of Data Ingestion Strategies

Strategy	Description	Benefits	Example Use Case
ETL	Batch processing of data extraction, transformation, and loading	Robust data transformation and quality control	Loading historical sales data into a graph database
Change Data Capture	Incremental updates by monitoring data changes	Minimal latency, near real-time updates	Financial transaction updates, inventory management
Streaming Data	Continuous ingestion using streaming platforms	Real-time analytics, dynamic graph updates	Social media data, IoT sensor streams
API-Driven Ingestion	Using APIs to pull data from external sources	Easy integration with cloud services, flexibility	Integrating third-party reviews, market data feeds

Code Example: Basic ETL with Python and NetworkX

Below is a simple Python code example that simulates an ETL process to load e-commerce data into a graph using the `networkx` library.

```python
python

import networkx as nx
import csv

# Create an empty graph
G = nx.DiGraph()

# Simulate Extract: Read data from CSV files (here we define
data inline for demonstration)
customers = [
    {"id": "C001", "name": "John Doe", "email":
"john@example.com"},
    {"id": "C002", "name": "Jane Smith", "email":
"jane@example.com"}
```

```
]

orders = [
    {"order_id": "O1001", "customer_id": "C001", "date":
"2025-01-15", "total": 250},
    {"order_id": "O1002", "customer_id": "C002", "date":
"2025-01-16", "total": 150}
]

# Transform and Load: Add customers as nodes and orders as
nodes/edges
for customer in customers:
    G.add_node(customer["id"], type="Customer",
name=customer["name"], email=customer["email"])

for order in orders:
    G.add_node(order["order_id"], type="Order",
date=order["date"], total=order["total"])
    # Create edge from customer to order
    G.add_edge(order["customer_id"], order["order_id"],
relationship="places")

# Visualize the graph
import matplotlib.pyplot as plt
plt.figure(figsize=(8, 6))
pos = nx.spring_layout(G)
nx.draw(G, pos, with_labels=True, node_color='lightgreen',
edge_color='gray', node_size=2000, font_size=10)
edge_labels = nx.get_edge_attributes(G, 'relationship')
nx.draw_networkx_edge_labels(G, pos, edge_labels=edge_labels,
font_color='red')
plt.title("ETL Example: Customers and Orders")
plt.show()
```

Explanation:

- **Extract:**
  Data is simulated with inline lists for customers and orders.
- **Transform:**
  Data fields are mapped to node properties (e.g., customer ID, name, email).
- **Load:**
  Customers and orders are added as nodes, and an edge labeled "places" connects customers to their orders.
- **Visualization:**
  The graph is visualized using Matplotlib to confirm that the data has been ingested correctly.

Summary of 8.2

Effective data ingestion and integration strategies are critical for building robust graph-based systems. Whether using batch ETL processes, real-time streaming, CDC, or API-driven ingestion, it is essential to ensure data quality, consistency, and timeliness. These strategies enable the creation of a unified, up-to-date graph that accurately reflects the underlying data sources.

8.3 Storage Solutions: Native Graph Databases vs. Multi-Model Approaches

Overview

Choosing the right storage solution is fundamental to the performance and scalability of a graph-based system. Two primary approaches are:

- **Native Graph Databases:**
  Databases designed specifically for storing and querying graph data.
- **Multi-Model Databases:**
  Databases that support multiple data models (e.g., graph, document, key-value) within a single system.

Native Graph Databases

Description:
Native graph databases are purpose-built for handling graph structures. They optimize storage, indexing, and querying for nodes and relationships.

Key Features:

- **Efficient Graph Traversal:**
  Optimized for complex queries involving deep relationships.
- **Flexible Schema:**
  Schema-less or schema-flexible, allowing easy evolution of the data model.
- **Examples:**
  Neo4j, GraphDB, Amazon Neptune.

Pros:

- High performance for graph-specific operations.
- Rich graph query languages (e.g., Cypher for Neo4j, SPARQL for RDF-based systems).

Cons:

- May require a separate system for non-graph data.
- Specialized knowledge required to manage and optimize.

Multi-Model Databases

Description:
Multi-model databases support multiple data models within a single system. They offer the flexibility to store graph data alongside other types (e.g., documents, key-values).

Key Features:

- **Versatility:**
  Ability to handle different data types in one platform.
- **Unified Querying:**
  Support for querying across models, often with a unified query language or API.
- **Examples:**
  ArangoDB, OrientDB, Microsoft Azure Cosmos DB.

Pros:

- Simplifies architecture by reducing the number of separate systems.
- Facilitates integration of diverse data types.

Cons:

- May not be as highly optimized for graph operations compared to native graph databases.
- Complexity in tuning performance for different models.

Comparison Table: Native Graph Databases vs. Multi-Model Approaches

Aspect	Native Graph Databases	Multi-Model Databases
Performance	Highly optimized for graph queries and traversals	Versatile but may not match native graph performance
Schema Flexibility	Very flexible and schema-less	Flexible across multiple models
Query Languages	Specialized (Cypher, SPARQL)	Unified or multiple query languages (e.g., AQL for ArangoDB)
Integration	Focused on graph data	Supports various data types in a single platform
Complexity	Requires expertise in graph databases	May involve trade-offs between models

Code Example: Querying with Neo4j (Native Graph Database) vs. ArangoDB (Multi-Model)

Below is a conceptual example that demonstrates how one might query a native graph database (Neo4j) using Cypher and a multi-model database (ArangoDB) using AQL.

Neo4j Cypher Query Example:

```cypher
cypher

// Neo4j: Find all customers who placed orders for products
in the Electronics category
MATCH (c:Customer)-[:PLACES]->(o:Order)-[:CONTAINS]-
>(p:Product)-[:BELONGS_TO]->(cat:Category {name:
"Electronics"})
RETURN c.name AS Customer, o.orderId AS OrderID, p.name AS
Product
```

ArangoDB AQL Query Example:

```aql
aql

// ArangoDB: Query the graph for customers and their orders
with products in Electronics category
```

```
FOR customer IN Customers
  FOR order IN Orders
    FILTER customer._id == order.customerId
    FOR product IN Products
      FILTER order._id IN product.orderIds
      FOR category IN Categories
        FILTER product.categoryId == category._id AND
category.name == "Electronics"
        RETURN {Customer: customer.name, OrderID:
order.orderId, Product: product.name}
```

Explanation:

- **Neo4j Example:**
  The Cypher query uses pattern matching to traverse the graph from customers to orders, products, and categories, returning the relevant information.
- **ArangoDB Example:**
  The AQL query demonstrates how to join across different collections (representing different models) and filter by category name. It shows the versatility of a multi-model database in handling graph-like queries.

Summary of 8.3

Choosing between native graph databases and multi-model databases depends on the specific requirements and constraints of your project. Native graph databases offer superior performance and specialized features for graph processing, while multi-model databases provide versatility and integration across various data types. Evaluating the trade-offs between performance, complexity, and integration needs is key to selecting the right storage solution for your graph-based system.

8.4 Middleware, APIs, and Service Layers

Overview

In a modern graph-based system, middleware, APIs, and service layers play a critical role in connecting the graph database to client applications and external systems. They serve as the glue that integrates various components, ensuring seamless data flow, abstraction of underlying complexities, and consistent access to data. In this section, we explore the functions, benefits, and best practices associated with these components.

Middleware

Definition:
Middleware is software that acts as an intermediary between different applications, databases, and services. It facilitates communication, data transformation, and process management.

Key Roles of Middleware in Graph-Based Systems:

- **Data Transformation and Integration:**
  Middleware can transform data from various sources into the format required by the graph database. For example, it may convert data from a relational database into a set of nodes and edges.
- **Routing and Orchestration:**
  It manages the routing of requests between clients and backend services. In an event-driven system, middleware can also handle message brokering.
- **Caching and Performance Optimization:**
  Middleware can cache frequent queries or results to reduce latency and improve response times.

Common Middleware Solutions:

- Apache Kafka for event streaming and real-time data integration.
- Enterprise Service Bus (ESB) solutions like MuleSoft or Apache Camel for orchestrating service interactions.
- Custom middleware developed in languages such as Node.js, Python, or Java that leverages RESTful services.

APIs (Application Programming Interfaces)

Definition:
APIs are sets of rules and protocols for building and interacting with software applications. They provide an abstraction layer that allows client applications to interact with the graph database without knowing its internal details.

Types of APIs for Graph Systems:

- **REST APIs:**
  Use HTTP methods (GET, POST, PUT, DELETE) to expose endpoints that perform specific operations on graph data.
- **GraphQL:**
  A query language that enables clients to request exactly the data they need, often resulting in reduced data transfer overhead.
- **SPARQL Endpoints:**
  Specialized APIs that allow querying of RDF-based graph databases using the SPARQL language.

Benefits of Using APIs:

- **Abstraction:**
  Hides the complexity of the underlying graph structure and query language.
- **Standardization:**
  Promotes consistency in how data is accessed and manipulated.
- **Interoperability:**
  Allows integration with external systems, mobile applications, and web clients.

Service Layers

Definition:
Service layers are logical layers in a software architecture that encapsulate business logic and provide a clear interface between the presentation (client) layer and the data access layer (graph database).

Key Functions:

- **Business Logic Implementation:**
  Encapsulates domain-specific rules and operations. For instance, calculating recommendations based on graph traversals.
- **Abstraction:**
  Provides a higher-level API that abstracts the details of graph queries and data manipulation.
- **Security and Validation:**
  Implements authentication, authorization, and input validation before data reaches the graph database.

- **Aggregation:**
  Combines data from multiple sources or services to deliver a unified response to the client.

Architectural Diagram (Conceptual)

Below is a textual representation of the architectural flow involving middleware, APIs, and service layers:

pgsql

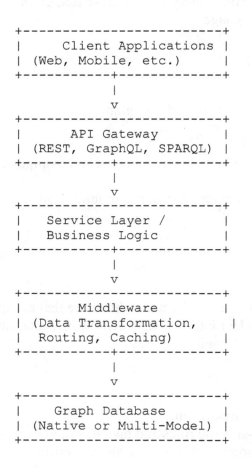

```
        +------------------------+
        |    Client Applications |
        |  (Web, Mobile, etc.)   |
        +-----------+------------+
                    |
                    v
        +------------------------+
        |     API Gateway        |
        |  (REST, GraphQL, SPARQL) |
        +-----------+------------+
                    |
                    v
        +--------------------------+
        |    Service Layer /       |
        |    Business Logic        |
        +-----------+------------+
                    |
                    v
        +------------------------+
        |      Middleware        |
        |  (Data Transformation, |
        |   Routing, Caching)    |
        +-----------+------------+
                    |
                    v
        +------------------------+
        |    Graph Database      |
        |  (Native or Multi-Model) |
        +------------------------+
```

Best Practices

- **Keep APIs Consistent:**
  Design APIs that follow a consistent naming and versioning strategy to ensure backward compatibility.

- **Use Standard Protocols:**
  Where possible, use widely adopted protocols (e.g., REST, GraphQL, SPARQL) to promote interoperability.
- **Implement Caching:**
  Leverage caching mechanisms at the middleware or API gateway level to reduce query load and improve performance.
- **Enforce Security:**
  Integrate authentication and authorization mechanisms within the service layer to protect sensitive data.

Code Example: Simple REST API for a Graph-Based System

Below is an example using Python's Flask framework to create a simple REST API that interacts with a graph database (using a simulated in-memory graph with NetworkX).

```python
python

from flask import Flask, jsonify, request
import networkx as nx

app = Flask(__name__)

# Create an example graph representing a simple social
network
G = nx.Graph()
G.add_node("Alice", type="Person")
G.add_node("Bob", type="Person")
G.add_edge("Alice", "Bob", relationship="friend_of")

@app.route("/api/person/<name>", methods=["GET"])
def get_person(name):
    if name in G.nodes:
        node_data = G.nodes[name]
        # Get neighbors (friends)
        friends = list(G.neighbors(name))
        return jsonify({
            "name": name,
            "attributes": node_data,
            "friends": friends
        })
    else:
        return jsonify({"error": "Person not found"}), 404

@app.route("/api/friendship", methods=["POST"])
def add_friendship():
    data = request.get_json()
```

```
    person1 = data.get("person1")
    person2 = data.get("person2")
    if person1 in G.nodes and person2 in G.nodes:
        G.add_edge(person1, person2,
relationship="friend_of")
        return jsonify({"message": "Friendship added"}), 201
    else:
        return jsonify({"error": "One or both persons not
found"}), 404

if __name__ == "__main__":
    app.run(debug=True)
```

Explanation:

- **API Endpoints:**
  Two endpoints are defined:
  - `GET /api/person/<name>` retrieves a person's details and friends.
  - `POST /api/friendship` adds a friendship between two people.
- **Middleware and Service Layer:**
  While this example is simplified, the Flask application acts as an API gateway and service layer, abstracting direct graph interactions.
- **Graph Database Simulation:**
  NetworkX simulates a graph database for demonstration purposes. In a production system, you would connect to a native graph database via an appropriate driver.

8.5 Security, Privacy, and Compliance Considerations

Overview

Security, privacy, and compliance are critical factors in designing any system that handles sensitive data. In graph-based systems, these considerations are especially important due to the interconnected nature of data, which can amplify the impact of vulnerabilities or breaches. This section discusses the key areas to address and strategies to implement robust security measures.

Key Security Considerations

1. **Authentication and Authorization:**
   - **Authentication:**
     Verify the identity of users or systems accessing the API and graph data.
   - **Authorization:**
     Define and enforce access control policies to ensure that users can only access data they are permitted to view or modify.
   - **Best Practices:**
     Use standards such as OAuth 2.0, OpenID Connect, or JWT (JSON Web Tokens) for authentication. Implement role-based access control (RBAC) to manage permissions.
2. **Data Encryption:**
   - **At Rest:**
     Encrypt data stored in the graph database to protect against unauthorized access if the storage media is compromised.
   - **In Transit:**
     Use TLS/SSL encryption for data transmitted over networks, ensuring that API calls and data exchanges are secure.
3. **Data Masking and Anonymization:**
   - **Definition:**
     Apply techniques to mask or anonymize sensitive data (e.g., personally identifiable information) to minimize risks in case of a data breach.
   - **Best Practices:**
     Ensure that sensitive fields are encrypted or replaced with pseudonymous identifiers where appropriate.
4. **Auditing and Monitoring:**
   - **Definition:**
     Implement logging and monitoring to track access and modifications to the graph data.
   - **Best Practices:**
     Use audit trails and real-time monitoring systems to detect and respond to suspicious activities.

Privacy Considerations

1. **Compliance with Regulations:**
   - **Regulatory Requirements:**
     Ensure compliance with data protection laws such as GDPR (General Data Protection Regulation), HIPAA (Health

Insurance Portability and Accountability Act), or CCPA (California Consumer Privacy Act).

- o **Best Practices:**
  Implement data retention policies, obtain explicit user consent, and provide mechanisms for data deletion or correction.

2. **Data Minimization:**
   - o **Definition:**
     Collect and retain only the data necessary for the system's operation.
   - o **Best Practices:**
     Regularly review data collection practices and remove any unnecessary or outdated data.

3. **User Transparency:**
   - o **Definition:**
     Clearly communicate to users what data is being collected, how it is used, and how it is protected.
   - o **Best Practices:**
     Provide privacy policies and user dashboards that allow users to view and control their data.

Compliance Considerations

1. **Standards and Certifications:**
   - o **Industry Standards:**
     Adhere to standards such as ISO/IEC 27001 for information security management.
   - o **Certifications:**
     Pursue certifications that demonstrate compliance with security and privacy standards.

2. **Regular Security Assessments:**
   - o **Penetration Testing:**
     Conduct regular security testing and vulnerability assessments to identify and remediate potential risks.
   - o **Compliance Audits:**
     Schedule audits to ensure that the system adheres to relevant regulatory requirements and internal policies.

\Table: Key Security, Privacy, and Compliance Measures

Measure	Description	Implementation
Authentication/Authorization	Ensure only authorized users can access data	OAuth 2.0, JWT, RBAC
Data Encryption	Protect data both at rest and in transit	TLS/SSL for transmission, AES for storage encryption
Data Masking/Anonymization	Obscure sensitive data to protect user privacy	Pseudonymization, redaction techniques
Auditing/Monitoring	Log and monitor access to detect suspicious activities	Audit trails, SIEM systems
Regulatory Compliance	Adhere to legal and regulatory requirements (GDPR, HIPAA, etc.)	Data retention policies, regular audits
User Transparency	Inform users about data usage and control mechanisms	Privacy policies, user dashboards

Code Example: Implementing Basic JWT Authentication in a Flask API

Below is a simplified example using Python's Flask framework to demonstrate basic JWT authentication for securing an API endpoint.

```python
from flask import Flask, request, jsonify
import jwt
import datetime
from functools import wraps

app = Flask(__name__)
app.config['SECRET_KEY'] = 'your_secret_key_here'
```

```python
# Decorator for verifying the JWT token
def token_required(f):
    @wraps(f)
    def decorated(*args, **kwargs):
        token = request.headers.get('x-access-token')
        if not token:
            return jsonify({'message': 'Token is missing!'}),
403
        try:
            data = jwt.decode(token,
app.config['SECRET_KEY'], algorithms=["HS256"])
            current_user = data['username']
        except Exception as e:
            return jsonify({'message': 'Token is invalid!',
'error': str(e)}), 403
        return f(current_user, *args, **kwargs)
    return decorated


# Endpoint to generate a token
@app.route('/login', methods=['POST'])
def login():
    auth_data = request.get_json()
    username = auth_data.get('username')
    password = auth_data.get('password')
    # Here, add real user verification logic; using a dummy
check for demonstration
    if username == 'admin' and password == 'password':
        token = jwt.encode({'username': username, 'exp':
datetime.datetime.utcnow() + datetime.timedelta(hours=1)},
                           app.config['SECRET_KEY'],
algorithm="HS256")
        return jsonify({'token': token})
    return jsonify({'message': 'Invalid credentials'}), 401


# Secured API endpoint
@app.route('/api/secure-data', methods=['GET'])
@token_required
def secure_data(current_user):
    return jsonify({'message': f'Hello, {current_user}. This
is secure data.'})


if __name__ == "__main__":
    app.run(debug=True)
```

Explanation:

- **JWT Setup:**
  The secret key is defined for encoding and decoding JWT tokens.

- **Token Generation:**
  The `/login` endpoint generates a token after validating user credentials (dummy check in this case).
- **Token Verification:**
  The `token_required` decorator checks for the presence of a valid token in the request header before allowing access to secured endpoints.
- **Secured Endpoint:**
  The `/api/secure-data` endpoint is protected, ensuring that only authenticated users can access it.

Summary of 8.5

Security, privacy, and compliance are fundamental aspects of designing graph-based systems. Key measures include robust authentication and authorization, data encryption, auditing, and adherence to regulatory requirements. By implementing these measures and using industry-standard tools and practices, organizations can protect sensitive data, build user trust, and ensure compliance with legal and regulatory frameworks.

Chapter 9: Scalability, Performance, and Maintenance

In graph-based systems, the complexity and interconnected nature of data demand careful planning for scalability, performance, and ongoing maintenance. This chapter discusses strategies and techniques to ensure that your graph-based system can grow to handle increasing data volumes and user loads while remaining efficient and responsive. We cover three main topics:

1. **Scaling Graph Databases and Distributed Systems**
2. **Performance Tuning and Optimization Techniques**
3. **Caching, Indexing, and Query Optimization**

9.1 Scaling Graph Databases and Distributed Systems

Overview

As data volume and query complexity grow, scaling a graph-based system becomes essential. Scaling can be achieved vertically (enhancing the capacity of a single machine) or horizontally (distributing data and processing across multiple machines). In distributed systems, data is partitioned across nodes to support concurrent operations and high availability.

Vertical Scaling vs. Horizontal Scaling

- **Vertical Scaling (Scaling Up):**
  - **Definition:**
    Increasing the resources (CPU, memory, storage) of a single machine.
  - **Advantages:**
    Simplicity in deployment and management.
  - **Limitations:**
    There is a physical limit to how much a single machine can be upgraded, and it can become a single point of failure.

- **Horizontal Scaling (Scaling Out):**
  - **Definition:**
    Distributing data and workload across multiple machines.
  - **Advantages:**
    Provides better fault tolerance, enables load balancing, and allows near-linear scalability.
  - **Challenges:**
    Requires mechanisms for data partitioning (sharding), replication, and consistency management.

Distributed Graph Databases

Modern graph databases often offer distributed architectures. Examples include:

- **Neo4j Fabric:**
  Enables horizontal scaling by partitioning data across multiple Neo4j instances.
- **Amazon Neptune:**
  A fully managed graph database that supports both RDF and Property Graph models with built-in clustering.
- **JanusGraph:**
  An open-source distributed graph database that can leverage various storage backends such as Apache Cassandra, HBase, or Google Cloud Bigtable.

Sharding and Replication

- **Sharding:**
  Dividing the graph data into smaller, manageable pieces (shards) that are distributed across multiple nodes. Each shard handles a subset of nodes and edges.
- **Replication:**
  Storing copies of data across different nodes to ensure high availability and fault tolerance. Replication can help in load balancing read operations and improving resilience.

Table: Vertical vs. Horizontal Scaling

Scaling Type	Definition	Advantages	Limitations
Vertical Scaling	Upgrading a single machine with more resources	Simpler to manage and deploy	Physical resource limits, single point of failure
Horizontal Scaling	Distributing data and workload across multiple machines	Improved fault tolerance, better scalability	Increased complexity in data partitioning and consistency management

Example Scenario: Scaling an E-commerce Graph Database

Imagine an e-commerce platform that uses a graph database to manage customers, products, and orders. As the number of users and transactions grows:

- **Sharding:**
  The customer and order data can be partitioned by geographic region, reducing the load on any single node.
- **Replication:**
  Data is replicated across multiple nodes to ensure that if one node fails, others can continue to serve queries.
- **Distributed Query Processing:**
  A distributed graph engine processes queries across shards, combining results to deliver near real-time responses.

9.2 Performance Tuning and Optimization Techniques

Overview

Performance tuning is a continuous process that involves monitoring, analyzing, and adjusting various aspects of a graph-based system to improve its responsiveness and efficiency. Key areas include query optimization, resource management, and configuration tuning.

Key Performance Tuning Areas

1. **Query Optimization:**
   o **Definition:**
     Improving the efficiency of graph queries to reduce response times and resource consumption.
   o **Techniques:**
     - Analyze query patterns to identify bottlenecks.
     - Refactor queries to minimize unnecessary traversals.
     - Use query profiling tools to understand performance characteristics.
2. **Resource Allocation:**
   o **Definition:**
     Ensuring that the system has sufficient CPU, memory, and I/O resources to handle the workload.
   o **Techniques:**
     - Adjust memory allocation parameters for the graph database.
     - Use load balancing to distribute query processing.
     - Monitor resource usage and scale up or out as needed.
3. **Configuration Tuning:**
   o **Definition:**
     Adjusting the configuration settings of the graph database and the underlying infrastructure to optimize performance.
   o **Techniques:**
     - Tuning cache sizes and timeouts.
     - Configuring garbage collection settings in JVM-based systems.
     - Optimizing disk I/O by selecting appropriate storage solutions.

Best Practices for Performance Tuning

- **Profiling and Benchmarking:**
  Regularly profile queries and benchmark system performance to identify areas for improvement.
- **Incremental Adjustments:**
  Make small, incremental changes to configuration settings and monitor the effects.
- **Automation:**
  Use automated monitoring and alerting tools to detect performance degradation and trigger scaling actions.

Code Example: Query Profiling in Neo4j (Using Cypher)

Below is an example of using Neo4j's built-in query profiling to analyze a query's performance.

```cypher
cypher

// Profile a query in Neo4j to analyze performance
PROFILE MATCH (c:Customer)-[:PLACES]->(o:Order)-[:CONTAINS]-
>(p:Product)
RETURN c.name, o.orderId, p.name
```

Explanation:

- **PROFILE Command:**
  The PROFILE command in Neo4j executes the query and provides detailed statistics about each operation, including execution time and resource usage.
- **Usage:**
  By examining the output, developers can identify which parts of the query are most expensive and optimize them accordingly.

9.3 Caching, Indexing, and Query Optimization

Overview

Caching and indexing are crucial for reducing query latency and improving the responsiveness of graph-based systems. Query optimization involves leveraging these techniques to speed up data retrieval and minimize computational overhead.

Caching Strategies

- **Result Caching:**
  - **Definition:**
    Store the results of frequently executed queries to avoid re-computation.
  - **Implementation:**
    Use in-memory caches such as Redis or built-in caching mechanisms in the graph database.

- **Object Caching:**
  - **Definition:**
    Cache individual nodes or subgraphs that are often accessed.
  - **Implementation:**
    Apply caching at the application level to reduce database load.

Indexing Techniques

- **Node Indexing:**
  - **Definition:**
    Create indexes on frequently queried node properties (e.g., customer ID, product name).
  - **Benefits:**
    Significantly speeds up lookup operations and filtering.
- **Edge Indexing:**
  - **Definition:**
    Index the properties of edges if they are used in query predicates.
  - **Benefits:**
    Improves performance for relationship-centric queries.

Query Optimization Techniques

1. **Optimized Query Patterns:**
   - **Practice:**
     Structure queries to reduce the number of nodes and relationships traversed.
   - **Example:**
     Use targeted match patterns in Cypher instead of broad searches.
2. **Selective Filtering:**
   - **Practice:**
     Apply filters early in the query to limit the dataset.
   - **Example:**
     Use WHERE clauses to restrict nodes based on indexed properties.
3. **Lazy Loading:**
   - **Practice:**
     Retrieve only the necessary data initially, and load additional details on demand.

o **Benefits:**
Reduces the amount of data transferred and processed.

Table: Caching and Indexing Techniques

Technique	Description	Benefits	Example
Result Caching	Storing the output of frequently executed queries	Reduces repetitive computation	Using Redis to cache a product recommendation query
Object Caching	Caching individual nodes or subgraphs	Lowers database load	Caching customer profile data in the application
Node Indexing	Creating indexes on node properties	Speeds up lookups and filtering	Indexing customer IDs and product names
Edge Indexing	Creating indexes on edge properties	Enhances performance of relationship queries	Indexing order date on relationships

Code Example: Creating an Index in Neo4j

Below is an example of how to create an index on a node property in Neo4j using Cypher.

cypher

```
// Create an index on the 'email' property of Customer nodes
in Neo4j
CREATE INDEX ON :Customer(email);
```

Explanation:

- **Index Creation:**
  The above Cypher command creates an index on the `email` property for nodes labeled as `Customer`.
- **Impact:**
  With this index, queries filtering on customer email will execute much faster.

9.4 Monitoring and Troubleshooting Graph Systems

Overview

Monitoring and troubleshooting are critical activities for maintaining the health and performance of graph-based systems. Given the complexity and interconnected nature of graph databases, it is essential to continuously track system metrics, diagnose issues, and resolve them promptly. In this section, we cover key monitoring metrics, common tools and techniques, and troubleshooting strategies tailored to graph systems.

Key Metrics to Monitor

Monitoring involves tracking various performance and health metrics that provide insight into how well your graph-based system is operating. Some key metrics include:

- **Query Performance:**
  - **Latency:** Time taken to execute queries.
  - **Throughput:** Number of queries processed per second.
  - **Query Execution Plan:** Detailed breakdown of the steps taken to execute a query.
- **Resource Utilization:**
  - **CPU Usage:** Percentage of CPU resources used by the graph database processes.
  - **Memory Usage:** Amount of RAM consumed by active operations, caching, and indexing.
  - **Disk I/O:** Rate of read and write operations to disk, crucial for systems that perform frequent data updates.
- **Network Performance:**
  - **Latency and Bandwidth:** Time and capacity for data transfer between distributed nodes, especially important in horizontally scaled systems.
- **Error Rates and Logs:**
  - **Application and System Logs:** Collection of errors, warnings, and informational messages that can indicate problems.
  - **Error Rates:** Frequency of failed queries or system errors.
- **Cache Hit/Miss Ratios:**

o **Cache Performance:** Metrics showing how often queries are served from cache versus hitting the underlying database.

Tools for Monitoring Graph Systems

Several tools can help monitor graph systems effectively:

- **Prometheus and Grafana:**
  Widely used for real-time monitoring and visualization. Prometheus collects metrics from the database and other system components, while Grafana provides dashboards for analysis.
- **ELK Stack (Elasticsearch, Logstash, Kibana):**
  Useful for aggregating, searching, and visualizing logs and error messages.
- **Built-in Monitoring Tools:**
  Many graph databases (e.g., Neo4j, Amazon Neptune) include native monitoring and management interfaces that display critical metrics and performance graphs.
- **Custom Scripts:**
  Tailored Python or shell scripts can periodically check system health and log key metrics.

Troubleshooting Techniques

When performance issues or errors arise, a systematic troubleshooting approach is essential:

1. **Analyze Query Performance:**
   - o Use profiling tools (e.g., Neo4j's PROFILE or EXPLAIN commands) to inspect query execution plans.
   - o Identify slow query parts, such as excessive node traversals or inefficient pattern matching.
2. **Examine Resource Utilization:**
   - o Monitor CPU, memory, and disk I/O to detect resource bottlenecks.
   - o Check for spikes in resource usage during peak loads and correlate them with specific queries or events.
3. **Review Logs and Error Messages:**
   - o Use log aggregation tools (e.g., ELK Stack) to search for recurring errors or warnings.

- o Pay attention to network errors, timeouts, or security-related messages.
4. **Test Network Performance:**
   - o For distributed graph systems, verify the network latency between nodes.
   - o Use tools like `ping`, `traceroute`, or dedicated network monitoring software.
5. **Check Cache Efficiency:**
   - o Analyze cache hit/miss ratios. Poor cache performance may indicate that queries are not optimized for caching.
   - o Consider increasing cache sizes or adjusting caching policies.

Table: Example Metrics and Their Importance

Metric	Description	Importance	Tool/Method
Query Latency	Time to execute a query	Indicates efficiency of query execution	Prometheus, Neo4j PROFILE
CPU Usage	Percentage of CPU utilization	High usage can indicate performance bottlenecks	System monitoring tools
Memory Usage	Amount of RAM consumed	Insufficient memory can slow down processing	Grafana, OS monitoring tools
Disk I/O	Read/write operations per second	Critical for systems with heavy write loads	I/O monitoring tools
Error Rate	Frequency of query or system errors	Helps detect issues in application logic or configuration	ELK Stack, log analysis
Cache Hit/Miss Ratio	Ratio of served requests from cache vs. actual database queries	High cache miss rate may require tuning caching strategies	Application logs, monitoring tools

Code Example: Basic Monitoring Script with Python

Below is a simple Python script using the `psutil` library to monitor CPU and memory usage, which can be adapted for graph database processes:

```python
import psutil
import time

def monitor_system(interval=5):
    print("Monitoring CPU and Memory usage. Press Ctrl+C to
stop.")
    try:
        while True:
            cpu_usage = psutil.cpu_percent(interval=1)
            memory_info = psutil.virtual_memory()
            print(f"CPU Usage: {cpu_usage}%")
            print(f"Memory Usage: {memory_info.percent}%
(Used: {memory_info.used // (1024 * 1024)} MB, Total:
{memory_info.total // (1024 * 1024)} MB)")
            time.sleep(interval)
    except KeyboardInterrupt:
        print("Monitoring stopped.")

if __name__ == "__main__":
    monitor_system()
```

Explanation:

- **psutil Library:**
  Used to fetch real-time system metrics such as CPU and memory usage.
- **Interval Parameter:**
  Determines how frequently the metrics are printed.
- **Usage:**
  This script can be run on a server hosting the graph database to monitor resource consumption and identify potential bottlenecks.

9.5 Strategies for Continuous Maintenance and Upgrades

Overview

Continuous maintenance and regular upgrades are essential to keep a graph-based system operating efficiently, secure, and aligned with evolving business needs. This involves proactive monitoring, regular backups, incremental updates, and version control. In this section, we discuss strategies for continuous maintenance and upgrade practices.

Key Maintenance Strategies

1. **Regular Backups and Disaster Recovery:**
    o **Backup Scheduling:**
      Implement automated backup procedures (e.g., daily, weekly) to create snapshots of the graph database.
    o **Disaster Recovery Planning:**
      Develop and test a disaster recovery plan that includes restoring data from backups in case of failures.
    o **Example:**
      Use built-in backup tools provided by the graph database (e.g., Neo4j's backup utilities) and store backups in a secure, offsite location.
2. **Schema and Data Versioning:**
    o **Version Control:**
      Use version control systems (e.g., Git) to manage changes in the graph schema and data models.
    o **Migration Scripts:**
      Develop migration scripts to update the schema or transform data during upgrades.
    o **Example:**
      Create a Git repository to track ontology changes and use migration tools to apply updates to production databases.
3. **Incremental Upgrades:**
    o **Rolling Upgrades:**
      Upgrade parts of the system incrementally to avoid downtime. This is particularly important for distributed systems.
    o **Blue-Green Deployments:**
      Maintain two production environments (blue and green) to allow seamless switching during upgrades.
    o **Example:**
      Deploy new features to the green environment, test thoroughly, then switch traffic from the blue environment once validation is complete.
4. **Automated Monitoring and Alerting:**
    o **Proactive Alerts:**
      Set up automated alerts based on predefined thresholds (e.g., high CPU usage, slow query response times) to trigger maintenance actions.

o **Usage:**
  Integrate monitoring tools (e.g., Prometheus, Grafana) with alerting systems (e.g., PagerDuty) to ensure rapid response to issues.

5. **Performance Regression Testing:**
   o **Regular Testing:**
     Implement performance regression tests to ensure that new changes do not degrade system performance.
   o **Benchmarking:**
     Maintain benchmarks for key queries and operations, and compare results before and after upgrades.

Best Practices for Maintenance and Upgrades

- **Documentation:**
  Keep comprehensive documentation of the system architecture, configurations, and maintenance procedures. This helps in troubleshooting and ensures continuity.
- **Change Management:**
  Follow a structured change management process that includes review, testing, and approval of updates.
- **Automation:**
  Automate routine maintenance tasks, such as backups, monitoring, and migrations, to reduce manual errors and improve efficiency.
- **Stakeholder Communication:**
  Communicate planned maintenance windows and upgrade schedules with stakeholders to minimize business disruptions.

Table: Maintenance and Upgrade Strategies

Strategy	Description	Benefits	Example/Tool
Regular Backups	Scheduled snapshots of the graph database for disaster recovery	Protects data integrity, ensures recoverability	Neo4j backup utilities, AWS Backup
Schema and Data Versioning	Version control for ontology and data schema changes	Facilitates incremental updates, rollback capabilities	Git, migration scripts

Strategy	Description	Benefits	Example/Tool
Incremental Upgrades	Rolling or blue-green deployments to update the system without downtime	Minimizes disruption, allows gradual rollout	Kubernetes rolling updates, blue-green deployment strategies
Automated Monitoring & Alerting	Proactive system monitoring with automated alerts for performance anomalies	Rapid issue detection and response	Prometheus, Grafana, PagerDuty
Performance Regression Testing	Regular testing to benchmark system performance before and after upgrades	Ensures new updates do not degrade performance	Automated test scripts, benchmarking tools

Code Example: Scheduling a Backup Script (Python)

Below is an example of a simple Python script that can be scheduled (using cron or a task scheduler) to perform a backup of a graph database directory.

```python
import os
import shutil
import datetime

def backup_graph_db(source_dir, backup_dir):
    # Generate a timestamp for the backup folder name
    timestamp =
datetime.datetime.now().strftime("%Y%m%d_%H%M%S")
    destination = os.path.join(backup_dir,
f"backup_{timestamp}")

    try:
        shutil.copytree(source_dir, destination)
        print(f"Backup successful: {destination}")
    except Exception as e:
        print(f"Backup failed: {str(e)}")

# Example usage
if __name__ == "__main__":
    # Source directory of the graph database (change as
needed)
    source_directory = "/path/to/graph_database"
```

```
# Backup directory where the backups will be stored
backup_directory = "/path/to/backup_folder"

backup_graph_db(source_directory, backup_directory)
```

Explanation:

- **shutil.copytree:**
  Copies the entire source directory (graph database files) to a new
  backup directory with a timestamp.
- **Scheduling:**
  This script can be scheduled via cron on Linux or Task Scheduler on
  Windows to run automatically at defined intervals.

Summary of 9.5

Continuous maintenance and upgrades are essential for ensuring the
longevity, performance, and security of graph-based systems. Strategies
include:

- Regular backups and disaster recovery planning.
- Versioning and incremental schema upgrades.
- Automated monitoring, alerting, and performance regression testing.

Implementing these practices minimizes downtime, protects data integrity,
and enables seamless system evolution in response to changing requirements
and technological advancements.

Chapter 10: Integrating RAG into Graph-Based Systems

Integrating Retrieval-Augmented Generation (RAG) into graph-based systems combines the strengths of structured data retrieval with advanced natural language generation. This integration enhances the ability of systems to produce contextually relevant, fact-based, and insightful responses by grounding generated content in data stored in graph databases.

10.1 Overview of Retrieval-Augmented Generation (RAG)

What is RAG?

Retrieval-Augmented Generation (RAG) is an approach that combines two powerful paradigms in artificial intelligence:

- **Retrieval:**
  A component that searches a large corpus or structured data source (such as a graph database) to retrieve relevant documents, records, or data snippets.
- **Generation:**
  A generative model (typically based on transformer architectures such as GPT) that produces natural language output. The generative process is augmented by the context provided by the retrieval component.

Key Idea:
By retrieving pertinent information from a knowledge base and feeding it into a generative model, RAG systems produce responses that are not only fluent but also factually grounded and contextually relevant.

Why RAG is Important

- **Improved Accuracy:**
  Pure generative models can sometimes produce plausible-sounding

but incorrect or outdated information. RAG systems mitigate this by anchoring responses in a reliable data source.

- **Contextual Richness:**
  The retrieved data enriches the context, enabling the generation of detailed and nuanced answers.
- **Adaptability:**
  RAG systems can dynamically incorporate updated information, making them well-suited for domains where data changes frequently.

Components of RAG

- **Retrieval Module:**
  Uses algorithms to identify and extract relevant data. In a graph-based system, this module may leverage graph traversals, indexing, or SPARQL queries.
- **Generative Module:**
  A language model that takes the retrieved context and the original query as input to generate a comprehensive response.
- **Fusion Mechanism:**
  Integrates the outputs of the retrieval and generative modules to produce the final response.

Table: Comparison of Pure Generation vs. RAG

Aspect	Pure Generation	Retrieval-Augmented Generation (RAG)
Data Source	Only learned from training data	Augmented with external, real-time data sources
Factual Accuracy	Can produce hallucinated or outdated facts	Grounded in external data, reducing errors
Contextual Detail	Limited to patterns learned during training	Enhanced with detailed and specific retrieved context
Adaptability	Static knowledge cutoff	Dynamically incorporates updated information

Pseudocode Example: RAG Workflow

Below is a high-level pseudocode example illustrating a basic RAG process:

```python
```

```python
def retrieve_context(query, graph_db):
    """
    Retrieve relevant data from the graph database based on
    the query.
    """
    # Use an appropriate graph query (e.g., SPARQL or a graph
    traversal)
    context_data = graph_db.query(query)
    return context_data

def generate_response(query, context_data, language_model):
    """
    Generate a response using a language model, augmented
    with retrieved context.
    """
    # Combine query and context into a single input
    combined_input = f"{query}\nContext:\n{context_data}"
    response = language_model.generate_text(combined_input)
    return response

def rag_pipeline(query, graph_db, language_model):
    # Step 1: Retrieve relevant context from the graph
    context_data = retrieve_context(query, graph_db)

    # Step 2: Generate a response using the augmented context
    final_response = generate_response(query, context_data,
language_model)

    return final_response

# Example usage
query = "What are the key features of the latest smartphone?"
final_answer = rag_pipeline(query, graph_database,
generative_model)
print(final_answer)
```

Explanation:

- **retrieve_context:**
  Retrieves relevant data from the graph database using a query.
- **generate_response:**
  Feeds the query along with the retrieved context to a generative
  language model.
- **rag_pipeline:**
  Integrates both steps to produce a final, contextually enriched
  response.

10.2 Architectural Considerations for RAG Integration

Overview

When integrating RAG into a graph-based system, the architecture must support both efficient data retrieval from the graph and effective communication with the generative model. This section discusses key architectural considerations to ensure seamless integration.

Key Considerations

1. **Separation of Concerns:**
   - **Retrieval Module:**
     Dedicated component responsible for querying the graph database. It should be optimized for fast, accurate data extraction.
   - **Generative Module:**
     Runs independently, often as a microservice or part of a larger language model infrastructure, responsible for text generation.
   - **Fusion Layer:**
     Acts as an intermediary, combining outputs from the retrieval and generative modules.
2. **Latency and Throughput:**
   - **Low Latency:**
     RAG systems must return responses quickly. Optimize the retrieval queries and consider asynchronous processing where possible.
   - **High Throughput:**
     Ensure that both retrieval and generation modules can handle high volumes of requests simultaneously. Scale horizontally if needed.
3. **Scalability and Fault Tolerance:**
   - **Distributed Architecture:**
     Consider deploying the retrieval module on a distributed graph database cluster to handle large-scale data.
   - **Resiliency:**
     Implement fallback mechanisms if the retrieval component fails or if the generative model is temporarily unavailable.

4. **Data Consistency and Freshness:**
   - **Real-Time Updates:**
     Ensure that the graph database reflects the most current data, especially if the system is used in dynamic environments.
   - **Caching Strategies:**
     Use caching to speed up frequent retrievals, but balance this with the need for up-to-date information.
5. **Security and Compliance:**
   - **Data Access Control:**
     Ensure that the retrieval module enforces strict access controls, particularly when handling sensitive data.
   - **Secure Communication:**
     Use encrypted channels (e.g., TLS) for communication between modules and external clients.

Architectural Diagram (Conceptual Description)

Imagine the architecture as a series of layers:

- **Client Layer:**
  Where user queries are received.
- **API Gateway:**
  Routes requests to appropriate modules.
- **Retrieval Module:**
  Queries the graph database.
- **Generative Module:**
  Processes the combined input (query + retrieved context).
- **Fusion Layer:**
  Merges outputs and returns the final response.
- **Graph Database:**
  Stores structured, interconnected data.
- **Monitoring & Logging Layer:**
  Ensures performance tracking and troubleshooting.

Table: Key Architectural Considerations

Aspect	Consideration	Implementation Strategy
Separation of Concerns	Isolate retrieval, generation, and fusion functions	Modular microservices architecture

Aspect	Consideration	Implementation Strategy
Latency & Throughput	Minimize response time and handle high request volumes	Optimize queries, use asynchronous processing, scale horizontally
Scalability	System must handle growing data and users	Distributed graph databases, load balancing
Data Freshness	Ensure retrieved data is up-to-date	Real-time data synchronization, minimal caching latency
Security	Protect sensitive data and ensure secure communications	Enforce strict access controls, use TLS encryption

Pseudocode: Integrating Retrieval and Generation (Expanded)

Below is a more detailed pseudocode example illustrating how the integration might be implemented within a service-oriented architecture:

```python
def retrieve_from_graph(query, graph_db, cache=None):
    """
    Retrieve data from the graph database with optional
caching.
    """
    # Check cache first
    if cache and query in cache:
        return cache[query]

    # Execute query on the graph database
    context_data = graph_db.execute_query(query)

    # Optionally cache the result
    if cache:
        cache[query] = context_data

    return context_data

def generate_augmented_response(query, context_data,
language_model):
    """
    Generate a response using a language model augmented with
context.
    """
```

```
    combined_input = f"Query: {query}\nContext:
{context_data}"
    return language_model.generate(combined_input)

def process_rag_request(query, graph_db, language_model,
cache=None):
    """
    Process a RAG request by integrating retrieval and
generation.
    """
    # Retrieve context from graph
    context = retrieve_from_graph(query, graph_db, cache)

    # Generate response using language model
    response = generate_augmented_response(query, context,
language_model)

    return response

# Example usage:
query = "What are the latest features of the new smartphone
model?"
final_response = process_rag_request(query, graph_database,
generative_model, cache=my_cache)
print(final_response)
```

Explanation:

- **Caching Option:**
  The `retrieve_from_graph` function optionally uses caching to speed up frequent queries.
- **Separation of Concerns:**
  The functions clearly separate retrieval and generation responsibilities.
- **Integration:**
  The `process_rag_request` function orchestrates the complete RAG pipeline.

10.3 Data Flow: From Graph Storage to Augmented Retrieval

Overview

Understanding the data flow from graph storage to augmented retrieval is critical for designing an efficient RAG system. This section outlines the end-to-end process of how data is stored in a graph, retrieved, and then used to augment generative responses.

Data Flow Process

1. **Data Storage in the Graph Database:**
   o **Graph Structure:**
     Data is stored in the graph database as nodes (entities) and edges (relationships). This data is often enriched with attributes and semantic annotations.
   o **Example:**
     In an e-commerce graph, customer information, product details, and transaction histories are stored as interconnected nodes.
2. **Data Retrieval:**
   o **Query Execution:**
     When a query is received, the retrieval module executes a query against the graph database. This might involve traversing relationships, filtering by node properties, or aggregating related data.
   o **Retrieval Tools:**
     Utilize query languages such as SPARQL for RDF-based graphs or Cypher for property graphs.
   o **Example Query:**
     "Find all products purchased by customers from a specific region" might involve traversing customer nodes to order nodes and then to product nodes.
3. **Augmenting the Retrieval:**
   o **Context Extraction:**
     The raw data retrieved from the graph is processed to extract relevant context, summaries, or key facts.
   o **Data Transformation:**
     Transform the retrieved data into a format suitable for feeding into a generative model. This may involve formatting the data

as structured text, JSON, or another intermediary representation.
4. **Generative Processing:**
   o **Input Combination:**
     The original query is combined with the retrieved context to create a comprehensive input for the language model.
   o **Generation:**
     The generative module processes the combined input and produces a natural language response that integrates the augmented data.
5. **Response Delivery:**
   o **Final Output:**
     The system returns the generated response to the user or client application.
   o **Feedback Loop:**
     Monitoring and feedback mechanisms capture performance data and user feedback for continuous improvement.

Flow Diagram (Described in Text)

Imagine the following sequential data flow:

- **Step 1:**
  Graph Database: Data is stored as nodes and edges.
- **Step 2:**
  Retrieval Module: Executes a query on the graph database to obtain relevant data.
- **Step 3:**
  Context Processor: Formats and cleans the retrieved data.
- **Step 4:**
  Generative Module: Receives combined input (original query + context) and generates a response.
- **Step 5:**
  API Gateway: Returns the final response to the user.

Table: Data Flow Stages and Their Functions

Stage	Function	Example/Tool
Data Storage	Store data as nodes and edges in a graph database	Neo4j, Amazon Neptune, JanusGraph

Stage	Function	Example/Tool
Data Retrieval	Query the graph to extract relevant information	SPARQL (for RDF), Cypher (for property graphs)
Context Extraction	Process and format retrieved data for augmentation	Custom transformation scripts, ETL tools
Generative Processing	Combine query with context and generate response	GPT-based models, Transformer architectures
Response Delivery	Return the final augmented response to the client	API Gateway, Web or mobile application interfaces

Pseudocode Example: Complete Data Flow in a RAG System

Below is a detailed pseudocode example that illustrates the data flow from graph storage to augmented retrieval:

```python
def query_graph(query_string, graph_db):
    """
    Execute a query on the graph database to retrieve
relevant data.
    """
    # Execute a graph query (e.g., using Cypher or SPARQL)
    result = graph_db.execute(query_string)
    return result

def process_retrieved_data(raw_data):
    """
    Process and format the raw data into a usable context.
    """
    # Example: Convert the raw result into a structured text
summary
    context = "\n".join([str(record) for record in raw_data])
    return context

def combine_input(query, context):
    """
    Combine the original query with the retrieved context.
    """
    return f"Query: {query}\nRetrieved Context:\n{context}"

def generate_augmented_text(combined_input, language_model):
    """
    Generate text using the language model, augmented with
the retrieved context.
    """
```

```python
    return language_model.generate(combined_input)

def rag_data_flow_pipeline(query, graph_db, language_model):
    # Step 1: Retrieve data from graph
    raw_data = query_graph(query, graph_db)

    # Step 2: Process the retrieved data
    context = process_retrieved_data(raw_data)

    # Step 3: Combine the original query with the context
    combined_input = combine_input(query, context)

    # Step 4: Generate the augmented response
    augmented_response =
generate_augmented_text(combined_input, language_model)

    return augmented_response

# Example usage:
query = "What are the latest smartphone features?"
final_output = rag_data_flow_pipeline(query, graph_database,
generative_model)
print(final_output)
```

Explanation:

- **Graph Query:**
  The function `query_graph` retrieves relevant data from the graph database based on the query.
- **Context Processing:**
  The `process_retrieved_data` function transforms raw data into a coherent context.
- **Input Combination:**
  The `combine_input` function merges the query and context.
- **Text Generation:**
  The `generate_augmented_text` function passes the combined input to the language model, which generates the final response.
- **Pipeline Integration:**
  The `rag_data_flow_pipeline` function integrates all steps into a complete data flow from graph storage to final output.

10.4 Enhancing Search and Recommendations with RAG

Overview

Search and recommendation systems are critical components in many applications, from e-commerce to social networks. Integrating Retrieval-Augmented Generation (RAG) into these systems improves both the accuracy and the richness of the responses. By combining structured graph data with a generative model, RAG enhances search relevance and delivers personalized recommendations that are grounded in factual data.

Enhancing Search with RAG

Traditional Search Limitations:

- **Keyword Matching:**
  Conventional search engines often rely on keyword matching, which may overlook the semantic relationships between entities.
- **Static Results:**
  Standard search systems return static results that may not reflect the most current data or user context.

RAG-Enhanced Search:

- **Dynamic Retrieval:**
  The retrieval module queries the graph database to gather the most relevant and up-to-date information based on the query context.
- **Contextual Augmentation:**
  The generative model uses the retrieved context to produce more comprehensive search results or summaries.
- **Personalization:**
  By incorporating user-specific data from the graph (e.g., past behavior or preferences), RAG can tailor search results to the individual.

Example Workflow for Search:

1. **User Query:**
   A user enters a query such as "latest smartphone features."

2. **Graph Retrieval:**
   The retrieval module queries the graph for nodes and relationships related to smartphones, product updates, and customer reviews.
3. **Context Processing:**
   The retrieved data is processed into a summary or list of key attributes.
4. **Generation:**
   The generative module combines the user query with the context to generate a rich, natural language response that highlights the latest features.
5. **Output:**
   The final response is delivered to the user, integrating both factual data and context.

Enhancing Recommendations with RAG

Traditional Recommendation Systems:

- Often rely on collaborative filtering or content-based filtering.
- May suffer from cold-start issues or provide generic suggestions.

RAG-Enhanced Recommendations:

- **Contextual Recommendations:**
  By retrieving detailed context from the graph—such as user behavior, product attributes, and social connections—the system can generate recommendations that are highly personalized.
- **Explanation Generation:**
  RAG can generate natural language explanations for recommendations, enhancing user trust and transparency.
- **Dynamic Adaptation:**
  The system can incorporate real-time data, allowing recommendations to evolve with user interactions and trends.

Example Workflow for Recommendations:

1. **User Profile Query:**
   A recommendation request is made, such as "Recommend products for me."
2. **Graph Retrieval:**
   The retrieval module gathers relevant information from the user's profile, past orders, product ratings, and social interactions.

3. **Context Synthesis:**
   The system synthesizes this information to extract key themes and preferences.
4. **Response Generation:**
   The generative model creates a personalized recommendation list with explanations, such as "Based on your recent purchase of a smartphone, you might like these accessories because…"
5. **Output:**
   The final augmented recommendation is delivered to the user.

Table: Enhancements with RAG in Search and Recommendations

Aspect	Traditional Approach	RAG-Enhanced Approach
Search Results	Keyword matching; static, list-based results	Dynamic retrieval with context; natural language summaries and explanations
Personalization	Limited personalization using historical data	Real-time, context-aware personalization by leveraging graph relationships and user behavior
Recommendation Explanations	Minimal or no explanation provided	Detailed natural language explanations that build trust and user engagement
Adaptability	Static results based on fixed data sets	Continuously updated responses that incorporate the latest graph data and user interactions

Code Example: Simulated RAG-Enhanced Search Function (Python)

Below is a simplified Python example using pseudocode to simulate the integration of RAG in a search function.

```python
def retrieve_search_context(query, graph_db):
    """
```

Simulate retrieval of relevant context from a graph
database based on a search query.
    """
    # For demonstration, we return a simulated context
string.
    # In a real system, this function would execute a graph
query (e.g., using SPARQL or Cypher).
    context = "Found nodes: Smartphone (latest model),
Reviews (positive feedback), Features (high-resolution
camera, long battery life)"
    return context

def generate_search_response(query, context, language_model):
    """
    Generate a rich search result using a language model with
augmented context.
    """
    # Combine the query and context
    combined_input = f"Search Query: {query}\nContext:
{context}"
    # Simulate generating a response with a language model
    response = language_model.generate_text(combined_input)
    return response

# Simulated usage:
query = "latest smartphone features"
graph_db = None   # In an actual implementation, this would be
a connection to a graph database.
language_model = type("SimulatedModel", (), {"generate_text":
lambda self, inp: "Augmented Search Result: The latest
smartphone features include a high-resolution camera, long
battery life, and fast processing."})()

# Retrieve context and generate response
context = retrieve_search_context(query, graph_db)
final_search_result = generate_search_response(query,
context, language_model)
print(final_search_result)
```

**Explanation:**

- **Retrieval:**
  The `retrieve_search_context` function simulates querying a graph
  database.
- **Generation:**
  The `generate_search_response` function simulates combining the
  query with the retrieved context and generating a natural language
  response using a language model.
```

- **Output:**
  The final search result is an augmented, detailed response that integrates the retrieved context.

10.5 Hybrid Systems: Merging Graph Data with ML Pipelines

Overview

Hybrid systems that merge graph data with machine learning (ML) pipelines leverage the strengths of both structured data and advanced analytical models. These systems integrate graph-based representations with ML techniques to enable predictive analytics, personalized recommendations, and enhanced decision-making.

Why Merge Graph Data with ML Pipelines?

- **Rich Feature Extraction:**
  Graph data provides rich features through relationships and connectivity that can be fed into ML models.
- **Improved Predictions:**
  Incorporating graph-derived features (e.g., centrality, clustering coefficients) can enhance the accuracy of predictions.
- **Enhanced Personalization:**
  Graph data can capture complex user behaviors and relationships, enabling more personalized ML-driven recommendations.
- **Explainability:**
  The structured nature of graph data supports better interpretability of ML model outputs.

Architectural Considerations

1. **Data Preprocessing:**
   - **Graph Embeddings:**
     Transform graph data into numerical vectors using techniques such as Node2Vec, DeepWalk, or Graph Neural Networks (GNNs). These embeddings capture the structural properties of the graph.

- o **Feature Engineering:**
  Extract additional graph features (e.g., degree, PageRank) to enhance the ML model's input.
2. **Integration Pipeline:**
   - o **Data Flow:**
     Create a pipeline where graph data is continuously extracted, processed into embeddings or features, and fed into ML models.
   - o **Batch vs. Real-Time Processing:**
     Determine whether the integration will occur in batch mode (e.g., daily retraining) or real-time (e.g., streaming updates).
3. **Model Training and Inference:**
   - o **Training:**
     Train ML models on the enriched feature set derived from graph data.
   - o **Inference:**
     Use the trained model to generate predictions or recommendations, integrating real-time graph data if needed.

Example Use Case: Product Recommendation

Scenario:

- **Graph Data:**
  The system stores customer interactions, product details, and purchase histories as a graph.
- **ML Model:**
  A recommendation model is trained using features derived from the graph (e.g., product embeddings, customer clusters).
- **Hybrid Approach:**
  The ML model predicts product recommendations, which are then further refined using real-time graph queries to incorporate the latest customer behavior and trends.

Table: Steps in a Hybrid System Pipeline

Step	Description	Example Tool/Method
Data Extraction	Extract graph data from the database	SPARQL queries, Cypher queries
Graph Embedding Generation	Transform graph nodes into numerical vectors	Node2Vec, DeepWalk, Graph Neural Networks

Step	Description	Example Tool/Method
Feature Engineering	Compute additional graph metrics (e.g., degree, centrality)	Custom Python scripts, NetworkX functions
Model Training	Train an ML model on the extracted features	Scikit-learn, TensorFlow, PyTorch
Inference and Real-Time Updates	Generate predictions using the trained model and update with real-time data	Batch processing or streaming with Apache Kafka

Code Example: Generating Graph Embeddings Using Node2Vec (Python)

Below is an example of using the `node2vec` library to generate embeddings from a graph created with NetworkX. These embeddings can be used as features in an ML pipeline.

```python
import networkx as nx
from node2vec import Node2Vec

# Create a simple graph (e.g., representing customer-product
interactions)
G = nx.Graph()
G.add_edges_from([
    ("Customer1", "ProductA"),
    ("Customer1", "ProductB"),
    ("Customer2", "ProductB"),
    ("Customer2", "ProductC"),
    ("Customer3", "ProductA"),
    ("Customer3", "ProductC")
])

# Precompute walks using Node2Vec
node2vec = Node2Vec(G, dimensions=64, walk_length=30,
num_walks=200, workers=2)

# Generate embeddings
model = node2vec.fit(window=10, min_count=1)
embeddings = {node: model.wv[node] for node in G.nodes()}

# Print the embedding for one node
print("Embedding for Customer1:", embeddings["Customer1"])
```

Explanation:

- **Graph Creation:**
  A simple graph is constructed with customer-product interactions.
- **Node2Vec Initialization:**
  The `Node2Vec` object is created with specified parameters to generate random walks.
- **Embedding Generation:**
  The model computes embeddings for each node. These embeddings capture the structural context and can be used as features in an ML model for tasks such as recommendations.

Integrating with an ML Pipeline

Once embeddings and features are generated, they can be integrated into an ML pipeline. For instance, you could train a recommendation model using scikit-learn:

```python
import numpy as np
from sklearn.cluster import KMeans

# Example: Use embeddings for clustering customers
# Prepare embedding matrix for customers
customer_nodes = [node for node in G.nodes() if "Customer" in
node]
X = np.array([embeddings[node] for node in customer_nodes])

# Cluster customers into 2 segments using KMeans
kmeans = KMeans(n_clusters=2, random_state=42).fit(X)
labels = kmeans.labels_

# Print clustering result
for i, customer in enumerate(customer_nodes):
    print(f"{customer}: Cluster {labels[i]}")
```

Explanation:

- **Feature Matrix:**
  The embeddings of customer nodes are collected into a matrix.
- **Clustering:**
  KMeans clustering groups customers into segments, which can be used to tailor recommendations.

Summary of 10.5

Hybrid systems merge the structured information from graph databases with the predictive power of ML pipelines. By generating graph embeddings, performing feature engineering, and integrating these features into ML models, you can enhance applications such as product recommendations and predictive analytics. This approach leverages the rich relationships in graph data to produce more accurate and personalized results.

Chapter 11: Tools, Platforms, and Frameworks

Implementing graph-based systems requires choosing the right tools and platforms to suit your data, use cases, and technical requirements. In this chapter, we will explore the following topics:

1. **Survey of Leading Graph Databases:**
   An overview of popular graph databases such as Neo4j, GraphDB, AWS Neptune, and others.
2. **Comparison of Open-Source vs. Proprietary Tools:**
   A discussion on the benefits and trade-offs between using open-source and proprietary solutions.
3. **Integration Frameworks and Middleware Solutions:**
   An examination of frameworks and middleware options that facilitate the integration of graph databases with other systems.

11.1 Survey of Leading Graph Databases (Neo4j, GraphDB, AWS Neptune, etc.)

Overview

Graph databases are specialized systems designed to store, process, and query graph data—data that is inherently interconnected. In this section, we explore several leading graph databases, each with its own strengths and ideal use cases.

Key Graph Databases

1. **Neo4j**
   - **Description:**
     Neo4j is one of the most popular native graph databases, known for its ease of use and powerful query language, Cypher. It is well-suited for complex traversals and relationship-centric queries.
   - **Features:**
     - Native graph storage and processing

- Cypher query language
  - High performance for transactional and analytical workloads
  - Extensive community support and enterprise features
- **Ideal Use Cases:**
  Social networks, recommendation systems, fraud detection

2. **GraphDB**
   - **Description:**
     GraphDB is an RDF-based graph database that specializes in handling semantic data. It supports SPARQL for querying and is widely used in scenarios requiring strict adherence to Semantic Web standards.
   - **Features:**
     - RDF data model and SPARQL support
     - Reasoning and inferencing capabilities
     - Integration with linked data
     - Scalable for large datasets
   - **Ideal Use Cases:**
     Knowledge graphs, semantic search, content management

3. **Amazon Neptune**
   - **Description:**
     Amazon Neptune is a fully managed graph database service provided by AWS. It supports both property graph and RDF models, allowing flexibility in how data is represented and queried.
   - **Features:**
     - Managed service with high availability and security
     - Supports both Apache TinkerPop Gremlin (for property graphs) and SPARQL (for RDF)
     - Seamless integration with other AWS services
     - Scalability and performance optimization
   - **Ideal Use Cases:**
     Enterprise applications, knowledge graphs, network security

4. **JanusGraph**
   - **Description:**
     JanusGraph is an open-source, distributed graph database that supports a variety of storage backends such as Apache Cassandra, HBase, and Google Cloud Bigtable.
   - **Features:**
     - Distributed architecture for scalability
     - Support for multi-backend storage solutions
     - Integration with Apache TinkerPop for querying

- o **Ideal Use Cases:**
  Big data analytics, IoT networks, large-scale social graphs

Table: Survey of Leading Graph Databases

Graph Database	Data Model	Query Language	Key Features	Ideal Use Cases
Neo4j	Property Graph	Cypher	Native graph storage, high performance, extensive community support	Social networks, recommendation systems, fraud detection
GraphDB	RDF (Semantic Web)	SPARQL	Reasoning/inferencing, semantic data management, linked data support	Knowledge graphs, semantic search, content management
Amazon Neptune	Property Graph & RDF	Gremlin / SPARQL	Managed service, high availability, integration with AWS, scalable	Enterprise applications, knowledge graphs, network security
JanusGraph	Property Graph	Gremlin	Distributed architecture, multi-backend support, open source	Big data analytics, IoT, large-scale social graphs

Code Example: Querying Neo4j Using Cypher

Below is a simple Python code example using the neo4j Python driver to query a Neo4j graph database:

```python
from neo4j import GraphDatabase

# Neo4j connection URI and credentials
uri = "bolt://localhost:7687"
username = "neo4j"
password = "your_password"
```

```
# Create a Neo4j driver instance
driver = GraphDatabase.driver(uri, auth=(username, password))

def get_customer_orders(tx, customer_name):
    query = (
        "MATCH (c:Customer)-[:PLACED]->(o:Order) "
        "WHERE c.name = $customer_name "
        "RETURN o.orderId AS orderId, o.date AS date, o.total
AS total"
    )
    result = tx.run(query, customer_name=customer_name)
    return [record for record in result]

with driver.session() as session:
    orders = session.read_transaction(get_customer_orders,
"John Doe")
    for order in orders:
        print(f"Order ID: {order['orderId']}, Date:
{order['date']}, Total: {order['total']}")

driver.close()
```

Explanation:

- **Driver Connection:**
  The script connects to a Neo4j database using the Bolt protocol.
- **Cypher Query:**
  The query matches customer nodes labeled `Customer` with outgoing
  `PLACED` relationships to `Order` nodes.
- **Transaction:**
  The query is executed in a read transaction, and the results are
  printed.

11.2 Comparison of Open-Source vs. Proprietary Tools

Overview

When selecting tools for graph-based systems, organizations must decide
between open-source and proprietary solutions. Each has its advantages and
trade-offs in terms of cost, flexibility, support, and innovation.

Open-Source Tools

Advantages:

- **Cost-Effective:**
  Generally free to use and modify.
- **Flexibility:**
  Source code access allows for customization to meet specific needs.
- **Community-Driven:**
  Active communities contribute improvements and plugins.
- **Transparency:**
  Open access to the codebase can enhance trust and security assessments.

Limitations:

- **Support:**
  May rely on community support rather than dedicated vendor support.
- **Integration:**
  May require more effort to integrate with existing enterprise systems.
- **Innovation Pace:**
  While often innovative, open-source tools might lack the comprehensive feature sets of proprietary tools.

Proprietary Tools

Advantages:

- **Vendor Support:**
  Comes with dedicated customer service, maintenance, and support.
- **Comprehensive Feature Sets:**
  Often include advanced features, integrations, and performance optimizations.
- **Reliability:**
  Tends to have rigorous testing and certification processes.
- **Ease of Integration:**
  May provide seamless integration with other enterprise tools and platforms.

Limitations:

- **Cost:**
  Licensing fees can be high.
- **Vendor Lock-In:**
  Dependence on a single vendor can limit flexibility and increase long-term costs.
- **Limited Customization:**
  Customization options may be restricted by the vendor's roadmap.

Table: Open-Source vs. Proprietary Tools

Aspect	Open-Source Tools	Proprietary Tools
Cost	Typically free; lower upfront costs	Licensing fees can be high
Support	Community-driven support; may require in-house expertise	Dedicated vendor support, service-level agreements
Flexibility	High; full access to source code; customizable	Limited customization; vendor-controlled feature set
Integration	May require additional effort to integrate with enterprise systems	Often provide seamless integration with other enterprise tools
Innovation	Rapid innovation through community contributions	Stable, thoroughly tested features; may lag behind cutting-edge advancements

Code Example: Evaluating Tool Options (Pseudocode)

Below is a simplified pseudocode that outlines decision criteria for choosing between open-source and proprietary graph tools:

```python
def choose_graph_tool(cost_sensitive, need_customization,
require_vendor_support):
    if cost_sensitive and need_customization:
        return "Consider an open-source tool like Neo4j
Community Edition or JanusGraph"
    elif require_vendor_support:
```

```
        return "Consider a proprietary solution like Neo4j
Enterprise or AWS Neptune"
    else:
        return "Evaluate based on integration capabilities
and long-term scalability needs"

# Example usage:
tool_decision = choose_graph_tool(cost_sensitive=True,
need_customization=True, require_vendor_support=False)
print("Tool Recommendation:", tool_decision)
```

Explanation:

- **Decision Criteria:**
  The pseudocode provides a simple decision-making process based on
  cost sensitivity, need for customization, and requirement for vendor
  support.
- **Output:**
  The function returns a recommendation based on the input criteria.

11.3 Integration Frameworks and Middleware Solutions

Overview

Integration frameworks and middleware solutions play a pivotal role in
connecting graph databases with various data sources, applications, and
services. They simplify data ingestion, transformation, and communication
between different system components, ensuring a cohesive architecture.

Key Integration Frameworks

1. **Apache Camel:**
   o **Description:**
     A versatile integration framework that supports various
     communication protocols and data formats.
   o **Features:**
     ▪ Provides a wide range of components for routing and
       mediation

- Supports integration with graph databases, relational databases, and messaging systems
  - o **Use Cases:**
    Data transformation pipelines, real-time messaging, and microservices integration.
2. **MuleSoft Anypoint Platform:**
   - o **Description:**
     A comprehensive integration platform that offers robust tools for API management, data integration, and orchestration.
   - o **Features:**
     - Drag-and-drop interface for designing integration flows
     - Pre-built connectors for various data sources, including graph databases
   - o **Use Cases:**
     Enterprise-grade integration, API-led connectivity, and service orchestration.
3. **Spring Integration:**
   - o **Description:**
     A lightweight framework for building enterprise integration solutions using the Spring ecosystem.
   - o **Features:**
     - Provides channels, transformers, and adapters for message routing
     - Seamless integration with Spring Boot applications
   - o **Use Cases:**
     Microservices communication, event-driven architectures, and integration with cloud services.

Middleware Solutions

Role of Middleware:

- **Data Transformation:**
  Convert data between different formats and models (e.g., converting relational data to graph structures).
- **Routing and Orchestration:**
  Direct data flows between systems and manage message passing.
- **Security and Logging:**
  Provide additional layers of security and monitoring for data transactions.

Table: Key Integration Frameworks and Middleware Solutions

Framework/Tool	Type	Key Features	Ideal Use Cases
Apache Camel	Integration Framework	Wide range of connectors, routing, and mediation capabilities	Data transformation, messaging systems, microservices integration
MuleSoft Anypoint	Integration Platform	Enterprise-grade API management, drag-and-drop design, pre-built connectors	Enterprise integration, API-led connectivity
Spring Integration	Integration Framework	Lightweight, Spring ecosystem integration, channels, and adapters	Microservices, event-driven architectures, cloud service integration
Custom Middleware	Custom/Ad-hoc Solutions	Tailored to specific needs, flexible and customizable	Specific use cases requiring bespoke integration logic

Code Example: Integrating a Graph Database with Apache Camel (Conceptual)

Below is a simplified example using Apache Camel's Java DSL to route messages between a graph database and a REST endpoint. (Note: This is a conceptual example and may need additional configuration for a full implementation.)

```java
import org.apache.camel.builder.RouteBuilder;

public class GraphIntegrationRoute extends RouteBuilder {
    @Override
    public void configure() throws Exception {
        // Define a route to poll data from a graph database
and expose it via a REST endpoint
        from("timer://graphDataPoller?period=60000")  // Poll
every 60 seconds
            .to("direct:queryGraph");
```

```
from("direct:queryGraph")
        .process(exchange -> {
                // Simulate querying the graph database
(e.g., using a Cypher query)
                String graphData = "Sample graph data: {
'nodes': [...], 'edges': [...] }";
                exchange.getIn().setBody(graphData);
        })
        .to("log:graphData?level=INFO")
        .to("direct:exposeData");

    from("direct:exposeData")

.to("restlet:http://localhost:8080/api/graphData?restletMetho
d=GET");
    }
}
```

Explanation:

- **Route Definition:**
  The route uses a timer to trigger data polling from the graph database
  at regular intervals.
- **Processing:**
  A processor simulates querying the graph database and setting the
  resulting data as the message body.
- **Logging and Exposure:**
  The data is logged and then exposed via a REST endpoint using
  Restlet.
- **Integration:**
  This route exemplifies how Apache Camel can integrate data flows
  between different components.

Summary of 11.3

Integration frameworks and middleware solutions are essential for building
cohesive, scalable, and maintainable graph-based systems. They facilitate
data transformation, routing, and secure communication between various
system components. By leveraging tools like Apache Camel, MuleSoft, and
Spring Integration, organizations can effectively connect graph databases
with other enterprise systems, ensuring smooth data flows and robust
application performance.

11.4 Case Study: Choosing the Right Technology Stack

Overview

Selecting the right technology stack for a graph-based system is a critical decision that affects performance, scalability, maintainability, and cost. In this case study, we walk through the process of evaluating requirements and making technology choices for an example application. We will consider factors such as data model, query needs, integration capabilities, scalability, and support.

Example Scenario

Scenario:
An e-commerce company plans to implement a recommendation system that leverages customer interactions, product data, and social relationships. The system should support complex relationship queries, real-time recommendations, and integration with existing enterprise services. The company is evaluating several graph database options along with integration frameworks and middleware.

Requirements Analysis

1. **Data Model and Query Complexity:**
   o The data is highly interconnected (customers, products, orders, reviews, social interactions).
   o The system requires support for complex traversals and relationship queries.
2. **Scalability and Performance:**
   o The system must handle high transaction volumes during peak shopping periods.
   o It should support both read-heavy and write-heavy workloads with low latency.
3. **Integration and Middleware:**
   o Integration with existing ERP systems and real-time data streams is essential.
   o A robust API layer and middleware to connect the graph database with web and mobile applications are required.
4. **Cost and Support:**

o Budget constraints favor open-source solutions; however, dedicated vendor support may be necessary for mission-critical components.

Evaluation of Technology Options

Based on these requirements, consider the following key components:

1. **Graph Database Options:**
   o **Neo4j (Open-Source Community Edition / Enterprise Edition):**
   Pros:
      - Native graph storage with powerful Cypher query language
      - Excellent performance for relationship queries
      - Strong community support and mature tooling
      Cons:
      - Enterprise features (e.g., clustering, advanced security) require the Enterprise Edition, which is proprietary
   o **Amazon Neptune:**
   Pros:
      - Fully managed service with high availability and scalability
      - Supports both property graph (Gremlin) and RDF (SPARQL) models
      - Seamless integration with AWS services
      Cons:
      - Higher ongoing operational costs compared to self-hosted solutions
   o **JanusGraph:**
   Pros:
      - Open-source and distributed, supports multiple storage backends (Cassandra, HBase)
      - Suitable for very large-scale deployments
      Cons:
      - Requires more complex configuration and management
      - Community support may be less comprehensive than Neo4j
2. **Integration Frameworks and Middleware:**

- o **Apache Camel:**
  Pros:
    - Flexible routing and data transformation capabilities
    - Supports a wide range of connectors and protocols
    Cons:
    - May require custom development to integrate with specific graph databases
- o **Spring Integration:**
  Pros:
    - Lightweight framework with excellent integration into Spring Boot applications
    - Well-suited for microservices architectures
    Cons:
    - Best for Java-centric environments; might require additional work for non-Java systems

3. **API and Service Layer:**
   - o **REST/GraphQL API Gateways:**
     Pros:
       - Provide abstraction over the graph database, making it easier for client applications to interact with the system
       - Facilitate versioning and security enforcement
       Cons:
       - Additional layer may introduce some latency if not optimized properly

Technology Stack Comparison Table

Component	Option 1	Option 2	Option 3	Key Considerations
Graph Database	Neo4j Community/Enterprise	Amazon Neptune	JanusGraph	Neo4j offers ease of use and mature tools; Neptune provides a fully managed solution within AWS; JanusGraph is ideal for large-

Component	Option 1	Option 2	Option 3	Key Considerations
				scale, distributed systems.
Integration Framework	Apache Camel	Spring Integration	Custom Middleware	Apache Camel is versatile and protocol-agnostic; Spring Integration fits well in Java environments; custom solutions offer tailored integration.
API Layer	REST/GraphQL Gateway	Custom API Layer	Hybrid Approach	Ensuring consistent, secure, and high-performance API access is critical. Consider the existing tech stack and team expertise when choosing the API solution.

Decision-Making Process

Using the evaluation criteria, the company may decide as follows:

- **Graph Database:**
  If the primary requirement is ease of use with strong community support and the company has a moderate scale, **Neo4j Enterprise Edition** may be the best choice despite its cost. For organizations

deeply integrated with AWS or requiring fully managed services, **Amazon Neptune** is a strong candidate. For very large-scale applications with the necessary in-house expertise, **JanusGraph** could be chosen.

- **Integration and Middleware:**
  If the development team is experienced with Java and Spring, **Spring Integration** may provide a smoother integration experience. Otherwise, **Apache Camel** offers flexibility across various languages and protocols.
- **API Layer:**
  A REST or GraphQL API gateway should be implemented to provide a consistent interface for client applications, with attention paid to performance and security.

After careful consideration, the company might choose a stack based on its current environment and future scalability needs. For example, if the company already leverages AWS heavily and values managed services, **Amazon Neptune** combined with a REST/GraphQL API and Apache Camel for integration could provide a robust and scalable solution. Conversely, if they prefer open-source and are comfortable managing their own infrastructure, **Neo4j Enterprise Edition** with Spring Integration and a custom API layer might be more appropriate.

11.5 Future Technologies and Emerging Tools

Overview

The landscape of graph-based systems is rapidly evolving, with new technologies and emerging tools continually reshaping the field. Staying informed about future trends helps organizations plan for long-term scalability, improved performance, and enhanced capabilities.

Emerging Technologies in Graph Databases

1. **Graph Neural Networks (GNNs):**
   - **Description:**
     GNNs are a class of machine learning models specifically designed to work with graph-structured data. They can learn

representations of nodes and edges, which are useful for tasks such as classification, link prediction, and clustering.
  - o **Potential Impact:**
    Integration of GNNs with traditional graph databases can lead to smarter, predictive systems that not only store data but also derive insights and detect patterns automatically.
2. **Federated Graph Querying:**
  - o **Description:**
    Techniques that allow queries to be executed across multiple, distributed graph databases seamlessly. This is especially relevant as organizations increasingly adopt polyglot persistence.
  - o **Potential Impact:**
    Improved interoperability and scalability by enabling a unified view over diverse data sources.
3. **Real-Time Graph Analytics Platforms:**
  - o **Description:**
    Platforms that support real-time analysis of graph data using in-memory processing and stream processing technologies.
  - o **Potential Impact:**
    Enhanced capabilities for dynamic systems such as fraud detection, network security, and personalized recommendations.

Emerging Integration and Middleware Tools

1. **Serverless Integration Platforms:**
  - o **Description:**
    Serverless architectures for integration, such as AWS Lambda and Azure Functions, can be used to build lightweight, event-driven data pipelines that interact with graph databases.
  - o **Potential Impact:**
    Lower operational overhead and improved scalability, especially for intermittent or bursty workloads.
2. **Enhanced API Management Solutions:**
  - o **Description:**
    Next-generation API management platforms that provide improved security, analytics, and developer experience for accessing graph-based services.
  - o **Potential Impact:**
    Streamlined development and better performance through caching, rate limiting, and dynamic scaling.

Future Trends in Tool Development

- **Convergence of Graph and ML Technologies:**
  As machine learning and graph data converge, we expect to see more platforms that natively support graph embeddings, hybrid analytics, and predictive modeling.
- **Increased Focus on Security and Privacy:**
  With growing data privacy regulations, future tools will likely incorporate advanced encryption, data masking, and compliance features directly into graph database management systems.
- **Integration with Blockchain and Decentralized Systems:**
  Some emerging tools are exploring the integration of graph databases with blockchain technology to provide immutable, decentralized data storage and provenance tracking.

Table: Future Technologies and Their Potential Impact

Technology/Tool	Description	Potential Impact
Graph Neural Networks (GNNs)	ML models for learning on graph data	Enhanced predictive analytics, intelligent feature extraction
Federated Graph Querying	Unified querying across distributed graph databases	Improved data integration and scalability
Real-Time Graph Analytics	In-memory and stream processing for graph data	Dynamic, real-time decision-making and monitoring
Serverless Integration Platforms	Event-driven, scalable integration without server management	Lower operational overhead, cost savings, scalability
Enhanced API Management	Advanced API gateways with improved security and analytics	Better developer experience, streamlined access to graph services
Blockchain Integration	Combining graph databases with blockchain technology	Immutable records, enhanced data provenance

Example: Conceptual Roadmap for Future Adoption

Imagine a company planning its technology roadmap for the next 3–5 years. The roadmap might include:

- **Short-Term:**
  Improve current graph systems by integrating advanced caching and monitoring tools.
- **Mid-Term:**
  Pilot projects integrating Graph Neural Networks to enhance recommendations and predictive analytics.
- **Long-Term:**
  Explore federated querying solutions and potential blockchain integrations for enhanced data security and provenance.

The future of graph-based systems is promising, with emerging technologies set to further enhance data analytics, machine learning integration, and system scalability. By staying informed about these trends and adopting new tools as they mature, organizations can maintain a competitive edge and build systems that are not only robust and scalable but also intelligent and adaptive to evolving business needs.

Chapter 12: Step-by-Step Implementation Guides

This chapter provides practical, hands-on guidance for implementing a graph-based system. We will walk through the process from setting up your development environment, ingesting raw data into a graph, and building a prototype knowledge graph that can be queried. These step-by-step instructions are designed to equip you with the skills to create a working knowledge graph system from scratch.

12.1 Setting Up Your Development Environment

Overview

Before developing a graph-based system, you need to set up your development environment with the necessary tools and frameworks. This setup includes installing a graph database, programming libraries, and development tools to facilitate building, testing, and deploying your application.

Key Components

1. **Graph Database Installation:**
   - **Neo4j Community Edition:**
     A popular open-source, native graph database that is easy to install and use for development and prototyping.
   - **Alternatives:**
     Other options include Amazon Neptune (for managed environments) or JanusGraph for distributed setups.
2. **Programming Language and Libraries:**
   - **Python:**
     Widely used for prototyping, with libraries such as `neo4j` for database connectivity, `networkx` for in-memory graph manipulation, and `pandas` for data processing.
   - **Installation Tools:**
     Use package managers like `pip` to install required libraries.

193

3. **Development Tools:**
   - **Integrated Development Environment (IDE):**
     Examples include Visual Studio Code, PyCharm, or any preferred text editor.
   - **Version Control:**
     Git for managing your codebase.
   - **Docker (Optional):**
     For containerizing your graph database and application for easier deployment and isolation.

Step-by-Step Setup

Step 1: Install Neo4j Community Edition

1. **Download Neo4j:**
   - Visit the Neo4j Download Center and select the Community Edition.
2. **Installation:**
   - Follow the installation instructions for your operating system (Windows, macOS, or Linux).
3. **Start the Neo4j Server:**
   - Launch Neo4j Desktop or use the command line to start the server.
   - Access the Neo4j Browser at `http://localhost:7474` and log in using the default credentials (username: `neo4j`, password: as set during installation).

Step 2: Set Up Your Python Environment

1. **Install Python (if not already installed):**
   - Download and install Python 3.x from python.org.
2. **Create a Virtual Environment:**

```bash
python -m venv graph-env
source graph-env/bin/activate  # On Windows: graph-env\Scripts\activate
```

3. **Install Required Libraries:**

```bash
```

```
pip install neo4j networkx pandas flask
```

- o `neo4j`: For connecting to the Neo4j database.
- o `networkx`: For in-memory graph processing and prototyping.
- o `pandas`: For data manipulation.
- o `flask`: (Optional) For creating API endpoints to interact with your graph.

Table: Development Environment Components

Component	Description	Installation/Resource
Neo4j Community Edition	Native graph database for development and prototyping	Neo4j Download Center
Python 3.x	Programming language for building and prototyping the system	python.org
Virtual Environment	Isolates dependencies for the project	`python -m venv graph-env`
Python Libraries	neo4j, networkx, pandas, flask for database connectivity and prototyping	Install via `pip install neo4j networkx pandas flask`
IDE	Code editor for development	Visual Studio Code, PyCharm, etc.

12.2 Data Ingestion: From Raw Data to Graph

Overview

Data ingestion involves the process of extracting raw data from various sources, transforming it into a format suitable for a graph model, and loading it into the graph database. In this section, we demonstrate a basic ETL (Extract, Transform, Load) process to ingest raw data into Neo4j.

Steps for Data Ingestion

1. **Extract:**
   o Collect raw data from sources such as CSV files, relational databases, or APIs.
2. **Transform:**
   o Clean the data, map fields to graph entities, and structure the data as nodes and relationships.
3. **Load:**
   o Insert the transformed data into the graph database using Cypher queries or import tools.

Example Scenario: Ingesting E-commerce Data

Suppose we have a CSV file containing customer and order information. We will ingest this data into Neo4j by creating nodes for Customers and Orders and relationships indicating which customer placed which order.

Sample CSV Data: `customers_orders.csv`

```
customer_id,customer_name,order_id,order_date,total
C001,John Doe,O1001,2025-01-15,250
C002,Jane Smith,O1002,2025-01-16,150
```

Python Script for Data Ingestion

Below is a complete Python script that reads the CSV file, transforms the data, and loads it into a Neo4j database using the `neo4j` driver.

```python
python

import csv
from neo4j import GraphDatabase

# Neo4j connection settings
uri = "bolt://localhost:7687"
username = "neo4j"
password = "your_password"

driver = GraphDatabase.driver(uri, auth=(username, password))
```

```python
def load_data_to_neo4j(csv_file_path):
    with driver.session() as session:
        with open(csv_file_path, 'r') as csvfile:
            reader = csv.DictReader(csvfile)
            for row in reader:
                # Create Customer node
                session.write_transaction(create_customer,
row['customer_id'], row['customer_name'])
                # Create Order node and relationship

session.write_transaction(create_order_and_relationship,
row['customer_id'], row['order_id'], row['order_date'],
row['total'])

def create_customer(tx, customer_id, customer_name):
    query = (
        "MERGE (c:Customer {id: $customer_id}) "
        "ON CREATE SET c.name = $customer_name"
    )
    tx.run(query, customer_id=customer_id,
customer_name=customer_name)

def create_order_and_relationship(tx, customer_id, order_id,
order_date, total):
    query = (
        "MERGE (c:Customer {id: $customer_id}) "
        "MERGE (o:Order {id: $order_id}) "
        "ON CREATE SET o.date = $order_date, o.total = $total
"
        "MERGE (c)-[:PLACED]->(o)"
    )
    tx.run(query, customer_id=customer_id, order_id=order_id,
order_date=order_date, total=float(total))

if __name__ == "__main__":
    csv_file_path = "customers_orders.csv"
    load_data_to_neo4j(csv_file_path)
    driver.close()
    print("Data ingestion completed successfully.")
```

Explanation:

- **CSV Reading:**
  The script reads from the CSV file using Python's `csv.DictReader`.
- **Data Transformation:**
  For each row, customer and order details are extracted.
- **Neo4j Transactions:**
  The functions `create_customer` and

`create_order_and_relationship` use Cypher queries with `MERGE` to create nodes and relationships in Neo4j.

- **Driver Management:**
  The Neo4j driver is used to manage the connection, and the session is closed after the data is loaded.

Table: ETL Process for Graph Data Ingestion

Step	Action	Tool/Method
Extract	Read raw data from CSV or other sources	Python `csv` module
Transform	Clean and map data fields to graph entities	Python scripting, data processing libraries (e.g., pandas)
Load	Insert nodes and relationships into Neo4j	Neo4j Cypher queries via `neo4j` Python driver

12.3 Building and Querying a Prototype Knowledge Graph

Overview

With the data ingested, the next step is to build a prototype knowledge graph and execute queries to validate the structure and relationships. In this section, we demonstrate how to construct a simple knowledge graph in Neo4j and query it using Cypher.

Building the Prototype

1. **Define the Graph Schema:**
   - **Nodes:**
     Create nodes for entities such as Customers and Orders.
   - **Relationships:**
     Define relationships such as `PLACED` between Customers and Orders.
2. **Populate the Graph:**
   - Use the data ingestion script (from Section 12.2) to populate the graph with sample data.

Querying the Prototype Knowledge Graph

After building the prototype, run several queries to validate and explore the data.

Example Queries

1. **Query: Retrieve All Customers and Their Orders**

   ```cypher
   cypher

   MATCH (c:Customer)-[:PLACED]->(o:Order)
   RETURN c.id AS CustomerID, c.name AS CustomerName, o.id
   AS OrderID, o.date AS OrderDate, o.total AS TotalAmount
   ```

   o **Explanation:**
     This query matches all Customer nodes connected to Order nodes via the PLACED relationship and returns relevant details.

2. **Query: Find Orders Above a Certain Total**

   ```cypher
   cypher

   MATCH (c:Customer)-[:PLACED]->(o:Order)
   WHERE o.total > 200
   RETURN c.name AS CustomerName, o.id AS OrderID, o.total
   AS TotalAmount
   ```

   o **Explanation:**
     Filters orders where the total amount exceeds 200, displaying the customer name and order details.

Code Example: Querying Using the Neo4j Python Driver

Below is a Python script that executes a query on the prototype knowledge graph and prints the results.

```python
python

from neo4j import GraphDatabase

# Neo4j connection settings (reuse from previous section)
uri = "bolt://localhost:7687"
username = "neo4j"
password = "your_password"
driver = GraphDatabase.driver(uri, auth=(username, password))
```

```
def query_customers_and_orders(tx):
    query = (
        "MATCH (c:Customer)-[:PLACED]->(o:Order) "
        "RETURN c.id AS CustomerID, c.name AS CustomerName,
o.id AS OrderID, o.date AS OrderDate, o.total AS TotalAmount"
    )
    result = tx.run(query)
    return [record for record in result]

with driver.session() as session:
    results =
session.read_transaction(query_customers_and_orders)
    for record in results:
        print(f"CustomerID: {record['CustomerID']}, Name:
{record['CustomerName']}, "
              f"OrderID: {record['OrderID']}, Date:
{record['OrderDate']}, Total: {record['TotalAmount']}")

driver.close()
```

Explanation:

- **Query Execution:**
  The `query_customers_and_orders` function runs a Cypher query to retrieve customer and order details.
- **Transaction Handling:**
  A read transaction is used to execute the query, ensuring proper handling of resources.
- **Result Processing:**
  The script prints each record's details, validating that the graph has been built correctly and the relationships are intact.

Table: Example Queries and Their Purposes

Query	Purpose	Expected Output
Retrieve all customers and their orders	Validate node creation and relationship mapping	List of customers with their corresponding orders
Find orders above a specified total	Filter and analyze order data based on a condition	Orders with totals greater than a set threshold

Overall Summary of Chapter 12

- **12.1 Setting Up Your Development Environment:**
  Detailed instructions were provided for installing Neo4j, setting up a Python virtual environment, and installing necessary libraries. A table summarized the components, ensuring that readers are prepared to start development.
- **12.2 Data Ingestion: From Raw Data to Graph:**
  We walked through an ETL process, using a CSV file containing customer and order data as an example. A complete Python script demonstrated how to extract, transform, and load data into Neo4j via Cypher queries, with a corresponding table outlining the ETL process.
- **12.3 Building and Querying a Prototype Knowledge Graph:**
  We explained how to construct a simple knowledge graph by defining nodes and relationships, then provided sample Cypher queries to validate the graph structure. A Python code example illustrated how to execute these queries using the Neo4j Python driver.

This comprehensive chapter equips you with practical, step-by-step guidance to set up your development environment, ingest raw data into a graph, and build a prototype knowledge graph that you can query and validate. By following these instructions and leveraging the provided examples, you can effectively implement a graph-based system tailored to your domain needs.

12.4 Incorporating RAG: Practical Integration Examples

Overview

Incorporating Retrieval-Augmented Generation (RAG) into your graph-based system involves integrating a retrieval module (to fetch relevant data from your graph database) with a generative language model (to produce natural language outputs). In this section, we provide practical examples that demonstrate how to integrate these components using Python. We will walk through the process step-by-step, from querying the graph database to generating augmented responses.

Key Steps in RAG Integration

1. **Query the Graph Database:**
   Retrieve contextually relevant information based on the user's query.
2. **Process and Format the Retrieved Data:**
   Transform raw graph data into a format suitable for input into the generative model.
3. **Combine the Query with the Retrieved Context:**
   Create a unified input that merges the original query and the contextual data.
4. **Generate the Final Response:**
   Use a generative language model to produce an answer that is augmented with the retrieved context.
5. **Return the Augmented Response:**
   Deliver the final output to the end-user.

Practical Example: RAG Integration Workflow

Below is a practical example that demonstrates each step in the RAG integration process using Python. In this example, we simulate a scenario where a user asks about the features of a new smartphone. The system queries a graph database, processes the retrieved context, and generates a final answer using a simulated language model.

Pseudocode Overview

1. **Retrieve Data from Graph:**
   The function `retrieve_context(query)` simulates querying the graph database.
2. **Process Retrieved Data:**
   The function `process_context(raw_data)` transforms the raw result into a summary.
3. **Combine Input for the Language Model:**
   The function `combine_inputs(query, context)` merges the query and processed context.
4. **Generate Augmented Response:**
   The function `generate_response(combined_input)` uses a language model to produce a final answer.
5. **Integration Pipeline:**
   The main function `rag_pipeline(query)` orchestrates the process.

Code Example: RAG Integration in Python

```python
python

# Simulated functions for a RAG system integration

def retrieve_context(query):
    """
    Simulate retrieving context data from a graph database.
    In a real implementation, this would execute a graph
query (e.g., using SPARQL or Cypher)
    to fetch relevant nodes and relationships.
    """
    # Example simulated data based on the query
    if "smartphone" in query.lower():
        raw_data = (
            "Smartphone: Model X, Features: high-resolution
camera, long battery life, "
            "fast processing, 5G connectivity, and an edge-
to-edge display."
        )
    else:
        raw_data = "No relevant data found."
    return raw_data

def process_context(raw_data):
    """
    Process and format the raw data retrieved from the graph.
    This function can perform additional cleaning or
summarization if needed.
    """
    # For this example, we assume the raw_data is already a
suitable summary.
    processed_context = raw_data.strip()
    return processed_context

def combine_inputs(query, context):
    """
    Combine the original query with the processed context
into a single input string.
    """
    combined_input = f"Query: {query}\nContext: {context}"
    return combined_input

def generate_response(combined_input):
    """
    Simulate generating a response using a generative
language model.
    In practice, this could call an API (e.g., OpenAI's GPT)
to generate the response.
    """
```

```python
        # For demonstration, we simulate a response based on the
combined input.
        # A real implementation would use a language model's
.generate() method.
    if "smartphone" in combined_input.lower():
        response = (
            "The latest smartphone, Model X, boasts a high-
resolution camera, "
            "long battery life, fast processing speeds, 5G
connectivity, and a stunning edge-to-edge display. "
            "These features make it an ideal choice for users
seeking performance and style."
        )
    else:
        response = "Sorry, I could not find relevant
information for your query."
    return response

def rag_pipeline(query):
    """
    Complete RAG integration pipeline: from retrieving
context from the graph to generating an augmented response.
    """
    raw_data = retrieve_context(query)
    context = process_context(raw_data)
    combined_input = combine_inputs(query, context)
    final_response = generate_response(combined_input)
    return final_response

# Example usage of the RAG pipeline
if __name__ == "__main__":
    user_query = "What are the key features of the new
smartphone?"
    answer = rag_pipeline(user_query)
    print("Augmented Response:")
    print(answer)
```

Explanation:

- **retrieve_context(query):**
  Simulates fetching relevant data from a graph database based on the query.
- **process_context(raw_data):**
  Cleans and prepares the retrieved data for use.
- **combine_inputs(query, context):**
  Merges the original query and the processed context into one string.
- **generate_response(combined_input):**
  Simulates a generative model's output using the combined input.

- **rag_pipeline(query):**
  Orchestrates the overall process and returns the final augmented response.

Table: RAG Integration Workflow Summary

Step	Function	Description
Data Retrieval	`retrieve_context(query)`	Simulates querying the graph database to fetch relevant data.
Context Processing	`process_context(raw_data)`	Cleans and formats the retrieved data.
Input Combination	`combine_inputs(query, context)`	Merges the query and context for the language model.
Response Generation	`generate_response(combined_input)`	Produces a natural language output based on the combined input.
Pipeline Orchestration	`rag_pipeline(query)`	Integrates all steps to provide the final augmented response.

12.5 Testing, Debugging, and Iterative Improvement

Overview

Testing, debugging, and iterative improvement are critical phases in the development of graph-based systems, especially when integrating complex components such as RAG. This section details strategies for ensuring your implementation is robust, efficient, and adaptable to changes.

Testing Strategies

1. **Unit Testing:**
   - **Definition:**
     Test individual functions or modules in isolation.
   - **Example:**
     Test functions like `retrieve_context()`, `process_context()`, and `combine_inputs()` with a variety of inputs to ensure they produce the expected output.
   - **Tools:**
     Python's `unittest` or `pytest` frameworks.
2. **Integration Testing:**
   - **Definition:**
     Test the complete pipeline (e.g., the `rag_pipeline()`) to ensure that all components interact correctly.
   - **Example:**
     Create test cases that simulate full end-to-end scenarios and verify that the final response is accurate.
   - **Tools:**
     End-to-end testing frameworks, API testing tools like Postman.
3. **Performance Testing:**
   - **Definition:**
     Assess the system's performance under load, including latency and throughput.
   - **Example:**
     Use stress testing tools to simulate multiple concurrent requests to the RAG pipeline.
   - **Tools:**
     Apache JMeter, Locust.

Debugging Techniques

1. **Logging and Monitoring:**
   - **Definition:**
     Implement logging at critical points in the code to track variable states and execution flow.
   - **Example:**
     Log the output of `retrieve_context()` and `process_context()` to verify that data is being correctly fetched and processed.

- o **Tools:**
  Python's `logging` module, ELK Stack for centralized logging.
2. **Interactive Debugging:**
   - o **Definition:**
     Use interactive debuggers to step through code and inspect variables at runtime.
   - o **Example:**
     Use Python's `pdb` module or IDE-integrated debuggers in Visual Studio Code or PyCharm.
   - o **Tips:**
     Set breakpoints in critical functions and monitor the flow of data.
3. **Automated Testing:**
   - o **Definition:**
     Use automated tests to quickly identify issues after changes are made.
   - o **Example:**
     Run unit tests automatically with every code commit using Continuous Integration (CI) tools.
   - o **Tools:**
     Jenkins, GitHub Actions, Travis CI.

Iterative Improvement Strategies

1. **Feedback Loops:**
   - o **Definition:**
     Continuously collect feedback from testing, user interactions, and monitoring systems.
   - o **Example:**
     Use performance metrics and error logs to identify bottlenecks or recurring issues.
   - o **Implementation:**
     Regularly review test results and iterate on the implementation to resolve issues.
2. **Refactoring:**
   - o **Definition:**
     Continuously improve code quality by refactoring inefficient or complex sections.
   - o **Best Practices:**
     Ensure that tests cover refactored code to maintain functionality.

3. **Version Control and Branching:**
   - **Definition:**
     Use version control to manage changes and experiment with improvements without affecting the production code.
   - **Example:**
     Use Git branches to develop new features or optimizations, then merge them into the main branch after thorough testing.

Table: Testing and Debugging Strategies

Strategy	Description	Tools/Techniques	Benefits
Unit Testing	Testing individual functions or modules in isolation	Python `unittest`, `pytest`	Early detection of bugs, code reliability
Integration Testing	Testing the complete pipeline for proper component interaction	Postman, Selenium, custom test scripts	Ensures end-to-end functionality
Performance Testing	Simulating load to measure latency and throughput	Apache JMeter, Locust	Identifies performance bottlenecks
Logging	Recording execution details for troubleshooting	Python `logging`, ELK Stack	Helps diagnose issues and monitor system health
Interactive Debugging	Stepping through code interactively	Python `pdb`, IDE debuggers	Provides real-time insights into code execution
Continuous Integration (CI)	Automating tests and builds with every code change	Jenkins, GitHub Actions, Travis CI	Ensures code quality and rapid feedback

Code Example: Unit Test for a RAG Component Using Pytest

Below is an example unit test for the `combine_inputs()` function using Pytest.

```python
```

```python
# File: test_rag.py
import pytest
from your_module import combine_inputs  # Replace
'your_module' with the actual module name

def test_combine_inputs():
    query = "What are the features of the new smartphone?"
    context = "Context: Model X with a high-resolution camera
and long battery life."
    expected_output = (
        "Query: What are the features of the new
smartphone?\n"
        "Context: Context: Model X with a high-resolution
camera and long battery life."
    )
    output = combine_inputs(query, context)
    assert output == expected_output

if __name__ == "__main__":
    pytest.main()
```

Explanation:

- **Test Function:**
  The function `test_combine_inputs()` tests whether
  `combine_inputs()` produces the expected output.
- **Assertion:**
  The `assert` statement verifies that the function's output matches the
  expected result.
- **Running Tests:**
  You can run the tests using the command `pytest test_rag.py` in
  your terminal.

Iterative Improvement Example: Refactoring and Testing

After initial tests, suppose you notice that `process_context()` needs
additional cleaning. You refactor it as follows:

python

```python
def process_context(raw_data):
    """
    Process and format the raw data into a usable context.
    Refactored to remove extra whitespace and handle missing
data.
    """
    if not raw_data:
```

```
    return "No context available."
# Remove extra whitespace and ensure clean formatting
processed_context = " ".join(raw_data.split())
return processed_context
```

- **Refactoring:**
  The function now checks for missing data and normalizes whitespace.
- **Retesting:**
  Run your unit tests again to ensure that the changes do not break existing functionality.

Summary of 12.5

Testing, debugging, and iterative improvement are critical for ensuring that your RAG-integrated graph-based system is robust, efficient, and reliable. By implementing unit and integration tests, using logging and interactive debuggers, and continuously refining your code based on feedback, you can maintain a high-quality system that evolves to meet user needs and performance requirements.

Chapter 13: Data Integration, ETL, and Pipeline Management

Effective data integration is vital for building robust graph-based systems. This chapter focuses on the key aspects of Extract, Transform, Load (ETL) processes and pipeline management. We will explore best practices for data extraction and transformation, review popular ETL tools and automation strategies, and discuss techniques to ensure high data quality through cleansing and validation.

13.1 Best Practices for Data Extraction and Transformation

Overview

Data extraction and transformation form the first two stages of the ETL process. Extraction involves gathering data from diverse sources, while transformation converts raw data into a format that aligns with your target data model (such as nodes, edges, and properties for graph databases). Following best practices in these steps is essential for ensuring that the data is accurate, consistent, and ready for analysis.

Best Practices for Data Extraction

1. **Source Identification and Prioritization:**
   - **Identify all data sources:**
     Determine which databases, files (e.g., CSV, JSON), APIs, or streams contain the relevant data.
   - **Assess data availability and frequency:**
     Prioritize sources based on their reliability and how frequently the data is updated.
2. **Data Connectivity:**
   - **Use robust connectors:**
     Use well-supported libraries or connectors (e.g., Python's `pandas`, `requests`, or specific database drivers) to interface with data sources.

- o **Handle authentication and security:**
  Ensure that connections use secure protocols (e.g., HTTPS) and proper authentication mechanisms.
3. **Incremental Extraction:**
   - o **Delta Loading:**
     Whenever possible, extract only the new or changed data since the last extraction to reduce load and processing time.
   - o **Timestamps and Change Data Capture (CDC):**
     Use timestamps or CDC mechanisms to track changes in source data.

Best Practices for Data Transformation

1. **Data Mapping:**
   - o **Field Mapping:**
     Map source data fields to the target graph schema. For example, map a CSV column "Customer_ID" to a node property "id" in a Customer node.
   - o **Consistent Naming Conventions:**
     Use clear and consistent naming conventions for fields to ensure clarity and maintainability.
2. **Data Normalization:**
   - o **Standardize Formats:**
     Convert dates, numbers, and other data types to a consistent format.
     Example: Convert all date strings to ISO 8601 format.
   - o **Remove Redundancy:**
     Eliminate duplicate entries and normalize data to reduce inconsistencies.
3. **Data Enrichment:**
   - o **Augment Data:**
     Enrich raw data with additional information where necessary.
     Example: Add derived attributes such as age from a birthdate.
   - o **Semantic Annotation:**
     Add metadata or link data to external ontologies to enhance context.
4. **Error Handling:**
   - o **Validation Checks:**
     Incorporate checks to validate data integrity during transformation (e.g., missing values, invalid formats).

o **Logging:**
Log any anomalies or transformation errors for later review and debugging.

Table: Best Practices for Data Extraction and Transformation

Practice	Description	Example/Tool
Source Identification	Identify and prioritize all relevant data sources	Inventory of databases, CSV files, APIs
Secure Connectivity	Use robust connectors and secure protocols (HTTPS, SSL/TLS)	Python `requests`, database drivers, ODBC/JDBC connectors
Incremental Extraction	Extract only new or changed data using delta loading or CDC	Using timestamps, CDC tools
Data Mapping	Map source data fields to target schema with consistent naming	Data dictionaries, mapping files
Data Normalization	Standardize formats and remove redundancy	Python `pandas` for data cleaning
Data Enrichment	Augment raw data with derived attributes and semantic annotations	Custom transformation scripts, integration with external ontologies
Error Handling and Logging	Validate data during transformation and log errors	Python logging, error handling frameworks

13.2 ETL Tools and Automation

Overview

ETL tools streamline the process of extracting data from various sources, transforming it to meet target specifications, and loading it into the graph database or data warehouse. Automation of these processes ensures that data integration is efficient, repeatable, and scalable.

Popular ETL Tools

1. **Apache NiFi:**
   - **Description:**
     A powerful, open-source ETL tool that supports data routing, transformation, and system mediation.
   - **Features:**
     - Visual interface for designing data flows
     - Real-time data processing
     - Integration with various data sources and formats
   - **Use Cases:**
     Suitable for complex workflows and real-time streaming data integration.
2. **Talend:**
   - **Description:**
     A comprehensive ETL and data integration platform that offers both open-source and enterprise versions.
   - **Features:**
     - Drag-and-drop interface
     - Extensive connector library
     - Data quality and governance capabilities
   - **Use Cases:**
     Ideal for organizations requiring robust, scalable data integration solutions with data quality management.
3. **Informatica PowerCenter:**
   - **Description:**
     A widely used proprietary ETL tool known for its scalability, reliability, and support for large enterprises.
   - **Features:**
     - Advanced transformation capabilities
     - Built-in data cleansing and profiling tools
     - Enterprise-level support and integration
   - **Use Cases:**
     Suitable for large-scale, enterprise data integration projects.
4. **Custom ETL Scripts:**
   - **Description:**
     Lightweight, custom-built ETL solutions using programming languages such as Python.
   - **Features:**
     - Highly customizable
     - Can be tailored to specific data formats and requirements

o **Use Cases:**
  Ideal for small to medium-sized projects or as a supplement to existing ETL tools.

Automation Strategies

- **Scheduling and Orchestration:**
  o Use tools like Apache Airflow or Cron jobs to schedule and orchestrate ETL workflows.
- **Monitoring and Alerting:**
  o Implement monitoring tools to track ETL job performance and trigger alerts for failures.
- **Scalability:**
  o Design ETL processes that can scale horizontally to handle increasing data volumes.

Table: Comparison of ETL Tools

Tool	Type	Key Features	Ideal Use Cases
Apache NiFi	Open-source	Visual interface, real-time processing, data routing	Complex, real-time streaming data integration
Talend	Open-source/Enterprise	Drag-and-drop design, extensive connectors, data quality tools	Robust ETL in medium to large organizations
Informatica PowerCenter	Proprietary	Advanced transformations, enterprise support, data governance	Large-scale, enterprise-level ETL and integration
Custom Scripts	Custom-built	Highly customizable, lightweight, language-specific	Small to medium-sized projects or custom ETL needs

Code Example: A Simple ETL Process with Python

Below is an example Python script that demonstrates a basic ETL process using Pandas to extract data from a CSV file, transform it, and print it out as a precursor to loading it into a graph database.

```python
python

import pandas as pd

def extract_data(file_path):
    """
    Extract data from a CSV file.
    """
    df = pd.read_csv(file_path)
    return df

def transform_data(df):
    """
    Transform data by standardizing date formats and renaming
columns.
    """
    # Convert 'order_date' column to datetime in ISO format
    df['order_date'] =
pd.to_datetime(df['order_date']).dt.strftime('%Y-%m-%d')
    # Rename columns to match the graph schema
    df.rename(columns={'customer_id': 'CustomerID',
'customer_name': 'CustomerName',
                       'order_id': 'OrderID', 'order_date':
'OrderDate', 'total': 'TotalAmount'},
             inplace=True)
    return df

def load_data(df):
    """
    Simulate loading data by printing the transformed
DataFrame.
    In a real scenario, this function would insert data into
a graph database.
    """
    print(df.head())

if __name__ == "__main__":
    file_path = "customers_orders.csv"
    raw_data = extract_data(file_path)
    transformed_data = transform_data(raw_data)
    load_data(transformed_data)
```

Explanation:

- **Extract:**
  The `extract_data()` function reads a CSV file using Pandas.
- **Transform:**
  The `transform_data()` function standardizes date formats and renames columns to match the target schema.

- **Load:**
  The `load_data()` function prints the DataFrame to simulate loading data. In a production scenario, this step would involve inserting the data into a graph database using appropriate APIs or drivers.

13.3 Data Quality and Cleansing Techniques

Overview

Ensuring data quality is crucial for the accuracy and reliability of a graph-based system. Data cleansing techniques help remove errors, inconsistencies, and redundancies in raw data before it is ingested into the system.

Key Techniques for Data Quality and Cleansing

1. **Data Validation:**
   - **Definition:**
     Verify that data meets predefined rules and formats.
   - **Techniques:**
     - Check for missing or null values
     - Validate data types and ranges (e.g., dates, numeric values)
   - **Example:**
     Ensuring that order dates are valid and within expected timeframes.
2. **Data Normalization:**
   - **Definition:**
     Standardize data formats and units across the dataset.
   - **Techniques:**
     - Convert date formats to a standard (e.g., ISO 8601)
     - Normalize text data (e.g., converting all text to lowercase)
   - **Example:**
     Standardizing customer names and addresses to avoid duplicates due to formatting differences.
3. **Duplicate Removal:**
   - **Definition:**
     Identify and remove duplicate records that may cause redundancy.

- o **Techniques:**
  - Use unique identifiers to detect duplicates
  - Apply fuzzy matching for records with minor differences
- o **Example:**
  Removing duplicate customer entries that have slightly different spellings.

4. **Data Enrichment:**
   - o **Definition:**
     Enhance data by adding missing information or linking to external datasets.
   - o **Techniques:**
     - Use external APIs or databases to fill in missing values
     - Append additional attributes based on existing data
   - o **Example:**
     Adding geographical data to customer addresses.

5. **Error Correction:**
   - o **Definition:**
     Identify and correct errors or inconsistencies in data.
   - o **Techniques:**
     - Manual review or automated correction algorithms
     - Cross-referencing with reliable data sources
   - o **Example:**
     Correcting misspelled product names based on a master product list.

Table: Data Quality and Cleansing Techniques

Technique	Description	Implementation Example
Data Validation	Verify that data meets quality rules and formats	Checking for null values in order_date columns
Data Normalization	Standardize data formats and units	Converting all dates to ISO 8601, lowercasing text
Duplicate Removal	Identify and remove duplicate records	Using unique customer IDs to filter duplicates
Data Enrichment	Enhance data by filling in missing information	Adding geographic coordinates to addresses
Error Correction	Identify and fix errors in data	Correcting typos in product names based on a reference

Code Example: Data Cleansing with Pandas

Below is a Python script that demonstrates data validation, normalization, duplicate removal, and basic error correction using Pandas.

```python
python

import pandas as pd

def clean_data(file_path):
    # Extract data from CSV
    df = pd.read_csv(file_path)

    # Data Validation: Check for missing values in critical
columns
    if df['order_date'].isnull().any():
        print("Warning: Missing order_date values detected.")
        df['order_date'].fillna('1970-01-01', inplace=True)
# Default value or alternative handling

    # Data Normalization: Standardize date formats and
lowercase text data
    df['order_date'] = pd.to_datetime(df['order_date'],
errors='coerce').dt.strftime('%Y-%m-%d')
    df['customer_name'] = df['customer_name'].str.lower()

    # Duplicate Removal: Drop duplicate records based on a
unique identifier (customer_id and order_id)
    df.drop_duplicates(subset=['customer_id', 'order_id'],
inplace=True)

    # Error Correction: Example - correcting common typos in
product names (this can be expanded)
    df['product_name'] =
df['product_name'].replace({'smrtphone': 'smartphone',
'headphnes': 'headphones'})

    return df

if __name__ == "__main__":
    file_path = "customers_orders_products.csv"  # Assume CSV
has columns: customer_id, customer_name, order_id,
order_date, total, product_name
    cleaned_data = clean_data(file_path)
    print("Cleaned Data Sample:")
    print(cleaned_data.head())
```

Explanation:

- **Data Extraction:**
  The CSV file is read into a Pandas DataFrame.
- **Validation:**
  The script checks for missing values in the `order_date` column and fills them with a default value.
- **Normalization:**
  Dates are converted to ISO 8601 format, and customer names are converted to lowercase.
- **Duplicate Removal:**
  Duplicates are dropped based on `customer_id` and `order_id`.
- **Error Correction:**
  Common typos in product names are corrected using the `replace` method.

Summary of 13.3

Ensuring data quality through validation, normalization, duplicate removal, enrichment, and error correction is critical for the success of any ETL process. By implementing robust data cleansing techniques, you ensure that the data loaded into your graph-based system is accurate, consistent, and ready for analysis.

13.4 Real-Time vs. Batch Processing in Graph Systems

Overview

In data integration and ETL processes for graph systems, two primary processing paradigms exist: real-time processing and batch processing. Each approach has its advantages, trade-offs, and ideal use cases. Understanding these differences is essential for designing a system that meets your application's performance, latency, and data freshness requirements.

Real-Time Processing

Definition:
Real-time processing refers to the immediate ingestion, transformation, and loading of data as soon as it is generated or received. This approach is essential when up-to-date information is critical for decision-making.

Key Characteristics:

- **Low Latency:**
  Data is processed almost immediately, allowing for instantaneous insights and actions.
- **Continuous Flow:**
  Data flows continuously through the system, often using streaming technologies.
- **Use Cases:**
  - Real-time analytics (e.g., fraud detection, social media monitoring)
  - Dynamic recommendations in e-commerce or content platforms
  - IoT sensor data processing

Common Tools and Technologies:

- **Apache Kafka:**
  A distributed streaming platform that allows real-time data ingestion and processing.
- **Apache Flink / Apache Spark Streaming:**
  Stream processing engines that support real-time analytics and ETL.
- **Change Data Capture (CDC):**
  Mechanisms that track and stream changes from data sources in real time.

Advantages:

- **Timely Insights:**
  Immediate processing provides the latest data for critical decisions.
- **Dynamic Responses:**
  Enables systems to react to events as they occur (e.g., triggering alerts).

Challenges:

- **Complexity:**
  Real-time systems can be more complex to design, implement, and maintain.
- **Resource Intensive:**
  Requires robust infrastructure to handle continuous data flow and high throughput.

Batch Processing

Definition:
Batch processing involves accumulating data over a period of time and processing it all at once. This method is suitable for tasks where immediate data freshness is not critical.

Key Characteristics:

- **High Throughput:**
  Processes large volumes of data in one go.
- **Scheduled Execution:**
  Typically run on a fixed schedule (e.g., nightly or weekly).
- **Use Cases:**
  - Periodic reporting and analytics
  - Data warehousing and archival
  - Bulk data migration or transformation tasks

Common Tools and Technologies:

- **Apache Airflow:**
  An orchestration tool for scheduling and managing batch workflows.
- **Talend and Informatica:**
  Comprehensive ETL platforms that support batch processing.
- **Custom Scripts:**
  Python or shell scripts scheduled via cron jobs for smaller-scale tasks.

Advantages:

- **Efficiency for Large Datasets:**
  Batch processing can efficiently handle and transform large amounts of data.
- **Simpler Error Handling:**
  Since processing occurs in defined intervals, errors can be isolated and addressed during scheduled runs.

Challenges:

- **Latency:**
  Data is not processed immediately; insights may be delayed until the next batch cycle.

- **Resource Peaks:**
  Batch jobs can lead to high resource consumption during execution periods.

Comparison Table: Real-Time vs. Batch Processing

Aspect	Real-Time Processing	Batch Processing
Latency	Low latency; near-instant processing	Higher latency; processing occurs at intervals
Data Freshness	Provides current, up-to-date information	May have delayed data, depending on batch frequency
Processing Model	Continuous stream of data	Accumulated data processed in large chunks
Use Cases	Real-time analytics, IoT, dynamic recommendations	Periodic reporting, data warehousing, bulk ETL
Tools/Technologies	Apache Kafka, Apache Flink, Spark Streaming, CDC	Apache Airflow, Talend, Informatica, custom cron jobs
Complexity	Generally more complex to implement and maintain	Simpler design; easier to manage in controlled intervals
Resource Utilization	Requires constant resource allocation	Can optimize resources during off-peak hours

Code Example: Real-Time vs. Batch Processing Simulation (Python)

Below is a simple Python example that demonstrates the basic difference between processing data in real time versus in batches. This example uses a simulated data stream and a simple function to process data.

```python
import time
import random

# Simulated data stream generator for real-time processing
```

```python
def generate_real_time_data():
    while True:
        data = random.randint(1, 100)
        yield data
        time.sleep(1)  # Simulate a data event every second

# Real-time processing function
def process_real_time():
    print("Real-Time Processing Started:")
    data_stream = generate_real_time_data()
    for _ in range(5):  # Process 5 events for demonstration
        data = next(data_stream)
        print(f"Processed real-time data: {data}")

# Batch processing function
def process_batch():
    print("Batch Processing Started:")
    # Simulate batch data collected over time
    batch_data = [random.randint(1, 100) for _ in range(10)]
    print(f"Batch data collected: {batch_data}")
    # Process the entire batch at once
    for data in batch_data:
        print(f"Processed batch data: {data}")

if __name__ == "__main__":
    # Simulate real-time processing
    process_real_time()
    print("\n")
    # Simulate batch processing
    process_batch()
```

Explanation:

- **Real-Time Simulation:**
  The generate_real_time_data() function simulates a continuous stream by yielding random data every second. The process_real_time() function processes a few events as they occur.
- **Batch Simulation:**
  The process_batch() function simulates accumulating data in a list and then processing the entire batch at once.
- **Output:**
  This example illustrates the difference in processing methods, where real-time processing handles data event-by-event, and batch processing handles a group of data at one time.

13.5 Case Studies on Successful Data Integration

Overview

Case studies offer valuable insights into real-world applications of data integration and ETL processes in graph-based systems. In this section, we present examples of successful data integration projects, highlighting the challenges, solutions, and benefits achieved.

Case Study 1: E-commerce Recommendation System

Background:

- **Scenario:**
  An e-commerce company sought to improve its product recommendation engine by integrating data from various sources, including customer interactions, purchase histories, and product metadata.
- **Challenge:**
  Data was scattered across multiple databases and file formats, leading to inconsistent and outdated recommendations.

Solution:

- **Data Integration Approach:**
  The company implemented a batch ETL process using Talend to extract data from relational databases, CSV files, and external APIs. Data was cleansed, normalized, and transformed into a unified graph structure.
- **Graph Database Implementation:**
  The integrated data was loaded into Neo4j, where relationships between customers, products, and transactions were modeled.
- **Outcome:**
  Enhanced recommendation accuracy, improved customer satisfaction, and a significant increase in sales due to personalized recommendations.

Key Takeaways:

- A robust ETL pipeline ensures data consistency and quality.
- Integrating diverse data sources into a graph enables more accurate relationship modeling.
- Batch processing can be effective for periodic updates in an e-commerce context.

Case Study 2: Real-Time Fraud Detection in Financial Services

Background:

- **Scenario:**
  A financial institution needed to detect fraudulent transactions in real time to prevent financial losses and maintain customer trust.
- **Challenge:**
  Traditional batch processing was too slow, and the data was too complex due to the interconnected nature of financial transactions.

Solution:

- **Data Integration Approach:**
  The institution implemented a real-time ETL pipeline using Apache Kafka and Spark Streaming to capture and process transaction data as it occurred.
- **Graph Database Implementation:**
  Data was loaded into Amazon Neptune, which provided low-latency graph querying capabilities for analyzing complex transaction networks.
- **Outcome:**
  Real-time fraud detection enabled rapid responses to suspicious activities, reducing financial losses and enhancing security.

Key Takeaways:

- Real-time data integration is critical for applications requiring immediate insights.
- Using streaming technologies and managed graph databases can meet high-performance and scalability demands.
- Continuous monitoring and rapid processing can dramatically improve fraud detection capabilities.

Case Study 3: Healthcare Knowledge Graph for Research and Patient Care

Background:

- **Scenario:**
  A healthcare provider aimed to build a knowledge graph that integrated patient records, clinical trial data, and medical research to support personalized patient care and advanced research.
- **Challenge:**
  Data was stored in heterogeneous systems, including legacy databases and unstructured medical texts, making it difficult to obtain a unified view.

Solution:

- **Data Integration Approach:**
  The provider used Apache NiFi to build a data pipeline that extracted, transformed, and loaded data from multiple sources into a unified format. Data cleansing and semantic enrichment techniques were applied to standardize medical terminologies.
- **Graph Database Implementation:**
  The integrated data was stored in GraphDB, leveraging its RDF-based model and SPARQL querying capabilities.
- **Outcome:**
  The knowledge graph enabled physicians to access comprehensive patient histories and research findings, leading to improved diagnoses and personalized treatment plans.

Key Takeaways:

- Combining batch and real-time ETL processes can address diverse data integration needs.
- Semantic enrichment is essential for integrating heterogeneous healthcare data.
- A well-designed knowledge graph can enhance both clinical decision-making and research capabilities.

Table: Summary of Case Studies

Case Study	Domain	Processing Mode	Key Technologies	Outcome/Benefit
E-commerce Recommendation System	Retail/E-commerce	Batch Processing	Talend, Neo4j	Improved recommendation accuracy, increased sales
Real-Time Fraud Detection	Financial Services	Real-Time Processing	Apache Kafka, Spark Streaming, Amazon Neptune	Rapid fraud detection, reduced financial losses
Healthcare Knowledge Graph	Healthcare	Hybrid (Batch & Real-Time)	Apache NiFi, GraphDB	Enhanced patient care, better research integration

Chapter 14: Querying, Analytics, and Visualization

Graph-based systems enable rich querying capabilities, in-depth analytics, and compelling visualizations to derive insights from complex, interconnected data. In this chapter, we explore advanced query techniques across various query languages, discuss methods for analyzing graph data, and review tools and techniques for effective visualization.

14.1 Advanced Query Techniques: SPARQL, Cypher, and GraphQL

Overview

Graph data can be queried using specialized languages designed to exploit its inherent structure. This section covers three widely used query languages:

- **SPARQL:**
  Designed for querying RDF data.
- **Cypher:**
  A declarative query language used primarily with Neo4j for property graphs.
- **GraphQL:**
  A query language for APIs that enables clients to request exactly the data they need, often used with graph-like data models.

SPARQL

Key Concepts:

- **Triple Patterns:**
  SPARQL queries are built around triple patterns that match subject–predicate–object triples.
- **Query Forms:**
  Common forms include SELECT (retrieve variables), ASK (boolean queries), CONSTRUCT (build new RDF graphs), and DESCRIBE (provide a description of resources).

Example SPARQL Query:

```sparql
sparql

PREFIX schema: <http://schema.org/>
PREFIX ex: <http://example.org/>

SELECT ?customer ?order ?total
WHERE {
  ?customer a schema:Person ;
            schema:name ?name .
  ?customer schema:places ?order .
  ?order schema:total ?total .
  FILTER(?total > 100)
}
```

Explanation:

- **PREFIX declarations:**
  Define namespaces for clarity.
- **Triple Patterns:**
  Match a customer who placed an order with a total greater than 100.
- **FILTER Clause:**
  Applies a condition to narrow down results.

Cypher

Key Concepts:

- **Pattern Matching:**
  Cypher uses ASCII-art-like syntax to describe graph patterns.
- **Declarative Syntax:**
  Focuses on what data to retrieve rather than how to retrieve it.

Example Cypher Query:

```cypher
cypher

// Find customers who placed orders with a total greater than
100
MATCH (c:Customer)-[:PLACED]->(o:Order)
WHERE o.total > 100
RETURN c.name AS CustomerName, o.orderId AS OrderID, o.total
AS TotalAmount
```

Explanation:

- **MATCH Clause:**
  Finds patterns in the graph.
- **WHERE Clause:**
  Filters orders with a total above 100.
- **RETURN Clause:**
  Specifies the data to be returned.

GraphQL

Key Concepts:

- **Flexible Data Retrieval:**
  Clients can specify exactly which fields they need.
- **Hierarchical Structure:**
  Reflects the nested nature of graph data.

Example GraphQL Query:

```graphql
{
  customer(id: "C001") {
    name
    orders {
      orderId
      date
      total
      products {
        name
        price
      }
    }
  }
}
```

Explanation:

- **Query Structure:**
  The query requests a customer by ID, along with their orders and details about the products in each order.
- **Field Selection:**
  Only the specified fields are returned, reducing over-fetching.

Comparison Table: SPARQL vs. Cypher vs. GraphQL

Feature	SPARQL	Cypher	GraphQL
Data Model	RDF triples	Property Graph	API-centric graph data (flexible schema)
Syntax Style	Triple patterns, similar to SQL-like queries	Pattern matching with ASCII art style	JSON-like query language
Primary Use Case	Semantic Web, knowledge graphs	Social networks, recommendation systems	Client-driven data fetching in web/mobile apps
Strength	Rich semantic reasoning, standardized	Intuitive for graph traversal	Precise, client-specified data retrieval

14.2 Analytics on Graph Data: Patterns, Trends, and Insights

Overview

Graph analytics involves uncovering patterns, trends, and insights from interconnected data. Advanced analytics can reveal hidden relationships, community structures, and influential nodes that traditional analytics might miss.

Key Graph Analytics Techniques

1. **Centrality Measures:**
   - **Degree Centrality:**
     The number of connections a node has. Indicates immediate influence.
   - **Betweenness Centrality:**
     Measures how often a node appears on the shortest paths between other nodes. Indicates control over information flow.
   - **Closeness Centrality:**
     Reflects how close a node is to all other nodes in the network.

- o **Example:**
  Identifying key influencers in a social network.
2. **Community Detection:**
   - o **Definition:**
     Algorithms to detect clusters or communities within a graph.
   - o **Techniques:**
     - ▪ **Louvain Method:**
       Optimizes modularity to find communities.
     - ▪ **Label Propagation:**
       Spreads labels based on majority voting.
   - o **Example:**
     Segmenting customers into communities based on shared interests or behaviors.
3. **Path Analysis:**
   - o **Definition:**
     Finding the shortest or most relevant paths between nodes.
   - o **Techniques:**
     - ▪ **Dijkstra's Algorithm:**
       For shortest path calculation.
     - ▪ **A* Search:**
       Heuristic-based path finding.
   - o **Example:**
     Determining the degree of separation between two entities in a network.
4. **Pattern Matching and Subgraph Extraction:**
   - o **Definition:**
     Identifying recurring substructures or motifs in the graph.
   - o **Techniques:**
     - ▪ **Graph Pattern Matching:**
       Using query languages like Cypher to detect specific patterns.
   - o **Example:**
     Detecting fraud rings in financial transactions.

Table: Key Graph Analytics Techniques and Their Applications

Technique	Description	Application Example
Centrality Measures	Identify influential nodes based on their connectivity	Identifying key influencers in social networks
Community Detection	Segment the graph into clusters or communities	Customer segmentation, fraud detection

Technique	Description	Application Example
Path Analysis	Calculate the shortest or most relevant paths	Determining degrees of separation in networks
Pattern Matching	Extract recurring subgraph structures	Detecting fraud patterns, network motifs

Code Example: Analyzing Graph Centrality Using NetworkX (Python)

Below is a Python code example using NetworkX to calculate and display degree centrality and betweenness centrality in a sample graph.

```python
import networkx as nx
import matplotlib.pyplot as plt

# Create a sample graph
G = nx.karate_club_graph()  # Using a built-in social network
graph for demonstration

# Calculate degree centrality and betweenness centrality
degree_centrality = nx.degree_centrality(G)
betweenness_centrality = nx.betweenness_centrality(G)

# Print centrality measures for a few nodes
print("Degree Centrality:")
for node, centrality in list(degree_centrality.items())[:5]:
    print(f"Node {node}: {centrality:.4f}")

print("\nBetweenness Centrality:")
for node, centrality in
list(betweenness_centrality.items())[:5]:
    print(f"Node {node}: {centrality:.4f}")

# Visualize the graph with node sizes based on degree
centrality
plt.figure(figsize=(8, 6))
node_sizes = [5000 * degree_centrality[node] for node in
G.nodes()]
nx.draw_networkx(G, node_size=node_sizes, with_labels=True,
node_color='skyblue', edge_color='gray')
plt.title("Graph Visualization with Degree Centrality")
plt.show()
```

Explanation:

- **Graph Creation:**
  The script uses NetworkX's built-in karate club graph.
- **Centrality Calculations:**
  Degree and betweenness centrality are computed.
- **Visualization:**
  Nodes are drawn with sizes proportional to their degree centrality, helping to visually identify influential nodes.

14.3 Visualization Tools and Techniques

Overview

Visualization is essential for understanding and communicating insights from graph data. Effective visualizations can reveal patterns, trends, and relationships that might not be apparent from raw data or tabular outputs.

Popular Visualization Tools

1. **Gephi:**
   - **Description:**
     An open-source network visualization and analysis tool.
   - **Features:**
     - Interactive visualization
     - Layout algorithms (e.g., ForceAtlas, Fruchterman-Reingold)
     - Rich filtering and clustering capabilities
   - **Ideal Use Cases:**
     Exploratory analysis and visual storytelling for complex networks.
2. **Cytoscape:**
   - **Description:**
     A platform for visualizing molecular interaction networks, but also applicable to general graph data.
   - **Features:**
     - Extensive plugins for analysis
     - Customizable layouts and styling
   - **Ideal Use Cases:**
     Bioinformatics, social network analysis, and general-purpose graph visualization.

3. **Neo4j Bloom:**
   - **Description:**
     A visualization tool provided by Neo4j for exploring and interacting with graph data.
   - **Features:**
     - Natural language search interface
     - Interactive exploration of graph data
     - Intuitive, user-friendly design
   - **Ideal Use Cases:**
     Business analytics, enterprise applications, and quick insights from graph data.
4. **D3.js:**
   - **Description:**
     A powerful JavaScript library for creating custom, dynamic data visualizations.
   - **Features:**
     - Highly customizable visualizations
     - Integration with web applications
   - **Ideal Use Cases:**
     Custom web-based visualizations, dashboards, and interactive applications.

Visualization Techniques

- **Force-Directed Layouts:**
  Use algorithms that simulate physical forces to position nodes in a visually appealing way that reveals clusters and connections.
- **Hierarchical Layouts:**
  Organize nodes in layers to represent hierarchical relationships.
- **Heat Maps and Node Coloring:**
  Color-code nodes and edges based on metrics such as centrality, community membership, or other attributes.
- **Interactive Dashboards:**
  Combine multiple visualizations (e.g., network graphs, bar charts, and line graphs) into interactive dashboards for comprehensive data exploration.

Code Example: Visualizing a Graph Using D3.js

Below is a simple HTML and JavaScript example using D3.js to create an interactive graph visualization.

html

```html
<!DOCTYPE html>
<html lang="en">
<head>
  <meta charset="UTF-8">
  <title>D3.js Graph Visualization</title>
  <script src="https://d3js.org/d3.v6.min.js"></script>
  <style>
    .node {
      stroke: #fff;
      stroke-width: 1.5px;
    }
    .link {
      stroke: #999;
      stroke-opacity: 0.6;
    }
  </style>
</head>
<body>
  <svg width="800" height="600"></svg>
  <script>
    const svg = d3.select("svg"),
          width = +svg.attr("width"),
          height = +svg.attr("height");

    // Sample data: nodes and links
    const graph = {
      "nodes": [
        {"id": "A"},
        {"id": "B"},
        {"id": "C"},
        {"id": "D"}
      ],
      "links": [
        {"source": "A", "target": "B"},
        {"source": "A", "target": "C"},
        {"source": "B", "target": "D"},
        {"source": "C", "target": "D"}
      ]
    };

    // Create a simulation for nodes and links
    const simulation = d3.forceSimulation(graph.nodes)
      .force("link", d3.forceLink(graph.links).id(d =>
d.id).distance(100))
      .force("charge", d3.forceManyBody().strength(-300))
      .force("center", d3.forceCenter(width / 2, height /
2));

    // Draw links
```

```
const link = svg.append("g")
  .attr("class", "links")
  .selectAll("line")
  .data(graph.links)
  .enter().append("line")
  .attr("class", "link");

// Draw nodes
const node = svg.append("g")
  .attr("class", "nodes")
  .selectAll("circle")
  .data(graph.nodes)
  .enter().append("circle")
  .attr("class", "node")
  .attr("r", 10)
  .call(d3.drag()
    .on("start", dragstarted)
    .on("drag", dragged)
    .on("end", dragended));

// Add labels
const label = svg.append("g")
  .attr("class", "labels")
  .selectAll("text")
  .data(graph.nodes)
  .enter().append("text")
  .attr("dy", -15)
  .text(d => d.id);

simulation.on("tick", () => {
  link
    .attr("x1", d => d.source.x)
    .attr("y1", d => d.source.y)
    .attr("x2", d => d.target.x)
    .attr("y2", d => d.target.y);
  node
    .attr("cx", d => d.x)
    .attr("cy", d => d.y);
  label
    .attr("x", d => d.x)
    .attr("y", d => d.y);
});

function dragstarted(event, d) {
  if (!event.active)
simulation.alphaTarget(0.3).restart();
  d.fx = d.x;
  d.fy = d.y;
}

function dragged(event, d) {
```

```
      d.fx = event.x;
      d.fy = event.y;
    }

    function dragended(event, d) {
      if (!event.active) simulation.alphaTarget(0);
      d.fx = null;
      d.fy = null;
    }
  </script>
</body>
</html>
```

Explanation:

- **Data Setup:**
  The graph data consists of nodes and links.
- **Simulation:**
  A force-directed simulation positions nodes based on physical forces.
- **SVG Elements:**
  Lines represent links and circles represent nodes, with labels added for clarity.
- **Interactivity:**
  Drag-and-drop behavior is implemented for node repositioning using D3's drag functions.

Summary of 14.3

Visualization tools like Gephi, Cytoscape, Neo4j Bloom, and D3.js offer diverse capabilities for representing graph data visually. Techniques such as force-directed layouts, hierarchical arrangements, and interactive dashboards help reveal complex patterns and insights. The provided D3.js example demonstrates how to create an interactive graph visualization that can be embedded in web applications.

Chapter 15: Deployment, Monitoring, and Maintenance

Deploying graph-based systems effectively is as important as designing them. This chapter discusses best practices and strategies for deploying graph databases and applications, comparing cloud and on-premises environments, and establishing robust CI/CD pipelines to enable continuous integration, testing, and deployment. These practices ensure that your graph-based system remains scalable, maintainable, and resilient in production.

15.1 Deployment Strategies for Graph-Based Systems

Overview

Deployment strategies determine how your graph-based system is rolled out and maintained in a production environment. The goal is to achieve high availability, scalability, and ease of maintenance. Key strategies include containerization, orchestration, and multi-region deployments.

Key Strategies

1. **Containerization:**
   - **Description:**
     Package your application and its dependencies into containers (e.g., Docker). Containers ensure that your system runs consistently across different environments.
   - **Benefits:**
     - Portability
     - Isolation of dependencies
     - Simplified version control and updates
   - **Example Tools:**
     - Docker
     - Podman
2. **Orchestration:**

- o **Description:**
  Manage the deployment, scaling, and operation of containers using orchestration platforms.
- o **Benefits:**
  - Automated scaling and load balancing
  - Rollbacks and self-healing capabilities
- o **Example Tools:**
  - Kubernetes
  - Docker Swarm

3. **Multi-Region and Multi-Availability Zone Deployments:**
   - o **Description:**
     Deploy your system across multiple geographic regions or availability zones to enhance fault tolerance and reduce latency.
   - o **Benefits:**
     - Increased resilience against regional outages
     - Improved response times for globally distributed users

4. **Blue-Green Deployments:**
   - o **Description:**
     Maintain two identical production environments (blue and green). Deploy updates to one environment while the other remains live, then switch traffic once the update is verified.
   - o **Benefits:**
     - Minimizes downtime
     - Simplifies rollback in case of issues

Table: Key Deployment Strategies

Strategy	Description	Benefits	Example Tools
Containerization	Package application with dependencies into containers	Portability, isolation, consistency	Docker, Podman
Orchestration	Manage container deployment, scaling, and operations	Automated scaling, load balancing, self-healing	Kubernetes, Docker Swarm
Multi-Region Deployments	Deploy across multiple regions/availability zones	Fault tolerance, reduced latency for global users	Cloud provider features (AWS, GCP, Azure)

Strategy	Description	Benefits	Example Tools
Blue-Green Deployments	Maintain parallel production environments	Zero downtime, easy rollback	Kubernetes, custom scripts

Code Example: Dockerfile for a Graph-Based Application

Below is an example of a Dockerfile for containerizing a simple graph-based application (e.g., a Python-based API interacting with a Neo4j database):

```dockerfile
# Use an official Python runtime as a parent image
FROM python:3.9-slim

# Set the working directory in the container
WORKDIR /app

# Copy the current directory contents into the container at /app
COPY . /app

# Install any needed packages specified in requirements.txt
RUN pip install --no-cache-dir -r requirements.txt

# Expose port 5000 for the application
EXPOSE 5000

# Define environment variable for Neo4j connection (example)
ENV NEO4J_URI=bolt://neo4j:7687
ENV NEO4J_USER=neo4j
ENV NEO4J_PASSWORD=your_password

# Run the application
CMD ["python", "app.py"]
```

Explanation:

- **FROM python:3.9-slim:**
  Uses a lightweight Python image.
- **WORKDIR /app:**
  Sets the working directory inside the container.
- **COPY and RUN:**
  Copies application files and installs dependencies.

- **EXPOSE:**
  Exposes port 5000.
- **ENV:**
  Sets environment variables for connecting to a Neo4j database.
- **CMD:**
  Runs the application.

15.2 Cloud vs. On-Premises Deployment

Overview

Choosing between cloud-based and on-premises deployment depends on various factors, including cost, scalability, security, and management overhead. Both options have their advantages and challenges.

Cloud Deployment

Advantages:

- **Scalability:**
  Cloud platforms provide auto-scaling and on-demand resources.
- **Managed Services:**
  Many cloud providers offer managed graph databases (e.g., Amazon Neptune, Azure Cosmos DB), reducing operational overhead.
- **Global Reach:**
  Easy deployment across multiple regions to serve a global audience.
- **Cost-Effective:**
  Pay-as-you-go pricing models can be more cost-effective for variable workloads.

Challenges:

- **Data Privacy:**
  Storing sensitive data on the cloud may raise compliance issues.
- **Vendor Lock-In:**
  Dependence on a single provider's ecosystem may limit flexibility.

On-Premises Deployment

Advantages:

- **Control:**
  Full control over hardware, data, and security configurations.
- **Customization:**
  Tailor the environment to specific performance or security requirements.
- **Compliance:**
  Easier to comply with strict data residency and privacy regulations.

Challenges:

- **Scalability:**
  Scaling on-premises systems can be costly and complex.
- **Maintenance:**
  Requires dedicated resources for hardware maintenance, updates, and security.
- **Upfront Costs:**
  Significant capital expenditure for hardware and infrastructure.

Comparison Table: Cloud vs. On-Premises Deployment

Aspect	Cloud Deployment	On-Premises Deployment
Scalability	Highly scalable with auto-scaling features	Limited by physical hardware; scaling can be expensive
Management	Managed services reduce operational overhead	Requires dedicated IT staff for maintenance and upgrades
Cost	Pay-as-you-go, operational expenditure	High upfront capital expenditure, fixed costs
Security & Compliance	May face data residency and compliance challenges	Full control over security configurations
Flexibility	Quick deployment across regions; vendor-dependent	Highly customizable; no vendor lock-in

Code Example: Deploying a Dockerized Application to AWS Elastic Container Service (ECS)

Below is an example of a simplified task definition JSON for deploying a Dockerized graph-based application to AWS ECS.

```json
json

{
  "family": "graph-app-task",
  "networkMode": "awsvpc",
  "containerDefinitions": [
    {
      "name": "graph-app",
      "image": "your-docker-repo/graph-app:latest",
      "essential": true,
      "portMappings": [
        {
          "containerPort": 5000,
          "hostPort": 5000,
          "protocol": "tcp"
        }
      ],
      "environment": [
        {
          "name": "NEO4J_URI",
          "value": "bolt://neo4j:7687"
        },
        {
          "name": "NEO4J_USER",
          "value": "neo4j"
        },
        {
          "name": "NEO4J_PASSWORD",
          "value": "your_password"
        }
      ]
    }
  ],
  "requiresCompatibilities": ["FARGATE"],
  "cpu": "256",
  "memory": "512"
}
```

Explanation:

- **Family:**
  Defines the task family.

- **ContainerDefinitions:**
  Specifies the container details, including the Docker image, port mappings, and environment variables.
- **RequiresCompatibilities:**
  Indicates the use of AWS Fargate (serverless container service).
- **CPU and Memory:**
  Allocates resources for the task.

15.3 Continuous Integration and Continuous Deployment (CI/CD)

Overview

CI/CD practices are critical for maintaining a high-quality, scalable, and agile development process. They enable frequent code integration, automated testing, and seamless deployment of updates, ensuring that your graph-based system remains robust and up-to-date.

Key Components of CI/CD

1. **Continuous Integration (CI):**
   - **Definition:**
     The practice of frequently merging code changes into a shared repository, where automated builds and tests are run.
   - **Benefits:**
     - Early detection of integration issues
     - Faster feedback on code quality
   - **Tools:**
     - Jenkins, GitHub Actions, GitLab CI, Travis CI
2. **Continuous Deployment (CD):**
   - **Definition:**
     Automating the deployment of code changes to production environments once they pass all tests.
   - **Benefits:**
     - Reduced manual intervention
     - Faster time-to-market
     - Consistent and reliable deployments
   - **Tools:**

- AWS CodePipeline, Kubernetes (with Helm), Azure DevOps

CI/CD Pipeline Workflow

1. **Code Commit:**
   Developers push code changes to a version-controlled repository (e.g., Git).
2. **Automated Build and Test:**
   The CI system automatically builds the application and runs tests.
3. **Deployment to Staging:**
   After passing tests, the code is deployed to a staging environment for further validation.
4. **Production Deployment:**
   Once validated, the code is automatically deployed to production.
5. **Monitoring and Rollback:**
   The system is monitored in production, and automated rollback is triggered if issues are detected.

Table: CI/CD Pipeline Stages

Stage	Description	Example Tools
Code Commit	Developers push code to the repository	Git, GitHub, GitLab
Build and Test	Automated build and unit/integration tests	Jenkins, GitHub Actions, Travis CI
Staging Deployment	Deploy code to a staging environment for further validation	Kubernetes, Docker Compose, AWS CodeDeploy
Production Deployment	Automatic deployment to the production environment	AWS CodePipeline, Azure DevOps
Monitoring and Rollback	Monitor system performance and automatically rollback on failure	Prometheus, Grafana, ELK Stack

Code Example: Simple CI/CD Pipeline with GitHub Actions

Below is an example GitHub Actions workflow file (`.github/workflows/ci-cd.yml`) for a Python-based graph application.

```yaml
yaml

name: CI/CD Pipeline

on:
  push:
    branches:
      - main
  pull_request:
    branches:
      - main

jobs:
  build:
    runs-on: ubuntu-latest

    steps:
    - name: Checkout Code
      uses: actions/checkout@v2

    - name: Set up Python
      uses: actions/setup-python@v2
      with:
        python-version: '3.9'

    - name: Install Dependencies
      run: |
        python -m venv venv
        . venv/bin/activate
        pip install --upgrade pip
        pip install -r requirements.txt

    - name: Run Tests
      run: |
        . venv/bin/activate
        pytest --maxfail=1 --disable-warnings -q

    - name: Build Docker Image
      run: |
        docker build -t graph-app .

  deploy:
    runs-on: ubuntu-latest
    needs: build

    steps:
    - name: Checkout Code
      uses: actions/checkout@v2

    - name: Deploy to Production
      run: |
```

```
echo "Deploying to production..."
        # Deployment commands, e.g., push Docker image to a
registry and update Kubernetes deployment
```

Explanation:

- **Triggers:**
  The workflow is triggered on code pushes and pull requests to the `main` branch.
- **Build Job:**
  The build job sets up Python, installs dependencies, and runs tests using Pytest. It also builds a Docker image.
- **Deploy Job:**
  The deploy job depends on the build job and executes deployment commands (which could involve pushing images to a registry and updating deployments in Kubernetes).

15.4 Monitoring Tools and Best Practices

Overview

Monitoring is a critical component in the lifecycle of any graph-based system. It enables you to track performance, identify potential issues before they become critical, and ensure that your system is operating efficiently. Effective monitoring combines the use of specialized tools, regular health checks, and well-defined best practices. This section explains the key metrics to monitor, the tools available for monitoring, and best practices to follow for a successful monitoring strategy.

Key Monitoring Metrics

Monitoring metrics help you assess the overall health and performance of your graph-based system. Important metrics include:

- **Query Performance:**
  - **Latency:** The time it takes to execute queries.
  - **Throughput:** The number of queries processed per unit time.
  - **Execution Plans:** Detailed steps of query execution that help in identifying bottlenecks.

- **Resource Utilization:**
  - o **CPU Usage:** Percentage of CPU resources in use.
  - o **Memory Usage:** The amount of RAM consumed.
  - o **Disk I/O:** The rate of read and write operations, crucial for systems with high data churn.
- **Network Performance:**
  - o **Latency and Bandwidth:** Especially important in distributed graph systems, these metrics indicate the speed and capacity of data transfer between nodes.
- **Error Rates and Logs:**
  - o **Application Logs:** To capture errors, warnings, and system events.
  - o **Error Rates:** Frequency of failed queries or operations.
- **Cache Efficiency:**
  - o **Cache Hit/Miss Ratio:** Indicates how often queries are served from cache compared to being executed against the database.

Popular Monitoring Tools

Several tools can help you monitor your graph-based system effectively:

- **Prometheus:**
  A popular open-source monitoring tool that collects time-series data. It is highly configurable and works well with Grafana for visualization.
- **Grafana:**
  A visualization platform that can create dashboards for real-time monitoring. It integrates with Prometheus and other data sources.
- **ELK Stack (Elasticsearch, Logstash, Kibana):**
  A set of tools that allows you to aggregate, search, and visualize logs and error data from your system.
- **Nagios:**
  A monitoring system that provides alerts and detailed monitoring for infrastructure components, including network performance and system resource usage.
- **Custom Scripts:**
  Lightweight monitoring scripts using Python (with libraries like `psutil`) can track system metrics on a server.

Best Practices for Monitoring

1. **Establish Baselines:**
   Understand normal system behavior to detect anomalies effectively.
2. **Set Alerts:**
   Configure alerts for critical metrics (e.g., high CPU usage, slow query responses) so that issues are promptly addressed.
3. **Implement Logging:**
   Ensure that all components of the system generate logs. Use centralized logging solutions to aggregate and analyze these logs.
4. **Use Dashboards:**
   Create interactive dashboards that provide real-time insights into system performance and health.
5. **Regular Reviews:**
   Periodically review the monitoring setup and update thresholds and alerts based on evolving system performance and business needs.

Table: Monitoring Tools and Best Practices

Aspect	Description	Example Tools/Techniques
Query Performance	Metrics related to query execution time and throughput	Prometheus, query profiling with Neo4j PROFILE/EXPLAIN
Resource Utilization	Monitoring CPU, memory, and disk I/O usage	Prometheus, Grafana, psutil in Python
Network Performance	Measuring latency and bandwidth between nodes in distributed systems	Network monitoring tools, built-in cloud provider metrics
Error Logging	Capturing and analyzing errors and warnings	ELK Stack, Nagios, custom logging with Python logging
Caching Efficiency	Evaluating cache hit/miss ratios to optimize query performance	Built-in cache monitoring features in graph databases
Alerts and Dashboards	Setting up real-time alerts and visual dashboards for monitoring	Grafana dashboards, Prometheus alerts

Code Example: Simple Monitoring Script Using Python

The following Python script uses the `psutil` library to monitor CPU and memory usage. This script can be adapted or extended to monitor additional metrics in your graph-based system.

```python
python

import psutil
import time

def monitor_system(interval=5):
    """
    Monitor CPU and memory usage at regular intervals.
    """
    print("Monitoring system performance. Press Ctrl+C to
stop.")
    try:
        while True:
            cpu_usage = psutil.cpu_percent(interval=1)
            memory_info = psutil.virtual_memory()
            print(f"CPU Usage: {cpu_usage}%")
            print(f"Memory Usage: {memory_info.percent}%
(Used: {memory_info.used // (1024 * 1024)} MB, Total:
{memory_info.total // (1024 * 1024)} MB)")
            time.sleep(interval)
    except KeyboardInterrupt:
        print("Monitoring stopped.")

if __name__ == "__main__":
    monitor_system()
```

Explanation:

- The script uses `psutil` to collect real-time CPU and memory usage.
- It prints these metrics every 5 seconds (configurable via the `interval` parameter).
- This basic monitoring script can be integrated into a larger monitoring system or used as a standalone tool during development.

15.5 Maintenance and Upgrading Your System

Overview

Maintenance and upgrades are vital to ensure that your graph-based system remains secure, efficient, and aligned with evolving business requirements. Regular maintenance helps prevent downtime and performance degradation, while systematic upgrades allow the system to evolve without significant disruptions.

Key Maintenance Strategies

1. **Regular Backups and Disaster Recovery:**
   - **Description:**
     Implement automated backup procedures to regularly snapshot your graph database.
   - **Best Practices:**
     - Schedule backups during off-peak hours.
     - Store backups in secure, offsite locations.
   - **Tools:**
     - Native backup utilities provided by your graph database (e.g., Neo4j backup tools).
2. **Version Control and Schema Management:**
   - **Description:**
     Use version control for your code, configuration files, and even schema definitions.
   - **Best Practices:**
     - Maintain a repository (e.g., Git) for schema changes and migration scripts.
     - Implement automated migration scripts to update the schema incrementally.
   - **Tools:**
     - Git, Liquibase (for database schema migrations).
3. **Performance Monitoring and Regular Updates:**
   - **Description:**
     Continuously monitor system performance and apply updates or patches regularly.
   - **Best Practices:**
     - Schedule regular maintenance windows.
     - Use monitoring tools to proactively identify performance issues.
   - **Tools:**
     - Prometheus, Grafana, ELK Stack.
4. **Incremental Upgrades and Blue-Green Deployments:**

- o **Description:**
  Upgrade components of your system incrementally to minimize downtime.
- o **Best Practices:**
  - Use blue-green deployment strategies to test new versions without affecting the live environment.
- o **Tools:**
  - Kubernetes for container orchestration and rolling updates.

Table: Maintenance and Upgrade Strategies

Strategy	Description	Benefits	Example Tools/Techniques
Regular Backups and Recovery	Scheduled data backups and disaster recovery plans	Ensures data integrity and quick recovery from failures	Neo4j backup utilities, cloud storage solutions
Version Control & Schema Management	Using version control to manage code and schema changes	Facilitates incremental upgrades and rollback capability	Git, Liquibase, Flyway
Performance Monitoring	Continuous tracking of system metrics and performance benchmarks	Early detection of issues, proactive maintenance	Prometheus, Grafana, ELK Stack
Incremental Upgrades/Blue-Green Deployments	Gradual deployment of new versions with minimal downtime	Reduces risk and downtime, smooth transition to new releases	Kubernetes, Helm, AWS CodeDeploy

Code Example: Simple Backup Script in Python

The following Python script demonstrates how to create a backup of a graph database directory. This script can be scheduled to run at regular intervals.

```python
```

```python
import os
import shutil
import datetime

def backup_graph_database(source_dir, backup_dir):
    """
    Create a backup of the graph database by copying the
    source directory to the backup directory with a timestamp.
    """
    # Generate a timestamp for the backup folder name
    timestamp =
    datetime.datetime.now().strftime("%Y%m%d_%H%M%S")
    destination = os.path.join(backup_dir,
    f"backup_{timestamp}")

    try:
        shutil.copytree(source_dir, destination)
        print(f"Backup successful: {destination}")
    except Exception as e:
        print(f"Backup failed: {str(e)}")

if __name__ == "__main__":
    source_directory = "/path/to/graph_database"
    backup_directory = "/path/to/backup_directory"
    backup_graph_database(source_directory, backup_directory)
```

Explanation:

- **shutil.copytree:**
  Recursively copies the entire graph database directory to a new
  backup directory, with the directory name containing a timestamp.
- **Scheduling:**
  This script can be scheduled using cron (on Linux) or Task Scheduler
  (on Windows) to run automatically at defined intervals.

Iterative Improvement and Upgrade Strategies

1. **Monitoring and Feedback:**
   - **Implementation:**
     Continuously monitor system performance and collect user
     feedback.
   - **Action:**
     Adjust configurations, apply patches, or refactor components
     based on feedback.
2. **Automated Testing and Continuous Integration:**

- o **Implementation:**
  Integrate automated tests and CI pipelines to ensure that changes do not introduce regressions.
- o **Action:**
  Use tools like GitHub Actions or Jenkins to run tests on each commit.

3. **Blue-Green Deployments:**
   - o **Implementation:**
     Maintain two production environments and switch traffic between them when deploying upgrades.
   - o **Action:**
     Use deployment tools and orchestration platforms like Kubernetes to facilitate seamless upgrades.

Summary of 15.5

Maintaining and upgrading your graph-based system requires a proactive and systematic approach. Regular backups, version-controlled schema changes, continuous performance monitoring, and incremental upgrades help ensure that your system remains reliable and efficient. By adopting best practices such as blue-green deployments and automated testing, you can minimize downtime and enhance the overall quality of your system.

.

Chapter 16: Advanced Graph Algorithms and Machine Learning Integration

Graph-based systems are not only powerful for storing and querying data; they also provide a rich substrate for advanced analytics and machine learning. In this chapter, we explore advanced graph algorithms used for pattern recognition and inference, discuss how to integrate Graph Neural Networks (GNNs) into your system, and examine various machine learning techniques that operate on graph data.

16.1 Graph Algorithms for Pattern Recognition and Inference

Overview

Graph algorithms are essential for extracting insights from interconnected data. They help identify patterns, detect communities, and perform inferencing by analyzing the structure and properties of the graph. Advanced graph algorithms can be broadly categorized into those used for pattern recognition and those used for inference.

Common Graph Algorithms

1. **Centrality Measures:**
   - **Degree Centrality:**
     Counts the number of edges connected to a node.
     Use Case: Identifying highly connected or influential nodes.
   - **Betweenness Centrality:**
     Measures how often a node appears on the shortest paths between other nodes.
     Use Case: Detecting nodes that act as bridges or bottlenecks in the network.
   - **Closeness Centrality:**
     Evaluates the average length of the shortest paths from a node to all other nodes.
     Use Case: Finding nodes that can quickly interact with all other nodes.

2. **Community Detection Algorithms:**
   o **Louvain Method:**
     Optimizes modularity to detect clusters or communities within the graph.
     Use Case: Customer segmentation or social group detection.
   o **Label Propagation:**
     Uses an iterative process where each node adopts the majority label of its neighbors until convergence.
     Use Case: Fast, scalable community detection.
3. **Path and Connectivity Algorithms:**
   o **Dijkstra's Algorithm:**
     Computes the shortest path between nodes in a weighted graph.
     Use Case: Route optimization in transportation networks.
   o **A* Search Algorithm:**
     A heuristic-based approach for pathfinding that can be more efficient in certain contexts.
   o **Connected Components:**
     Identifies isolated subgraphs within a network.
     Use Case: Detecting disconnected or weakly connected clusters.
4. **Pattern Matching and Subgraph Isomorphism:**
   o **Subgraph Matching:**
     Searches for a specific pattern or motif within a larger graph.
     Use Case: Fraud detection by identifying suspicious transaction patterns.

Table: Graph Algorithms for Pattern Recognition and Inference

Algorithm	Purpose	Example Use Case
Degree Centrality	Measure node connectivity	Identify influential users in social networks
Betweenness Centrality	Find nodes acting as bridges	Detect potential bottlenecks in communication networks
Closeness Centrality	Determine nodes with rapid reach	Identify nodes for efficient information dissemination
Louvain Method	Detect communities	Segment customers into groups based on purchasing behavior
Label Propagation	Quick community detection	Real-time clustering in social media analytics

Algorithm	Purpose	Example Use Case
Dijkstra's Algorithm	Shortest path finding	Optimize delivery routes in logistics
A* Search	Heuristic-based pathfinding	Efficient navigation in map applications
Subgraph Matching	Detect specific patterns or motifs	Identify fraud rings or recurring behavior patterns

Code Example: Calculating Centrality Measures with NetworkX (Python)

Below is an example that demonstrates how to calculate degree centrality and betweenness centrality for a sample graph using the NetworkX library.

```python
import networkx as nx
import matplotlib.pyplot as plt

# Create a sample graph using NetworkX's built-in Karate Club
graph
G = nx.karate_club_graph()

# Calculate degree centrality and betweenness centrality
degree_centrality = nx.degree_centrality(G)
betweenness_centrality = nx.betweenness_centrality(G)

# Print centrality measures for the first 5 nodes
print("Degree Centrality:")
for node, centrality in list(degree_centrality.items())[:5]:
    print(f"Node {node}: {centrality:.4f}")

print("\nBetweenness Centrality:")
for node, centrality in
list(betweenness_centrality.items())[:5]:
    print(f"Node {node}: {centrality:.4f}")

# Visualize the graph with node sizes proportional to degree
centrality
plt.figure(figsize=(8, 6))
node_sizes = [5000 * degree_centrality[node] for node in
G.nodes()]
nx.draw_networkx(G, node_size=node_sizes, with_labels=True,
node_color='lightgreen', edge_color='gray')
plt.title("Graph Visualization with Degree Centrality")
plt.show()
```

Explanation:

- **Graph Creation:**
  The Karate Club graph is used as a sample.
- **Centrality Calculation:**
  Both degree and betweenness centrality are computed.
- **Visualization:**
  Node sizes in the visualization are scaled based on degree centrality, providing a visual cue for node importance.

16.2 Integrating Graph Neural Networks (GNNs)

Overview

Graph Neural Networks (GNNs) extend deep learning techniques to graph-structured data. They can learn node representations (embeddings) that capture both feature and structural information, which can be used for a variety of tasks such as node classification, link prediction, and graph-level predictions.

Key Concepts in GNNs

1. **Node Embeddings:**
   o **Definition:**
   Low-dimensional vector representations that capture the properties and context of nodes.
   o **Techniques:**
   - **Node2Vec, DeepWalk:**
     Algorithms for generating node embeddings via random walks.
   - **Graph Convolutional Networks (GCNs):**
     Neural networks that aggregate feature information from neighbors.
2. **Message Passing:**
   o **Definition:**
   The process by which nodes aggregate and transform information from their neighbors.

o **Mechanism:**
Each node updates its embedding by combining its own
features with those of its neighbors.
3. **Model Architectures:**
   o **Examples:**
     ▪ **GCN:**
       Simplest form of graph neural network.
     ▪ **GraphSAGE:**
       Generates embeddings by sampling and aggregating
       features from a node's local neighborhood.
     ▪ **Graph Attention Networks (GATs):**
       Uses attention mechanisms to weigh neighbor
       contributions.

Integration Process

1. **Data Preparation:**
   o **Graph Construction:**
     Build a graph with nodes, edges, and features.
   o **Feature Extraction:**
     Normalize and prepare features for each node.
2. **Model Training:**
   o **Choose a GNN Architecture:**
     For example, use a GCN for node classification.
   o **Train the Model:**
     Use frameworks such as PyTorch Geometric or DGL (Deep
     Graph Library) to train the GNN.
3. **Inference:**
   o **Generate Node Embeddings:**
     Use the trained model to compute embeddings for
     downstream tasks.
   o **Apply to Applications:**
     Use embeddings for recommendations, anomaly detection, or
     clustering.

Code Example: Training a Simple GCN with PyTorch Geometric

Below is an example that demonstrates how to build and train a simple
Graph Convolutional Network (GCN) using PyTorch Geometric for a node
classification task.

```python
import torch
import torch.nn.functional as F
from torch_geometric.nn import GCNConv
from torch_geometric.datasets import Planetoid
from torch_geometric.data import DataLoader

# Load a sample dataset (e.g., Cora dataset)
dataset = Planetoid(root='/tmp/Cora', name='Cora')

class GCN(torch.nn.Module):
    def __init__(self, num_features, num_classes):
        super(GCN, self).__init__()
        self.conv1 = GCNConv(num_features, 16)
        self.conv2 = GCNConv(16, num_classes)

    def forward(self, data):
        x, edge_index = data.x, data.edge_index
        x = self.conv1(x, edge_index)
        x = F.relu(x)
        x = F.dropout(x, training=self.training)
        x = self.conv2(x, edge_index)
        return F.log_softmax(x, dim=1)

# Initialize model, optimizer, and dataset loader
device = torch.device('cuda' if torch.cuda.is_available() else 'cpu')
model = GCN(dataset.num_features,
dataset.num_classes).to(device)
data = dataset[0].to(device)
optimizer = torch.optim.Adam(model.parameters(), lr=0.01,
weight_decay=5e-4)

# Training loop
model.train()
for epoch in range(200):
    optimizer.zero_grad()
    out = model(data)
    loss = F.nll_loss(out[data.train_mask],
data.y[data.train_mask])
    loss.backward()
    optimizer.step()
    if epoch % 20 == 0:
        print(f'Epoch {epoch}, Loss: {loss.item():.4f}')

# Inference and evaluation
model.eval()
_, pred = model(data).max(dim=1)
```

```
correct =
int(pred[data.test_mask].eq(data.y[data.test_mask]).sum().ite
m())
accuracy = correct / int(data.test_mask.sum())
print(f'Test Accuracy: {accuracy:.4f}')
```

Explanation:

- **Dataset:**
  The Cora dataset is loaded using PyTorch Geometric's Planetoid class.
- **GCN Model:**
  A simple two-layer GCN is defined for node classification.
- **Training Loop:**
  The model is trained for 200 epochs using negative log likelihood loss.
- **Evaluation:**
  Test accuracy is computed on the test mask.

16.3 Machine Learning on Graph Data

Overview

Machine learning on graph data involves applying conventional ML techniques to features derived from graphs. This can include both unsupervised and supervised learning methods to solve tasks such as classification, clustering, link prediction, and regression.

Key Techniques

1. **Graph Embedding Generation:**
   - **Definition:**
     Convert nodes, edges, or entire graphs into fixed-size vector representations.
   - **Techniques:**
     - **Node2Vec/DeepWalk:**
       Generate embeddings using random walks.
     - **Autoencoders:**
       Learn latent representations in an unsupervised manner.

2. **Supervised Learning:**
    o **Task:**
    Train models to predict node labels, relationships, or other outcomes.
    o **Example:**
    Classifying nodes based on features derived from graph structure (using embeddings as features).
3. **Unsupervised Learning:**
    o **Task:**
    Cluster nodes or detect communities without labeled data.
    o **Example:**
    Using K-means clustering on node embeddings to identify communities.
4. **Link Prediction:**
    o **Definition:**
    Predict missing or future links between nodes.
    o **Techniques:**
    Use features such as node similarity, common neighbors, or learned embeddings.

Table: Machine Learning Techniques for Graph Data

Technique	Description	Application Example
Graph Embedding Generation	Transform graph elements into fixed-size vector representations	Node classification, clustering, recommendation
Supervised Learning	Train models on labeled graph data using embeddings as features	Predicting user interests, fraud detection
Unsupervised Learning	Identify patterns and clusters without labels	Community detection, anomaly detection
Link Prediction	Predict potential or missing relationships in the graph	Recommending new friends, predicting business connections

Code Example: Unsupervised Learning with Node2Vec and K-Means

Below is an example that generates node embeddings using Node2Vec and then applies K-means clustering to group nodes into communities.

```python
python

import networkx as nx
import numpy as np
from node2vec import Node2Vec
from sklearn.cluster import KMeans

# Create a sample graph using NetworkX
G = nx.karate_club_graph()

# Generate node embeddings using Node2Vec
node2vec = Node2Vec(G, dimensions=64, walk_length=30,
num_walks=200, workers=2)
model = node2vec.fit(window=10, min_count=1)
embeddings = np.array([model.wv[str(node)] for node in
G.nodes()])

# Apply K-Means clustering to the embeddings
kmeans = KMeans(n_clusters=2,
random_state=42).fit(embeddings)
labels = kmeans.labels_

# Print clustering results for the first 5 nodes
for i, node in enumerate(list(G.nodes())[:5]):
    print(f"Node {node}: Cluster {labels[i]}")

# Visualize clusters (using node color to represent clusters)
import matplotlib.pyplot as plt
pos = nx.spring_layout(G)
node_colors = [labels[i] for i in range(len(G.nodes()))]
nx.draw_networkx(G, pos, node_color=node_colors,
with_labels=True, cmap=plt.cm.Set1, node_size=500)
plt.title("K-Means Clustering on Node2Vec Embeddings")
plt.show()
```

Explanation:

- **Graph Creation:**
  The Karate Club graph is used as the sample graph.
- **Embedding Generation:**
  Node2Vec is applied to generate 64-dimensional embeddings for each node.
- **Clustering:**
  K-means clustering groups nodes into 2 clusters based on their embeddings.
- **Visualization:**
  Nodes are colored based on cluster labels, providing a visual representation of communities.

Summary of 16.3

Machine learning on graph data leverages techniques such as embedding generation, supervised and unsupervised learning, and link prediction to extract insights from graph-structured data. By applying these methods, you can build predictive models, identify communities, and uncover hidden relationships within your graph data.

16.4 Real-World Applications of Graph-Based ML

Overview

Graph-based machine learning (ML) leverages the interconnected structure of data to solve complex problems that traditional ML methods may struggle with. By utilizing graph algorithms and graph neural networks (GNNs), organizations can derive insights from data that is naturally represented as networks. In this section, we explore several real-world applications of graph-based ML across different industries.

Key Application Areas

1. **Social Network Analysis:**
   - **Description:**
     Graph-based ML is used to analyze social networks, identifying influential users, detecting communities, and recommending new connections.
   - **Techniques:**
     - Centrality measures to find key influencers
     - Community detection algorithms to segment users
     - Link prediction for friend recommendations
   - **Example:**
     Platforms like Facebook and LinkedIn utilize graph-based ML to suggest connections and highlight trending topics among users.
2. **Recommendation Systems:**
   - **Description:**
     Recommendations can be enhanced by analyzing the relationships between users, products, and interactions.
   - **Techniques:**

- Graph embeddings (e.g., Node2Vec, GNNs) to represent users and products
- Collaborative filtering enhanced with graph connectivity information
- Hybrid approaches combining content-based and collaborative filtering
  - **Example:**
  E-commerce platforms, such as Amazon, use graph-based ML to provide personalized product recommendations based on browsing history and social connections.
3. **Fraud Detection:**
   - **Description:**
   Graph-based ML can uncover complex patterns of fraudulent behavior by analyzing transaction networks.
   - **Techniques:**
     - Subgraph pattern matching to identify known fraud rings
     - Anomaly detection using graph embeddings
     - Community detection to isolate suspicious clusters
   - **Example:**
   Financial institutions use graph-based ML to detect and prevent fraudulent transactions by monitoring unusual patterns in transaction networks.
4. **Knowledge Graphs for Semantic Search and QA Systems:**
   - **Description:**
   Integrating graph-based ML into knowledge graphs improves semantic search, natural language query understanding, and question-answering (QA) systems.
   - **Techniques:**
     - Graph-based inference and reasoning
     - GNNs for learning relationships between concepts
     - Retrieval-Augmented Generation (RAG) for enhanced QA systems
   - **Example:**
   Google's Knowledge Graph and IBM Watson use graph-based ML techniques to deliver accurate search results and answer complex questions.
5. **Biological and Medical Networks:**
   - **Description:**
   Graph-based ML is used to analyze biological networks, such as protein–protein interactions, gene regulatory networks, and disease networks.

- o **Techniques:**
  - GNNs to predict drug–target interactions
  - Community detection to identify functional modules
  - Link prediction for discovering new relationships in biological data
- o **Example:**
  In bioinformatics, graph-based ML helps in identifying potential drug candidates by analyzing molecular interactions and disease pathways.

Table: Real-World Applications of Graph-Based ML

Application Area	Description	Key Techniques	Example
Social Network Analysis	Identifying influential users and communities	Centrality, community detection, link prediction	Friend recommendations on social media platforms
Recommendation Systems	Personalizing recommendations based on user-product interactions	Graph embeddings, collaborative filtering, hybrid methods	Product suggestions on e-commerce websites
Fraud Detection	Detecting anomalies and fraudulent behavior in transaction networks	Subgraph matching, anomaly detection, community detection	Fraud detection in financial transactions
Semantic Search & QA Systems	Enhancing search and question answering through semantic graphs	Graph-based inference, GNNs, RAG	Knowledge Graphs powering search engines and QA systems
Biological and Medical Networks	Analyzing molecular and disease networks	GNNs, community detection, link prediction	Drug discovery and disease pathway analysis in bioinformatics

Code Example: Using Graph-Based ML for Recommendation (Simplified)

Below is a simplified example demonstrating how to generate node embeddings using Node2Vec and then use them in a simple recommendation scenario with K-Means clustering. This example highlights how graph-based ML can be applied to segment users for personalized recommendations.

```python
import networkx as nx
import numpy as np
from node2vec import Node2Vec
from sklearn.cluster import KMeans

# Create a sample graph representing user-product
interactions
G = nx.Graph()
# Example edges: (User, Product)
edges = [
    ("User1", "ProductA"), ("User1", "ProductB"),
    ("User2", "ProductB"), ("User2", "ProductC"),
    ("User3", "ProductA"), ("User3", "ProductC"),
    ("User4", "ProductA"), ("User4", "ProductB"),
    ("User4", "ProductC")
]
G.add_edges_from(edges)

# Generate node embeddings using Node2Vec
node2vec = Node2Vec(G, dimensions=64, walk_length=30,
num_walks=200, workers=2)
model = node2vec.fit(window=10, min_count=1)

# Extract embeddings for user nodes only
users = [node for node in G.nodes() if "User" in node]
user_embeddings = np.array([model.wv[node] for node in
users])

# Apply K-Means clustering to group users
kmeans = KMeans(n_clusters=2,
random_state=42).fit(user_embeddings)
labels = kmeans.labels_

# Print clustering results
print("User Clustering Results:")
for i, user in enumerate(users):
    print(f"{user}: Cluster {labels[i]}")

# Visualize clustering results (optional)
```

```
import matplotlib.pyplot as plt
pos = nx.spring_layout(G)
user_colors = [labels[users.index(node)] if node in users
else 0 for node in G.nodes()]
nx.draw_networkx(G, pos, node_color=user_colors,
cmap=plt.cm.Set1, with_labels=True, node_size=500)
plt.title("User Clustering Based on Node2Vec Embeddings")
plt.show()
```

Explanation:

- **Graph Creation:**
  A simple graph is built to represent interactions between users and products.
- **Embedding Generation:**
  Node2Vec is used to generate embeddings that capture the graph structure.
- **Clustering:**
  K-Means clustering is applied to group users based on their embeddings, which can be used to drive personalized recommendations.
- **Visualization:**
  The graph is visualized with node colors representing different clusters.

16.5 Challenges and Future Directions

Overview

While graph-based ML and advanced graph algorithms have significant potential, several challenges must be addressed to fully leverage these technologies. Additionally, emerging trends and future directions promise to further enhance the capabilities of graph-based systems.

Key Challenges

1. **Scalability and Performance:**
   o **Challenge:**
     Graph-based systems often face challenges when scaling to

handle very large graphs with millions or billions of nodes and edges.
- o **Potential Solutions:**
    - ▪ Distributed computing architectures
    - ▪ Improved indexing and caching strategies
    - ▪ Optimization of graph query languages

2. **Complexity of Graph Data:**
   - o **Challenge:**
     Graphs inherently have complex, non-linear relationships that can be difficult to model, analyze, and visualize.
   - o **Potential Solutions:**
     - ▪ Advanced visualization tools
     - ▪ Improved algorithms for graph pattern recognition and inference

3. **Integration with Machine Learning:**
   - o **Challenge:**
     Effectively integrating traditional ML techniques with graph data requires specialized methods (e.g., graph embeddings, GNNs) that are still under active research.
   - o **Potential Solutions:**
     - ▪ Development of standardized frameworks for graph-based ML
     - ▪ Enhanced tools for generating and using graph embeddings

4. **Data Quality and Heterogeneity:**
   - o **Challenge:**
     Graph-based systems often integrate data from diverse sources, leading to issues with data quality, inconsistency, and missing values.
   - o **Potential Solutions:**
     - ▪ Robust ETL processes and data cleansing techniques
     - ▪ Semantic enrichment to standardize heterogeneous data sources

5. **Interpretability and Explainability:**
   - o **Challenge:**
     As ML models (especially deep learning models like GNNs) become more complex, their decisions can become difficult to interpret.
   - o **Potential Solutions:**
     - ▪ Development of explainable AI techniques tailored to graph data

- Visualization tools that can illustrate model behavior on graph structures

Future Directions

1. **Enhanced Graph Neural Networks:**
   - **Trend:**
     Continued research into GNN architectures (e.g., Graph Attention Networks, Graph Convolutional Networks) promises more accurate and scalable models.
   - **Future Impact:**
     Improved performance on tasks such as node classification, link prediction, and graph-level prediction.
2. **Federated Learning on Graphs:**
   - **Trend:**
     Applying federated learning principles to graph data, enabling distributed training of ML models without centralized data collection.
   - **Future Impact:**
     Enhanced data privacy and scalability, particularly important in domains like healthcare and finance.
3. **Real-Time Graph Analytics:**
   - **Trend:**
     Increasing focus on real-time processing and analytics of graph data using streaming technologies.
   - **Future Impact:**
     More responsive systems capable of dynamic decision-making, such as real-time fraud detection or adaptive recommendations.
4. **Integration with Emerging Technologies:**
   - **Trend:**
     Combining graph-based systems with other emerging technologies, such as blockchain for immutable data storage and IoT for processing sensor data.
   - **Future Impact:**
     Broader applicability and increased robustness in complex, interconnected environments.
5. **Improved Tooling and Standardization:**
   - **Trend:**
     Ongoing efforts to standardize graph data models, query languages, and ML integration frameworks.

- **Future Impact:**
  Easier adoption and interoperability across different systems, fostering innovation and collaboration.

Table: Challenges and Future Directions in Graph-Based ML

Challenge	Description	Potential Solutions/Future Trends
Scalability and Performance	Handling large-scale, complex graphs	Distributed architectures, optimized indexing, and caching
Complexity of Graph Data	Modeling and visualizing non-linear, interconnected data	Advanced visualization tools, improved pattern recognition algorithms
Integration with ML	Combining traditional ML with graph data	Standardized graph ML frameworks, enhanced GNN architectures
Data Quality and Heterogeneity	Managing inconsistent and diverse data sources	Robust ETL and data cleansing, semantic enrichment
Interpretability and Explainability	Understanding the decisions of complex ML models	Explainable AI techniques tailored for graphs, enhanced model visualization
Future Directions	Enhanced GNNs, federated learning, real-time analytics, emerging tech integration, improved tooling	Ongoing research, new standards, cross-domain collaborations

Example Scenario: Future Roadmap for a Graph-Based ML System

Imagine a company using graph-based ML for fraud detection. Their roadmap might include:

- **Short-Term:**
  Optimize existing graph queries and implement advanced caching.
- **Mid-Term:**
  Pilot a GNN-based model for improved fraud detection accuracy.

- **Long-Term:**
  Explore federated learning to train models across multiple branches without centralizing sensitive data, and integrate real-time analytics for immediate response.

While graph-based ML offers significant advantages for analyzing complex relationships, several challenges remain, particularly in scalability, data integration, and interpretability. Future research and emerging technologies promise to address these challenges, leading to more powerful, efficient, and transparent graph-based systems.

Chapter 17: Deep Dive into Retrieval-Augmented Generation (RAG)

Retrieval-Augmented Generation (RAG) is an innovative paradigm that fuses the strengths of information retrieval and generative language models. By incorporating external data into the generation process, RAG systems produce responses that are not only fluent and contextually relevant but also grounded in up-to-date, factual information. In this chapter, we examine advanced RAG concepts, explore use cases and performance optimizations, discuss applications in NLP and AI, consider hybrid approaches that blend rule-based and data-driven methods, and review techniques for evaluating and benchmarking RAG systems.

17.1 Advanced Concepts in RAG

Overview

Advanced RAG concepts build on the basic idea of augmenting generative models with retrieved data. This section explores the deeper mechanics of RAG, including its modular components, fusion strategies, and approaches to manage the balance between retrieval and generation.

Key Components and Concepts

1. **Modular Architecture:**
   - **Retrieval Module:**
     Responsible for identifying and fetching relevant documents or data snippets from a large corpus or a structured knowledge base (such as a graph database).
   - **Generative Module:**
     A language model (e.g., GPT-based) that uses the retrieved context along with the original query to generate natural language responses.
   - **Fusion Mechanism:**
     The strategy used to integrate retrieved information into the generative process. Approaches can be as simple as

concatenation or more complex methods involving attention mechanisms.

2. **Context Integration:**
   o **Static vs. Dynamic Context:**
     Static context involves using a fixed knowledge base, whereas dynamic context can include real-time data updates.
   o **Weighting Mechanisms:**
     Advanced RAG models may weight the retrieved context differently based on its relevance, often using attention or gating mechanisms to modulate the influence of retrieved content.

3. **End-to-End Training vs. Decoupled Training:**
   o **End-to-End Training:**
     The entire RAG system is trained simultaneously so that the retrieval and generative components are optimized jointly.
   o **Decoupled Training:**
     The retrieval module is trained separately from the generative model, which may simplify training but can reduce overall coherence.

Table: Advanced RAG Components

Component	Description	Key Considerations
Retrieval Module	Fetches relevant data based on the query	Efficiency, relevance scoring, use of graph queries
Generative Module	Generates natural language output using augmented input	Fluency, coherence, integration of retrieved context
Fusion Mechanism	Combines query and retrieved context for generation	Attention mechanisms, gating, concatenation strategies
Training Paradigm	End-to-end vs. decoupled training approaches	Trade-off between integration and simplicity

Code Example: Simple Fusion via Concatenation

Below is a simplified Python pseudocode example that demonstrates a basic fusion mechanism by concatenating the retrieved context with the query before passing it to a generative model.

```python
def simple_fusion(query, retrieved_context):
    """
    Combine the user query with the retrieved context by
    simple concatenation.
    """
    combined_input = f"Query: {query}\nContext:
{retrieved_context}"
    return combined_input

# Example usage:
query = "What are the main features of the new smartphone?"
retrieved_context = "The new smartphone includes a high-
resolution camera, long battery life, and 5G connectivity."
combined_input = simple_fusion(query, retrieved_context)
print("Combined Input for Generation:")
print(combined_input)
```

Explanation:

- The function `simple_fusion` demonstrates one basic approach to integrate context: concatenation. This method is easy to implement but may be further enhanced by weighting mechanisms in more advanced systems.

17.2 Use Cases and Performance Optimization

Overview

RAG systems have been applied in various domains to improve the accuracy, relevance, and contextual richness of generated content. This section explores specific use cases and discusses strategies to optimize the performance of RAG implementations.

Use Cases

1. **Customer Support:**
   o **Scenario:**
     An AI chatbot that retrieves information from a company's knowledge base to provide accurate, context-aware responses to customer inquiries.

- o **Benefits:**
  Reduced support costs and improved customer satisfaction.
2. **Content Summarization:**
   - o **Scenario:**
     Generating summaries of long documents or articles by retrieving key information and synthesizing it into concise summaries.
   - o **Benefits:**
     Enhanced readability and efficient information consumption.
3. **Search and Recommendation:**
   - o **Scenario:**
     Augmenting search results or recommendations with real-time data, improving personalization and accuracy.
   - o **Benefits:**
     Higher engagement and conversion rates in e-commerce and content platforms.

Performance Optimization Strategies

1. **Caching Retrieved Context:**
   - o **Technique:**
     Cache frequently retrieved data to reduce latency and improve response times.
   - o **Consideration:**
     Implement cache invalidation strategies to maintain data freshness.
2. **Query Optimization in the Retrieval Module:**
   - o **Technique:**
     Optimize graph queries (e.g., using indexes, limiting result sets) to speed up data retrieval.
   - o **Consideration:**
     Use profiling tools to analyze query performance.
3. **Parallel Processing:**
   - o **Technique:**
     Execute multiple retrieval queries in parallel to leverage multi-core processing capabilities.
   - o **Consideration:**
     Ensure that parallelization does not compromise the consistency of the retrieved context.
4. **Efficient Fusion Mechanisms:**
   - o **Technique:**
     Optimize the fusion process (e.g., through attention

mechanisms) to balance the influence of the query and context.
- o **Consideration:**
  Evaluate the impact on generation quality and adjust parameters accordingly.

Table: Use Cases and Performance Optimizations

Use Case	Description	Performance Optimization Strategies
Customer Support	AI chatbots retrieving context for accurate answers	Caching, query optimization, parallel processing
Content Summarization	Summarizing lengthy documents using retrieved key info	Efficient fusion, query profiling, incremental context updates
Search and Recommendation	Enhancing search/recommendations with real-time data	Real-time retrieval optimization, hybrid caching, load balancing

Code Example: Caching Retrieved Context with Python

Below is an example that demonstrates a simple caching mechanism using Python's `functools.lru_cache` decorator to cache the results of the retrieval function.

```python
from functools import lru_cache

@lru_cache(maxsize=100)
def cached_retrieve_context(query):
    """
    Simulate retrieval of context data from a graph database
with caching.
    """
    # In a real implementation, perform the query on the
graph database.
    # Here, we simulate with a fixed response.
    simulated_context = "Simulated context data for query: "
+ query
```

```
    return simulated_context

# Example usage:
query = "What features does the new smartphone have?"
context1 = cached_retrieve_context(query)
print("First retrieval:", context1)
context2 = cached_retrieve_context(query)
print("Cached retrieval:", context2)
```

Explanation:

- **Caching Decorator:**
  The `lru_cache` decorator caches the result of
  `cached_retrieve_context` for up to 100 unique queries.
- **Usage:**
  The first call retrieves the context and caches it; subsequent calls with
  the same query fetch the cached result, improving performance.

17.3 RAG in Natural Language Processing and AI

Overview

RAG has significant implications in natural language processing (NLP) and
broader AI applications. By incorporating retrieval mechanisms, RAG
systems enhance the factual accuracy and context sensitivity of language
models. This section examines the applications of RAG in NLP and
discusses how it improves AI performance.

Applications in NLP and AI

1. **Question Answering (QA) Systems:**
   - **Scenario:**
     RAG systems can retrieve relevant passages from knowledge
     bases to support accurate answers in QA tasks.
   - **Benefits:**
     More precise and context-aware responses.
2. **Conversational Agents and Chatbots:**

- o **Scenario:**
  Chatbots that use RAG can provide detailed, fact-based answers by integrating real-time data retrieval.
- o **Benefits:**
  Improved user satisfaction and reduced support costs.
3. **Content Generation and Summarization:**
   - o **Scenario:**
     Generating summaries or news articles that incorporate up-to-date information from reliable sources.
   - o **Benefits:**
     Enhanced relevance and factual grounding of generated content.
4. **Language Translation and Paraphrasing:**
   - o **Scenario:**
     RAG can assist in translating text by retrieving context from bilingual corpora, leading to more accurate translations.
   - o **Benefits:**
     Improved translation quality and consistency.

Table: RAG Applications in NLP

Application	Description	Benefits
Question Answering (QA)	Retrieve relevant information to support accurate answers	Enhanced accuracy and context sensitivity
Conversational Agents	Integrate real-time data into chatbot responses	More engaging and informative interactions
Content Generation/Summarization	Generate summaries with up-to-date factual information	Increased relevance and factual correctness
Language Translation	Use retrieval to provide context for accurate translation	Improved translation quality and coherence

Example: Simulated QA System Using RAG (Pseudocode)

Below is a pseudocode example illustrating how a QA system might use RAG to generate an answer:

```python
python

def qa_system(query, graph_db, language_model):
    # Step 1: Retrieve relevant context from the graph
database
    context = retrieve_context(query, graph_db)

    # Step 2: Process the retrieved context (cleaning and
summarizing)
    processed_context = process_context(context)

    # Step 3: Combine the query with the processed context
    combined_input = combine_inputs(query, processed_context)

    # Step 4: Generate a final answer using the language
model
    answer = language_model.generate_response(combined_input)

    return answer

# Example usage:
query = "How does the new smartphone improve battery life?"
answer = qa_system(query, graph_database, generative_model)
print("QA System Answer:", answer)
```

Explanation:

- This pseudocode demonstrates a typical workflow in a QA system
  enhanced by RAG, where the query is enriched with context before
  generating a response.

17.4 Hybrid Architectures: Combining Rule-Based and Data-Driven Approaches

Overview

Hybrid architectures combine rule-based systems and data-driven (ML-based) approaches to leverage the strengths of both methods. Rule-based components provide deterministic, explainable outcomes, while data-driven models offer adaptability and improved performance in complex scenarios.

Benefits of Hybrid Architectures

- **Enhanced Accuracy:**
  Rule-based methods ensure that critical domain rules are always enforced, while ML components provide flexibility in handling variability.
- **Explainability:**
  Rules offer clear, understandable logic that can be explained to stakeholders, which complements the often "black-box" nature of ML models.
- **Robustness:**
  The system can fall back on rule-based logic in cases where data-driven models are uncertain or when training data is sparse.

Key Components of a Hybrid Architecture

1. **Rule-Based Module:**
   - **Function:**
     Implements explicit business logic and domain rules.
   - **Examples:**
     If a customer's purchase history meets certain criteria, apply a specific discount or recommendation rule.
2. **Data-Driven Module:**
   - **Function:**
     Uses machine learning to predict or classify based on historical data and learned patterns.
   - **Examples:**
     A neural network that predicts product recommendations based on user behavior.
3. **Fusion Layer:**
   - **Function:**
     Combines the outputs of the rule-based and data-driven modules.
   - **Techniques:**
     Weighted averaging, decision trees, or more sophisticated ensemble methods.

Table: Hybrid Architecture Components

Component	Function	Example Use Case
Rule-Based Module	Enforce deterministic rules and business logic	Apply fixed discount rules, validate customer data
Data-Driven Module	Predict outcomes using ML models	Generate personalized recommendations
Fusion Layer	Combine outputs from both modules	Integrate rule-based decisions with ML predictions

Code Example: Simple Hybrid Decision Fusion (Python Pseudocode)

Below is a simplified example that combines rule-based logic and ML predictions for a recommendation system.

```python
python

def rule_based_recommendation(user_data):
    """
    Apply deterministic rules to generate a basic
recommendation.
    """
    if user_data.get("loyalty") == "Gold":
        return "Recommend premium products"
    else:
        return "Recommend standard products"

def ml_based_recommendation(user_data, ml_model):
    """
    Use a machine learning model to predict a recommendation.
    """
    # Simulated prediction from ML model
    prediction = ml_model.predict(user_data)  # Assume this
returns a recommendation string
    return prediction

def hybrid_recommendation(user_data, ml_model, alpha=0.5):
    """
    Combine rule-based and ML-based recommendations using
weighted fusion.
    """
    rule_rec = rule_based_recommendation(user_data)
    ml_rec = ml_based_recommendation(user_data, ml_model)
```

```
    # For demonstration, we choose one of the recommendations
based on alpha threshold
    # In a real system, a more sophisticated fusion strategy
would be applied.
    if alpha > 0.5:
        return rule_rec
    else:
        return ml_rec

# Example usage:
user_data = {"loyalty": "Gold", "purchase_history":
["ProductA", "ProductB"]}
class DummyMLModel:
    def predict(self, data):
        return "Recommend ML-based suggestion"

ml_model = DummyMLModel()
final_recommendation = hybrid_recommendation(user_data,
ml_model, alpha=0.7)
print("Hybrid Recommendation:", final_recommendation)
```

Explanation:

- **Rule-Based Recommendation:**
  A simple function applies a deterministic rule.
- **ML-Based Recommendation:**
  A simulated ML model returns a prediction.
- **Hybrid Fusion:**
  The `hybrid_recommendation` function uses a simple weighted
  strategy (here simulated with an alpha threshold) to choose between
  the two outputs.

17.5 Evaluating and Benchmarking RAG Systems

Overview

Evaluating and benchmarking RAG systems is critical for understanding
their performance, accuracy, and overall effectiveness. This section discusses
methodologies for assessing RAG systems, including evaluation metrics,
benchmarking techniques, and practical considerations.

Evaluation Metrics

1. **Accuracy and Relevance:**
   - **Definition:**
     Measure how accurately the generated responses reflect the retrieved context and satisfy the query.
   - **Metrics:**
     - Precision, recall, and F1 score for QA tasks.
     - BLEU or ROUGE scores for language generation tasks.
2. **Latency:**
   - **Definition:**
     The time taken from receiving a query to delivering a final response.
   - **Importance:**
     Low latency is critical for real-time applications such as chatbots.
3. **Throughput:**
   - **Definition:**
     The number of queries processed per unit time.
   - **Importance:**
     A measure of scalability and performance under load.
4. **Resource Utilization:**
   - **Definition:**
     Monitor CPU, memory, and I/O usage during query processing.
   - **Importance:**
     Ensures that the system operates efficiently under various loads.
5. **User Satisfaction:**
   - **Definition:**
     Qualitative measure based on user feedback regarding the relevance and helpfulness of responses.
   - **Importance:**
     Ultimately determines the system's value in real-world applications.

Benchmarking Techniques

1. **A/B Testing:**
   - **Method:**
     Deploy two versions of the RAG system (e.g., with different

fusion strategies) to compare performance and user satisfaction.

- o **Example:**
  Compare a simple concatenation fusion method with a more advanced attention-based method.

2. **Load Testing:**
   - o **Method:**
     Simulate high query volumes to evaluate system throughput and latency.
   - o **Tools:**
     Apache JMeter, Locust, or custom scripts.

3. **Profiling:**
   - o **Method:**
     Use profiling tools to analyze query execution paths, module performance, and resource usage.
   - o **Tools:**
     Built-in database profilers, custom logging frameworks.

4. **User Surveys and Feedback:**
   - o **Method:**
     Collect user feedback to assess the relevance and clarity of generated responses.
   - o **Implementation:**
     Deploy feedback forms or interactive rating systems.

Table: Evaluation Metrics for RAG Systems

Metric	Description	Measurement Tools/Methods
Accuracy and Relevance	How closely responses match the expected output	Precision, Recall, F1, BLEU, ROUGE
Latency	Time taken to process and return a query	Application monitoring tools, logging
Throughput	Number of queries processed per unit time	Load testing tools (e.g., JMeter, Locust)
Resource Utilization	CPU, memory, and I/O usage during processing	Prometheus, Grafana, system monitoring scripts
User Satisfaction	Qualitative assessment based on user feedback	Surveys, feedback forms, user studies

Code Example: Benchmarking Latency in a RAG Pipeline (Python)

Below is an example of a simple Python script that benchmarks the latency of a RAG pipeline by timing the process.

```python
python

import time

def benchmark_rag_pipeline(query, rag_pipeline,
iterations=10):
    """
    Benchmark the RAG pipeline by measuring the average
latency over a specified number of iterations.
    """
    total_time = 0
    for _ in range(iterations):
        start_time = time.time()
        _ = rag_pipeline(query)
        elapsed_time = time.time() - start_time
        total_time += elapsed_time
        print(f"Iteration completed in {elapsed_time:.4f}
seconds")

    average_latency = total_time / iterations
    print(f"Average Latency: {average_latency:.4f} seconds")
    return average_latency

# Simulated RAG pipeline function for demonstration
def simulated_rag_pipeline(query):
    # Simulate processing time
    time.sleep(0.5)
    return "Simulated response for query: " + query

# Benchmark the simulated RAG pipeline
query = "What are the latest features of the new smartphone?"
benchmark_rag_pipeline(query, simulated_rag_pipeline,
iterations=5)
```

Explanation:

- **Benchmark Function:**
  The `benchmark_rag_pipeline` function measures the time taken to process a query over multiple iterations.
- **Latency Calculation:**
  It calculates and prints the average latency.

- **Simulated Pipeline:**
  A dummy `simulated_rag_pipeline` function is used to mimic processing delays, providing a basis for testing.

Future Considerations in Evaluation

- **Dynamic Benchmarking:**
  As systems evolve, continuously update benchmarks to reflect new optimizations.
- **Comprehensive Testing:**
  Evaluate not just the latency and throughput but also the qualitative aspects of generated responses through user studies.
- **Automated Reporting:**
  Integrate benchmarking into CI/CD pipelines to automatically report performance metrics after each deployment.

Chapter 18: Graph-Based Systems in AI, NLP, and Beyond

Graph-based systems have emerged as a powerful approach for organizing and leveraging structured knowledge. By representing data as interconnected nodes and edges, graph databases and algorithms enhance the capabilities of artificial intelligence (AI), natural language processing (NLP), and recommendation systems. In this chapter, we explore how structured knowledge from graphs can enhance AI, improve semantic search and NLP applications, and drive more effective recommendation engines.

18.1 Enhancing AI with Structured Knowledge

Overview

Structured knowledge in the form of knowledge graphs provides AI systems with a rich, interconnected data source that goes beyond unstructured text. By integrating structured knowledge, AI models can reason over relationships, infer missing information, and support complex decision-making tasks.

Key Benefits

1. **Contextual Understanding:**
   Graphs capture relationships between entities, allowing AI models to understand the context behind data. For example, a knowledge graph linking people, places, and events can help an AI system infer social or historical connections.
2. **Enhanced Reasoning:**
   Structured knowledge enables logical reasoning over relationships. AI systems can perform tasks such as question answering, anomaly detection, and predictive analysis by leveraging graph-based inference.
3. **Data Integration:**
   Graphs serve as a unifying structure to integrate heterogeneous data from multiple sources. This integration ensures that AI models have

access to comprehensive and consistent data, leading to more informed predictions.

Real-World Applications

- **Knowledge Graphs in Search Engines:**
  Search engines like Google use knowledge graphs to deliver rich, contextual search results by linking entities (e.g., people, places, concepts) and providing direct answers to user queries.
- **Intelligent Assistants:**
  Virtual assistants (e.g., Siri, Alexa) utilize structured knowledge to understand user intent and provide more relevant responses.

Table: Enhancing AI with Structured Knowledge

Benefit	Description	Example Application
Contextual Understanding	AI models gain insights from the relationships between entities	Knowledge graphs in search engines to provide context-aware answers
Enhanced Reasoning	Support for logical inference and decision-making	Fraud detection systems that infer relationships between transactions
Data Integration	Unify disparate data sources into a coherent structure	Healthcare systems integrating patient records, research, and clinical data

Code Example: Building a Simple Knowledge Graph for AI Enhancement Using NetworkX

Below is a Python example using NetworkX to build a simple knowledge graph. This graph can later be used to support AI tasks such as answering queries or inferring relationships.

```python
python

import networkx as nx
import matplotlib.pyplot as plt

# Create a new directed graph for a simple knowledge base
G = nx.DiGraph()

# Add nodes with attributes
```

```
G.add_node("Alice", type="Person", occupation="Researcher")
G.add_node("Bob", type="Person", occupation="Engineer")
G.add_node("University X", type="Institution", location="City
A")
G.add_node("Project Y", type="Project", field="AI Research")

# Add edges to represent relationships
G.add_edge("Alice", "University X", relation="studied_at")
G.add_edge("Alice", "Project Y", relation="leads")
G.add_edge("Bob", "Project Y", relation="collaborates_on")

# Visualize the knowledge graph
pos = nx.spring_layout(G)
nx.draw(G, pos, with_labels=True, node_color='lightblue',
edge_color='gray', node_size=2500, font_size=10)
edge_labels = nx.get_edge_attributes(G, 'relation')
nx.draw_networkx_edge_labels(G, pos, edge_labels=edge_labels,
font_color='red')
plt.title("Simple Knowledge Graph for AI Enhancement")
plt.show()
```

Explanation:

- **Graph Construction:**
  A directed graph is created where nodes represent entities (people, institutions, projects) with attributes.
- **Relationship Modeling:**
  Edges capture relationships (e.g., "studied_at", "leads", "collaborates_on"), providing context for AI inference.
- **Visualization:**
  The graph is visualized to illustrate how entities are interconnected, which can be used as a basis for further reasoning and analytics.

18.2 Natural Language Processing and Semantic Search

Overview

Natural Language Processing (NLP) and semantic search benefit greatly from graph-based systems by incorporating structured knowledge. Graphs enable the representation of semantic relationships between words, phrases, and entities, thereby enhancing the understanding of natural language.

Enhancing NLP with Graphs

1. **Semantic Relationships:**
   - Graphs can represent synonymy, hypernymy, and other semantic relationships.
   - **Example:**
     WordNet, a lexical database, is structured as a graph to support various NLP tasks such as word sense disambiguation.
2. **Contextual Retrieval:**
   - Semantic search leverages graphs to understand the context of a query, retrieving results that are semantically related even if they do not share the same keywords.
   - **Example:**
     A query for "physician" might also retrieve results for "doctor" if the graph captures the synonym relationship.
3. **Named Entity Recognition and Linking:**
   - Graphs help in identifying and linking named entities (e.g., people, organizations) to structured knowledge bases.
   - **Example:**
     In question answering systems, linking recognized entities to a knowledge graph improves the accuracy of responses.

Table: NLP and Semantic Search Enhancements with Graphs

Aspect	Description	Example Application
Semantic Relationships	Capturing synonyms, hypernyms, and other relations	WordNet for word sense disambiguation
Contextual Retrieval	Retrieving semantically related results	Semantic search engines that return conceptually related results
Named Entity Recognition	Identifying and linking entities to structured data	QA systems that use knowledge graphs for accurate answers

Code Example: Using a Graph for Semantic Search (Simplified Example)

Below is a Python pseudocode example that simulates a semantic search process using a knowledge graph built with NetworkX.

python

```python
def semantic_search(query, graph):
    """
    Simulate a semantic search by finding nodes that are
    semantically related to the query.
    """
    # For simplicity, assume the query is a term and we
    search for related terms in the graph
    related_nodes = []
    for node, data in graph.nodes(data=True):
        if query.lower() in node.lower() or query.lower() in
        data.get('synonyms', []):
            related_nodes.append(node)
    return related_nodes

# Build a simple knowledge graph with semantic relationships
G = nx.Graph()
G.add_node("doctor", synonyms=["physician", "medic"])
G.add_node("hospital")
G.add_edge("doctor", "hospital", relation="works_at")

# Simulate a semantic search for the term "physician"
query_term = "physician"
results = semantic_search(query_term, G)
print("Semantic Search Results:", results)
```

Explanation:

- **Graph Construction:**
  Nodes are added with additional attributes like synonyms to simulate semantic relationships.
- **Search Function:**
  The `semantic_search` function looks for nodes where the query term appears directly or within the synonyms list.
- **Output:**
  The search returns nodes semantically related to the query term.

18.3 The Role of Graphs in Recommendation Engines

Overview

Recommendation engines are a core application area for graph-based systems. Graphs naturally represent relationships between users, products, and interactions, making them ideal for powering personalized recommendations.

How Graphs Enhance Recommendation Engines

1. **Collaborative Filtering:**
   - **Graph-Based Approach:**
     Represent users and products as nodes with edges indicating interactions (e.g., purchases, ratings). Collaborative filtering leverages these relationships to recommend products based on similar user behaviors.
   - **Techniques:**
     - Graph traversal to find similar users or products
     - Node embeddings to capture latent features for similarity computation
2. **Content-Based Filtering:**
   - **Graph-Based Approach:**
     Use graph nodes to represent product features and attributes. Recommendations are generated by matching product features with user preferences.
   - **Techniques:**
     - Subgraph matching to identify products with similar features
     - Semantic enrichment to link similar products across different categories
3. **Hybrid Approaches:**
   - **Description:**
     Combine collaborative and content-based filtering using graph data to create a more comprehensive recommendation engine.
   - **Example:**
     Amazon and Netflix utilize hybrid approaches that merge behavioral data with product metadata to deliver personalized recommendations.

Table: Graph-Based Recommendation Techniques

Technique	Description	Example Use Case
Collaborative Filtering	Uses user-product interaction graphs to find similarities	Recommending products based on similar user behavior
Content-Based Filtering	Uses product attributes and semantic relationships	Suggesting items with similar features or genres
Hybrid Approaches	Combines both collaborative and content-based filtering	Personalized recommendations in e-commerce

Code Example: Building a Simple Graph-Based Recommendation System Using NetworkX

Below is an example that demonstrates how to generate recommendations by leveraging collaborative filtering in a graph.

```python
import networkx as nx
import numpy as np

# Create a sample graph representing user-product
interactions
G = nx.Graph()
# Example interactions: (User, Product)
interactions = [
    ("User1", "ProductA"),
    ("User1", "ProductB"),
    ("User2", "ProductB"),
    ("User2", "ProductC"),
    ("User3", "ProductA"),
    ("User3", "ProductC"),
    ("User4", "ProductA"),
    ("User4", "ProductB"),
    ("User4", "ProductC")
]
G.add_edges_from(interactions)

def recommend_products(user, graph, top_n=2):
    """
    Generate product recommendations for a given user based
on collaborative filtering.
    """
```

```
    # Find products the user has already interacted with
    user_products = set(graph.neighbors(user))

    # Compute scores for all products based on common
neighbors
    scores = {}
    for other_user in [n for n in graph.nodes() if
n.startswith("User") and n != user]:
        common_products =
user_products.intersection(set(graph.neighbors(other_user)))
        for product in
set(graph.neighbors(other_user)).difference(user_products):
            scores[product] = scores.get(product, 0) +
len(common_products)

    # Sort products based on scores and return top_n
recommendations
    recommended_products = sorted(scores.items(), key=lambda
x: x[1], reverse=True)[:top_n]
    return [product for product, score in
recommended_products]

# Example usage:
user = "User1"
recommendations = recommend_products(user, G)
print(f"Recommendations for {user}: {recommendations}")
```

Explanation:

- **Graph Construction:**
  A simple bipartite graph of users and products is created.
- **Recommendation Function:**
  The function `recommend_products` calculates recommendation scores based on the number of common product interactions between users.
- **Output:**
  The function returns a list of recommended products for a given user based on collaborative filtering.

18.4 Integrating IoT and Sensor Data into Graphs

Overview

The integration of Internet of Things (IoT) and sensor data into graph-based systems opens new avenues for real-time analytics, predictive maintenance, and intelligent automation. IoT devices generate large volumes of time-series and contextual data that, when combined with the relational power of graphs, can offer a holistic view of complex environments.

Benefits of Integrating IoT Data with Graphs

- **Contextual Relationship Mapping:**
  Graphs naturally capture relationships between sensors, devices, and the environment, enabling complex contextual queries.
- **Real-Time Analytics:**
  Graph-based systems can integrate streaming sensor data, supporting timely analysis and decision-making.
- **Anomaly Detection and Predictive Maintenance:**
  By modeling sensor networks as graphs, organizations can detect unusual patterns and predict failures before they occur.
- **Enhanced Visualization:**
  Graph visualizations can effectively represent sensor networks, displaying connections between devices and aggregated metrics such as signal strength or temperature variations.

Key Components for IoT Data Integration

1. **Data Ingestion:**
   - **Streaming Platforms:**
     Use tools like Apache Kafka or MQTT brokers to ingest sensor data in real time.
   - **Batch Ingestion:**
     For historical sensor data, use ETL pipelines to load data from databases or files.
2. **Data Transformation and Mapping:**
   - **Normalization:**
     Standardize sensor data formats (e.g., timestamp formats, units of measurement).
   - **Entity Mapping:**
     Map sensor IDs, device types, and location data to nodes and relationships in the graph.
   - **Temporal Attributes:**
     Attach time-series data as properties or create dedicated temporal nodes to support time-based queries.
3. **Storage in Graph Database:**

- o **Selection:**
  Use a graph database that supports real-time ingestion and time-series data, such as Neo4j, Amazon Neptune, or specialized time-series databases integrated with graph capabilities.
- o **Indexing:**
  Index frequently queried attributes such as device ID, location, and timestamp for improved performance.

Table: IoT Data Integration Components

Component	Description	Example Tools/Techniques
Data Ingestion	Capturing real-time and batch sensor data	Apache Kafka, MQTT, custom ETL scripts
Data Transformation	Normalizing and mapping sensor data to graph entities	Pandas, Apache NiFi, custom Python scripts
Graph Storage	Storing the integrated sensor data in a graph database	Neo4j, Amazon Neptune, JanusGraph
Temporal Data Handling	Managing time-series data and attaching timestamps to nodes/relationships	Time-series nodes, temporal indexes

Code Example: Ingesting IoT Data into a Graph Using Python and NetworkX

Below is a simplified Python example that simulates integrating sensor data into a graph using NetworkX. In a production system, data would be streamed and stored in a graph database.

```python
import networkx as nx
import datetime

# Create a directed graph to represent IoT sensor data
G = nx.DiGraph()

# Example sensor data (simulated)
sensor_data = [
    {"sensor_id": "S001", "value": 23.5, "timestamp": "2025-
02-01T10:00:00", "location": "Room 101"},
```

```
    {"sensor_id": "S002", "value": 19.8, "timestamp": "2025-
02-01T10:00:05", "location": "Room 102"},
    {"sensor_id": "S001", "value": 24.0, "timestamp": "2025-
02-01T10:00:10", "location": "Room 101"}
]

# Ingest sensor data into the graph
for entry in sensor_data:
    sensor_node = entry["sensor_id"]
    # Create or update sensor node with location info
    if not G.has_node(sensor_node):
        G.add_node(sensor_node, location=entry["location"])
    # Create a time-series node for each reading
    reading_node = f"{sensor_node}_{entry['timestamp']}"
    G.add_node(reading_node, value=entry["value"],
timestamp=entry["timestamp"])
    # Connect the sensor node to the reading node
    G.add_edge(sensor_node, reading_node, relation="reports")

# Visualize the graph
import matplotlib.pyplot as plt
pos = nx.spring_layout(G)
nx.draw_networkx(G, pos, with_labels=True,
node_color='lightblue', edge_color='gray', node_size=1500,
font_size=8)
plt.title("IoT Sensor Data Graph")
plt.show()
```

Explanation:

- **Graph Creation:**
  A directed graph is created to represent sensor data.
- **Data Ingestion:**
  Sensor readings are simulated and ingested, creating nodes for sensors and their time-stamped readings.
- **Relationships:**
  Edges connect each sensor to its corresponding readings.
- **Visualization:**
  The graph is visualized to show the structure of the sensor network.

18.5 Multimodal Data and Future Opportunities

Overview

Multimodal data refers to information that comes in multiple formats, such as text, images, audio, and video. Integrating multimodal data into graph-based systems can enrich knowledge graphs and open up new opportunities for advanced analytics and machine learning. This section explores the challenges and opportunities associated with multimodal data integration.

Benefits of Multimodal Data Integration

1. **Richer Context:**
   Combining different types of data provides a more comprehensive view of entities and relationships.
2. **Enhanced Insights:**
   Multimodal graphs can reveal correlations across modalities (e.g., linking textual descriptions with images), leading to more nuanced insights.
3. **Improved AI and ML Models:**
   Models trained on multimodal data can achieve better performance by leveraging diverse data sources.

Challenges

- **Data Heterogeneity:**
  Different modalities require distinct processing and representation methods.
- **Alignment and Fusion:**
  Integrating data from disparate sources requires alignment techniques to fuse information coherently.
- **Scalability:**
  Handling large volumes of multimodal data can be computationally intensive.

Integration Strategies

1. **Unified Data Model:**

- o **Description:**
  Develop a schema that can represent multiple data types in a unified manner. For example, nodes can have attributes for textual data, links to image files, or audio metadata.
2. **Feature Extraction and Embeddings:**
   - o **Technique:**
     Use specialized algorithms to extract features from each modality. For text, use NLP models; for images, use convolutional neural networks (CNNs); for audio, use signal processing techniques.
   - o **Fusion:**
     Combine these features into a single vector representation that can be attached to nodes in the graph.
3. **Cross-Modal Linking:**
   - o **Approach:**
     Establish relationships between nodes representing different modalities. For example, link a product description (text) to its image (visual) using a common identifier.
4. **Use of Multimodal Machine Learning Models:**
   - o **Implementation:**
     Leverage models that are designed to handle multimodal inputs, such as transformers that process both text and image data simultaneously.

Future Opportunities

- **Personalized Experiences:**
  Multimodal graphs can drive hyper-personalized recommendations by combining textual reviews, images, and user interaction data.
- **Enhanced Search and Discovery:**
  Semantic search systems can utilize multimodal data to provide richer, more accurate search results.
- **Advanced Analytics:**
  Opportunities in healthcare, entertainment, and smart cities where multimodal data integration can lead to breakthrough insights.

Table: Multimodal Data Integration Strategies

Strategy	Description	Benefits
Unified Data Model	Develop a schema to represent multiple data modalities	Consistent representation, easier integration
Feature Extraction	Extract features using modality-specific techniques	Richer node attributes, improved ML performance
Cross-Modal Linking	Establish relationships between different modalities	Enhanced insights, holistic view of data
Multimodal ML Models	Use models designed for multimodal inputs	Improved accuracy and personalization

Code Example: Combining Text and Image Features for a Product Node

Below is a simplified Python example that demonstrates how to extract textual features using TF-IDF and image features using a pre-trained CNN (using Keras), and then combine these features to represent a product node.

```python
python

import numpy as np
from sklearn.feature_extraction.text import TfidfVectorizer
from tensorflow.keras.applications import VGG16
from tensorflow.keras.preprocessing.image import load_img,
img_to_array
from tensorflow.keras.applications.vgg16 import
preprocess_input

# Example product description and image file path
product_description = "This is a state-of-the-art smartphone
with a high-resolution display and advanced camera features."
image_path = "path/to/product_image.jpg"

# Extract textual features using TF-IDF
vectorizer = TfidfVectorizer(max_features=50)
text_features =
vectorizer.fit_transform([product_description]).toarray()[0]

# Extract image features using VGG16 pre-trained model
model = VGG16(weights='imagenet', include_top=False,
pooling='avg')
image = load_img(image_path, target_size=(224, 224))
```

```
image_array = img_to_array(image)
image_array = np.expand_dims(image_array, axis=0)
image_array = preprocess_input(image_array)
image_features = model.predict(image_array)[0]

# Combine textual and image features into a single vector
combined_features = np.concatenate((text_features,
image_features))

print("Combined Features Shape:", combined_features.shape)
```

Explanation:

- **Textual Features:**
  TF-IDF is used to convert the product description into a numerical vector.
- **Image Features:**
  A pre-trained VGG16 model extracts features from the product image.
- **Feature Fusion:**
  The textual and image feature vectors are concatenated to create a comprehensive representation for the product node.
- **Outcome:**
  The combined feature vector can be stored as node attributes in a knowledge graph to support multimodal analysis.

Chapter 19: Future Trends, Challenges, and Research Directions

19.1 Evolving Standards and Technologies

Overview

The field of graph-based systems, particularly in relation to graph databases and RAG systems, is continually evolving. New standards and technologies emerge to address existing challenges and expand the capabilities of these systems.

Key Trends

1. **New Query Languages and Protocols:**
   o Continued development of more expressive query languages and improved interoperability standards.
2. **Enhanced Graph Data Models:**
   o Evolving from traditional property and RDF graphs to more flexible, hybrid models that incorporate time-series, spatial, and multimodal data.
3. **Integration of AI and ML:**
   o Tighter integration of graph analytics with machine learning, including built-in support for graph neural networks and advanced inference engines.

Future Impact

- **Interoperability:**
  Standardized protocols will enable easier data sharing across systems and platforms.
- **Performance:**
  Emerging technologies promise faster, more scalable graph processing.
- **Innovation:**
  New models and standards will unlock previously untapped applications in diverse domains.

19.2 Ethical Considerations and Data Governance

Overview

As graph-based systems become more prevalent, ethical considerations and robust data governance become critical. This section explores the importance of ensuring that data is used responsibly and in compliance with legal standards.

Key Areas of Focus

1. **Privacy and Data Protection:**
   o **Compliance:**
     Adherence to regulations such as GDPR, HIPAA, and CCPA.
   o **Techniques:**
     Data anonymization, encryption, and access control.
2. **Transparency and Accountability:**
   o **Explainability:**
     Ensuring that AI models, including those using graph data, can explain their decisions.
   o **Auditing:**
     Maintaining audit trails to track data access and modifications.
3. **Bias and Fairness:**
   o **Mitigation:**
     Identifying and mitigating biases in graph data and ML models.
   o **Evaluation:**
     Regular audits and fairness assessments.

Table: Ethical Considerations and Governance Practices

Focus Area	Key Considerations	Techniques/Tools
Privacy and Data Protection	Secure data storage and compliance with regulations	Data encryption, anonymization, access control
Transparency	Explainability of decisions made by AI systems	Explainable AI frameworks, audit logs

Focus Area	Key Considerations	Techniques/Tools
Bias and Fairness	Identification and mitigation of biases	Fairness audits, bias detection algorithms
Data Governance	Policies and procedures for data management	Governance frameworks, compliance monitoring tools

19.3 Scalability Challenges in Big Data Environments

Overview

Graph-based systems must scale to handle the ever-growing volume of data in today's big data environments. This section discusses the challenges and potential solutions for scaling graph databases and RAG systems.

Challenges

1. **Data Volume:**
   o Handling millions or billions of nodes and relationships.
2. **Query Complexity:**
   o Maintaining performance with increasingly complex queries and deep graph traversals.
3. **Distributed Processing:**
   o Managing data consistency and performance across distributed systems.

Potential Solutions

- **Distributed Graph Databases:**
  o Technologies such as JanusGraph and Amazon Neptune support distributed architectures.
- **Advanced Indexing and Caching:**
  o Techniques to improve query response times in large-scale graphs.
- **Parallel and Asynchronous Processing:**
  o Leveraging multi-core and distributed processing frameworks to improve throughput.

Table: Scalability Challenges and Solutions

Challenge	Description	Potential Solutions
Data Volume	Handling massive amounts of graph data	Distributed architectures, sharding, replication
Query Complexity	Slow performance on complex traversals	Advanced indexing, caching, optimized query algorithms
Distributed Processing	Data consistency and latency across nodes	Parallel processing frameworks, asynchronous processing

19.4 The Next Generation of Graph Databases and RAG Systems

Overview

The next generation of graph databases and RAG systems promises significant improvements in scalability, performance, and intelligence. This section discusses emerging technologies and innovations that are shaping the future of graph-based systems.

Emerging Innovations

1. **Next-Generation Graph Databases:**
   o **Features:**
   Increased scalability, built-in machine learning capabilities, and support for hybrid data models.
   o **Examples:**
   New iterations of platforms like Neo4j, as well as innovative solutions from cloud providers.
2. **Advanced RAG Systems:**
   o **Integration:**
   Deeper integration of RAG with graph databases to provide real-time, contextually enriched responses.
   o **Capabilities:**
   Enhanced fusion mechanisms, end-to-end training of retrieval and generation components, and improved performance through hardware acceleration.

Future Impact

- **Enhanced Capabilities:**
  More intelligent and responsive systems capable of handling dynamic, large-scale data.
- **Broader Adoption:**
  As systems become more user-friendly and performant, broader adoption in various industries is expected.

19.5 Open Research Questions and Opportunities

Overview

Despite significant progress, many open research questions remain in the field of graph-based systems and RAG. This section highlights key areas where further research is needed and discusses opportunities for innovation.

Open Research Questions

1. **Optimization of Fusion Mechanisms:**
   - **Question:**
     How can we further improve the integration of retrieval and generative components for more accurate and context-aware responses?
2. **Scalability in Extreme Data Environments:**
   - **Question:**
     What novel techniques can be developed to manage and query extremely large graphs efficiently?
3. **Interoperability and Standardization:**
   - **Question:**
     How can emerging standards be further developed to ensure seamless integration of graph-based systems across diverse domains?
4. **Ethical AI and Explainability:**
   - **Question:**
     How can we enhance the transparency and fairness of graph-

based ML models, especially in critical applications like healthcare and finance?

5. **Hybrid Architectures:**
   o **Question:**
      What is the optimal balance between rule-based and data-driven approaches in hybrid systems, and how can this be dynamically adjusted?

Future Opportunities

- **Innovative Applications:**
  New applications in areas such as autonomous systems, smart cities, and personalized healthcare.
- **Cross-Domain Integration:**
  Combining graph-based systems with blockchain, IoT, and other emerging technologies for enhanced data security and provenance.
- **Advanced ML Techniques:**
  Further research into GNNs and multimodal ML models that can leverage the full potential of graph data.

Table: Open Research Questions and Future Opportunities

Research Area	Open Question	Potential Opportunity
Fusion Mechanisms	How to optimize the integration of retrieval and generation?	Develop advanced attention-based and adaptive fusion methods
Scalability	How to efficiently manage extremely large graphs?	Novel distributed algorithms and parallel processing frameworks
Interoperability	How to standardize graph-based systems across domains?	Development of universal protocols and data models
Ethical AI	How to ensure transparency and fairness in graph-based ML?	Research into explainable AI techniques and fairness metrics
Hybrid Architectures	What is the optimal balance between rule-based and ML approaches?	Dynamic, adaptive systems that adjust based on data characteristics

The future of graph-based systems and RAG is filled with challenges and exciting opportunities. Continued research in fusion optimization, scalability, interoperability, ethical AI, and hybrid architectures will shape the next generation of intelligent systems. By addressing these open questions, researchers and practitioners can unlock new capabilities and drive innovation across industries.

Chapter 20: Enterprise Knowledge Graphs

Enterprise knowledge graphs are designed to consolidate, structure, and expose the wealth of data distributed across an organization. They provide a unified view of corporate knowledge that enhances decision-making, fosters collaboration, and drives digital transformation. This chapter explains how to build corporate knowledge bases, integrate legacy systems with modern graph technologies, presents a detailed case study of digital transformation in large enterprises, and outlines best practices for deploying enterprise knowledge graphs.

20.1 Building Corporate Knowledge Bases

Overview

Building a corporate knowledge base involves creating a unified, structured representation of an organization's information. This process encompasses understanding the domain, designing an ontology, and integrating data from various sources into a graph database.

Steps for Building Corporate Knowledge Bases

1. **Domain Analysis and Requirement Gathering:**
   - **Identify Key Domains:**
     Determine the critical business areas (e.g., finance, human resources, customer support) that will be represented.
   - **Stakeholder Engagement:**
     Interview subject matter experts to capture essential entities, relationships, and use cases.
   - **Define Use Cases:**
     Identify how different business units will use the knowledge base—for example, for decision support, collaboration, or reporting.
2. **Ontology and Data Model Design:**
   - **Entity and Relationship Identification:**
     Define primary entities such as Employee, Department, Project, Customer, Product, and how they relate (e.g., "works_in," "leads," "purchases").

- o **Schema Definition:**
  Establish attributes for each entity and specify the types of relationships. Leverage standard vocabularies (e.g., schema.org) where applicable.
- o **Iterative Refinement:**
  Validate the model with stakeholders and adjust based on feedback.
3. **Data Integration:**
   - o **Source Identification:**
     Identify data sources such as ERP systems, CRMs, spreadsheets, and external APIs.
   - o **ETL Process:**
     Extract, transform, and load (ETL) data into the graph database, ensuring normalization, cleansing, and semantic enrichment.
   - o **Consolidation:**
     Merge data from disparate sources into a cohesive, unified knowledge base.
4. **Implementation:**
   - o **Select a Graph Database:**
     Choose a database that meets enterprise needs (e.g., Neo4j, Amazon Neptune).
   - o **Prototype and Iterate:**
     Build an initial prototype and refine it based on user feedback and performance testing.

Table: Steps for Building Corporate Knowledge Bases

Step	Key Activities	Outcome
Domain Analysis	Identify key business domains, interview stakeholders, define use cases	Clear understanding of corporate knowledge requirements
Ontology and Data Model	Define entities, relationships, and attributes; design the schema	A formalized model representing organizational data
Data Integration	Extract data from various sources, transform and cleanse data	Unified and high-quality data ready for graph ingestion

Step	Key Activities	Outcome
Implementation	Choose graph database, prototype, and iteratively refine the solution	A working corporate knowledge base with continuous improvement

Code Example: Creating a Simple Corporate Knowledge Graph in Neo4j (Python)

The following Python script uses the Neo4j Python driver to create a basic corporate knowledge graph, including nodes for employees, departments, and projects.

```python
from neo4j import GraphDatabase

# Neo4j connection settings
uri = "bolt://localhost:7687"
username = "neo4j"
password = "your_password"
driver = GraphDatabase.driver(uri, auth=(username, password))

def create_corporate_knowledge_graph(tx):
    # Create Employee nodes
    tx.run("MERGE (e:Employee {id: 'E001', name: 'Alice'})")
    tx.run("MERGE (e:Employee {id: 'E002', name: 'Bob'})")

    # Create Department node
    tx.run("MERGE (d:Department {id: 'D001', name: 'Research
and Development'})")

    # Create Project node
    tx.run("MERGE (p:Project {id: 'P001', name: 'Project
X'})")

    # Create relationships
    tx.run("MATCH (e:Employee {id: 'E001'}), (d:Department
{id: 'D001'}) MERGE (e)-[:WORKS_IN]->(d)")
    tx.run("MATCH (e:Employee {id: 'E002'}), (d:Department
{id: 'D001'}) MERGE (e)-[:WORKS_IN]->(d)")
    tx.run("MATCH (e:Employee {id: 'E001'}), (p:Project {id:
'P001'}) MERGE (e)-[:LEADS]->(p)")
    tx.run("MATCH (e:Employee {id: 'E002'}), (p:Project {id:
'P001'}) MERGE (e)-[:COLLABORATES_ON]->(p)")

with driver.session() as session:
```

```
session.write_transaction(create_corporate_knowledge_graph)
driver.close()
print("Corporate knowledge graph created successfully.")
```

Explanation:

- **Graph Construction:**
  The script creates nodes for employees, a department, and a project.
- **Relationship Modeling:**
  Relationships such as WORKS_IN, LEADS, and COLLABORATES_ON are established.
- **MERGE Statement:**
  The MERGE clause ensures nodes and relationships are created only once.

20.2 Integrating Legacy Systems with Modern Graph Technologies

Overview

Large enterprises often face the challenge of integrating legacy systems with modern graph technologies. Legacy systems contain valuable historical data but may use outdated formats or be isolated in silos. Modern graph technologies, on the other hand, offer flexible data models and powerful analytics capabilities.

Integration Strategies

1. **Data Extraction and ETL:**
   o **Approach:**
     Develop ETL pipelines to extract data from legacy systems (e.g., relational databases, flat files), transform it to a modern schema, and load it into a graph database.
   o **Best Practices:**
     ▪ Implement robust data cleansing and normalization routines.
     ▪ Use middleware or ETL tools like Apache NiFi or Talend for consistent data transformation.

2. **API Wrappers and Adapters:**
   - **Approach:**
   Create API wrappers to expose legacy system data via modern RESTful or GraphQL interfaces.
   - **Best Practices:**
     - Secure API access.
     - Implement caching to reduce load on legacy systems.
3. **Data Federation:**
   - **Approach:**
   Use federation techniques to create a virtual view over legacy data without migrating all data to the new system.
   - **Best Practices:**
     - Use federated query engines that can access multiple data sources.
     - Ensure data consistency and real-time synchronization.
4. **Incremental Modernization:**
   - **Approach:**
   Gradually modernize legacy systems by integrating them into the graph-based architecture over time.
   - **Best Practices:**
     - Prioritize critical data sources and functionalities.
     - Monitor performance and adjust integration strategies as needed.

Table: Legacy Systems Integration Strategies

Strategy	Description	Benefits	Example Tools/Methods
Data Extraction & ETL	Extract, cleanse, and transform legacy data for the graph	Consolidates disparate data, improves data quality	Apache NiFi, Talend, custom ETL scripts
API Wrappers/Adapters	Expose legacy data via modern APIs	Seamless integration with minimal disruption	RESTful API development, GraphQL servers
Data Federation	Create a virtual unified view	Real-time access without full migration	Federated query engines,

Strategy	Description	Benefits	Example Tools/Methods
	over legacy systems		middleware solutions
Incremental Modernization	Gradually replace legacy systems with modern technologies	Low-risk, phased transition	Microservices, containerization, hybrid architectures

Code Example: Transforming Legacy Data with Python

Below is a Python script that extracts data from a CSV file simulating a legacy system, transforms it, and prepares it for loading into a modern graph database.

```python
import pandas as pd

def extract_legacy_data(file_path):
    """
    Extract data from a legacy CSV file.
    """
    df = pd.read_csv(file_path)
    return df

def transform_legacy_data(df):
    """
    Transform legacy data to align with the modern graph
schema.
    """
    # Rename columns to match the modern schema
    df.rename(columns={
        'cust_id': 'CustomerID',
        'cust_name': 'CustomerName',
        'order_num': 'OrderID',
        'order_dt': 'OrderDate',
        'amount': 'TotalAmount'
    }, inplace=True)

    # Normalize the date format
    df['OrderDate'] =
pd.to_datetime(df['OrderDate']).dt.strftime('%Y-%m-%d')

    return df
```

```
# Example usage:
legacy_file = "legacy_customers_orders.csv"  # CSV with
legacy data
legacy_data = extract_legacy_data(legacy_file)
transformed_data = transform_legacy_data(legacy_data)
print("Transformed Legacy Data Sample:")
print(transformed_data.head())
```

Explanation:

- **Data Extraction:**
  The CSV file is read using Pandas.
- **Transformation:**
  Column names are standardized, and date formats are normalized.
- **Outcome:**
  The transformed data is now ready for integration into a modern
  graph database.

20.3 Case Study: Digital Transformation in Large Enterprises

Overview

Digital transformation in large enterprises involves integrating diverse legacy systems into a unified, modern knowledge graph. This case study illustrates how a multinational corporation successfully transitioned to a graph-based architecture, overcoming challenges associated with data silos and legacy systems.

Scenario

- **Background:**
  A large enterprise with multiple legacy systems across various business units (finance, HR, supply chain) sought to create a unified view of corporate knowledge.
- **Challenges:**
    o Disparate data sources and formats
    o Inconsistent data schemas
    o High integration and maintenance costs in legacy systems

- **Solution:**
  The enterprise implemented a comprehensive ETL process to extract and transform data from legacy systems. They developed API adapters to integrate real-time data and built a corporate knowledge graph using a modern graph database (e.g., Neo4j or Amazon Neptune). Interactive dashboards and reporting tools were also deployed to enable data-driven decision-making.

Key Outcomes

- **Improved Data Accessibility:**
  Consolidated data from across the organization, breaking down silos.
- **Enhanced Decision-Making:**
  Real-time insights and analytics enabled better strategic decisions.
- **Operational Efficiency:**
  Reduced redundancy and streamlined data management processes.
- **Cost Savings:**
  Lowered operational costs through effective data integration and automation.

Table: Case Study Summary

Phase	Key Activities	Outcome/Benefit
Data Consolidation	Extract, cleanse, and integrate legacy data	Unified view of corporate data across business units
Knowledge Graph Construction	Design ontology and load data into a modern graph DB	Interconnected and enriched corporate knowledge
Integration and Access	Develop API adapters and dashboards for data access	Real-time analytics and informed decision-making
Operational Impact	Streamlined processes and reduced data redundancy	Enhanced efficiency and cost savings

Discussion

This case study demonstrates that digital transformation is not solely about technology replacement; it is about integrating legacy data into a coherent, modern framework that supports continuous innovation. The key to success lies in robust ETL processes, strategic use of modern graph technologies, and ongoing user training and support.

20.4 Best Practices for Enterprise Deployment

Overview

Deploying enterprise knowledge graphs requires careful planning to ensure scalability, security, and performance. This section outlines best practices for enterprise deployment, including infrastructure design, data governance, security measures, and ongoing support.

Best Practices

1. **Scalability and Performance:**
   - **Plan for Growth:**
     Design your system to scale horizontally, using distributed graph databases and load balancing.
   - **Performance Optimization:**
     Use indexing, caching, and query optimization techniques.
   - **Monitoring:**
     Continuously monitor system performance and resource utilization.
2. **Security and Data Governance:**
   - **Data Protection:**
     Implement strong access controls, encryption, and data anonymization.
   - **Compliance:**
     Ensure compliance with regulations such as GDPR, HIPAA, or CCPA.
   - **Audit Trails:**
     Maintain logs for data access and modifications for accountability.
3. **Integration and Interoperability:**
   - **API-Driven Architecture:**
     Develop standardized APIs to connect with other enterprise systems.
   - **Legacy Integration:**
     Use ETL and API adapters to incorporate legacy data.

- o **Standardized Ontologies:**
  Adopt industry standards and vocabularies to ensure consistency.
4. **Deployment Strategies:**
   - o **Containerization:**
     Use Docker and orchestration platforms like Kubernetes to simplify deployment.
   - o **CI/CD Pipelines:**
     Automate testing and deployment processes to ensure smooth updates.
   - o **Blue-Green Deployments:**
     Implement strategies to minimize downtime during upgrades.

Table: Best Practices for Enterprise Deployment

Best Practice	Description	Benefits	Example/Tools
Scalability and Performance	Design for horizontal scaling and optimize queries	High performance, low latency	Distributed graph DBs, caching, indexing
Security and Data Governance	Implement robust access control, encryption, and compliance measures	Secure and compliant data management	RBAC, TLS/SSL, data anonymization tools
Integration and Interoperability	Develop standardized APIs and integrate legacy systems	Seamless data flow across enterprise systems	RESTful APIs, ETL tools (Talend, Apache NiFi)
Deployment Strategies	Use containerization, CI/CD, and blue-green deployments	Minimized downtime, consistent updates	Docker, Kubernetes, Jenkins, GitHub Actions

Code Example: Docker Compose Configuration for Enterprise Deployment

Below is a sample `docker-compose.yml` file that demonstrates a basic configuration for deploying an enterprise knowledge graph system with a graph database (Neo4j) and an API service.

```yaml
```

```yaml
version: '3.8'
services:
  neo4j:
    image: neo4j:enterprise
    container_name: neo4j
    environment:
      - NEO4J_AUTH=neo4j/your_password
    ports:
      - "7474:7474"
      - "7687:7687"
    volumes:
      - neo4j_data:/data

  api:
    build: .
    container_name: graph-api
    environment:
      - NEO4J_URI=bolt://neo4j:7687
      - NEO4J_USER=neo4j
      - NEO4J_PASSWORD=your_password
    ports:
      - "5000:5000"
    depends_on:
      - neo4j

volumes:
  neo4j_data:
```

Explanation:

- **Neo4j Service:**
  Runs the Neo4j Enterprise edition with authentication enabled.
- **API Service:**
  Builds a custom API that connects to the Neo4j database.
- **Volumes:**
  Persist Neo4j data using Docker volumes.
- **Dependencies:**
  The API service depends on the Neo4j service, ensuring correct startup order.

Chapter 21: Domain-Specific Applications

Enterprise and specialized applications of knowledge graphs are transforming industries by integrating disparate data sources, enabling advanced analytics, and facilitating smarter decision-making. This chapter examines four key domains where knowledge graphs have demonstrated significant value.

21.1 Knowledge Graphs in Healthcare: Improving Patient Outcomes

Overview

In healthcare, knowledge graphs are used to integrate patient records, clinical research, treatment protocols, and even real-time monitoring data. By consolidating these diverse sources into a unified graph, healthcare providers can gain a holistic view of patient histories, identify correlations between symptoms and outcomes, and support personalized treatment strategies.

Benefits

- **Improved Diagnostics:**
  By integrating clinical data, imaging results, and research findings, healthcare providers can make more accurate diagnoses.
- **Personalized Treatment:**
  Knowledge graphs enable the analysis of individual patient data alongside broader clinical insights, leading to customized treatment plans.
- **Enhanced Research:**
  Researchers can discover new correlations and treatment pathways by exploring the interconnected data.
- **Operational Efficiency:**
  Streamlines administrative tasks by linking disparate systems such as EHRs, lab results, and prescription data.

Example Use Case

A hospital builds a knowledge graph that includes patient demographics, medical history, lab test results, and clinical trial data. The system can identify patients who meet specific criteria for clinical trials, suggest tailored treatment plans, and flag potential adverse reactions based on similar historical cases.

Table: Benefits and Challenges of Healthcare Knowledge Graphs

Aspect	Benefits	Challenges
Improved Diagnostics	Integrated data leads to more accurate diagnoses	Data privacy and regulatory compliance (e.g., HIPAA)
Personalized Treatment	Tailored treatment plans based on comprehensive patient data	Data integration from disparate, heterogeneous sources
Enhanced Research	Uncovers new treatment pathways and correlations	High data complexity and need for continuous updates
Operational Efficiency	Streamlines administrative processes	Legacy system integration and interoperability issues

Code Example: Building a Simple Healthcare Knowledge Graph

Below is an example using Python and NetworkX to build a simple healthcare knowledge graph that models patients, doctors, and treatments.

```python
import networkx as nx
import matplotlib.pyplot as plt

# Create a directed graph for healthcare data
G = nx.DiGraph()

# Add nodes: patients, doctors, and treatments
G.add_node("Patient: John Doe", type="Patient", age=45,
condition="Hypertension")
G.add_node("Doctor: Dr. Smith", type="Doctor",
specialty="Cardiology")
G.add_node("Treatment: Medication A", type="Treatment",
description="Antihypertensive medication")
```

```
# Add relationships
G.add_edge("Patient: John Doe", "Doctor: Dr. Smith",
relation="consults")
G.add_edge("Doctor: Dr. Smith", "Treatment: Medication A",
relation="prescribes")
G.add_edge("Patient: John Doe", "Treatment: Medication A",
relation="receives")

# Visualize the graph
pos = nx.spring_layout(G)
nx.draw(G, pos, with_labels=True, node_color='lightblue',
edge_color='gray', node_size=2500, font_size=10)
edge_labels = nx.get_edge_attributes(G, 'relation')
nx.draw_networkx_edge_labels(G, pos, edge_labels=edge_labels,
font_color='red')
plt.title("Healthcare Knowledge Graph Example")
plt.show()
```

Explanation:

- **Graph Construction:**
  Nodes represent a patient, a doctor, and a treatment.
- **Relationship Modeling:**
  Edges define relationships such as "consults," "prescribes," and "receives."
- **Visualization:**
  The graph visually demonstrates the interconnections, providing a basis for further analysis.

21.2 Financial Services: Risk Management and Fraud Detection

Overview

In financial services, knowledge graphs help organizations manage risk and detect fraudulent activities by linking transactions, customer data, and external data sources. The ability to model complex relationships in financial networks makes graphs particularly valuable for uncovering hidden patterns and anomalies.

Benefits

- **Enhanced Fraud Detection:**
  Graphs can identify unusual patterns and suspicious linkages between transactions that may indicate fraud.
- **Risk Management:**
  By visualizing and analyzing connections between entities (e.g., customers, accounts, transactions), financial institutions can assess risk more effectively.
- **Regulatory Compliance:**
  Provides a transparent view of data relationships that supports regulatory audits and reporting.

Example Use Case

A bank utilizes a knowledge graph to model customer transactions and relationships. By applying graph algorithms, the bank can detect fraud rings, identify high-risk entities based on centrality measures, and predict potential fraudulent behavior through link prediction.

Table: Financial Services Applications of Knowledge Graphs

Application Area	Description	Example Techniques
Fraud Detection	Identify and analyze suspicious transaction patterns	Subgraph matching, anomaly detection, centrality measures
Risk Management	Assess risk by mapping relationships between customers and accounts	Graph traversal, link prediction, clustering
Regulatory Compliance	Ensure transparent reporting of financial relationships	Data lineage tracking, audit trails, graph visualization

Code Example: Querying a Fraud Detection Graph in Neo4j (Cypher)

Below is a Cypher query example that could be used in Neo4j to identify potential fraud by detecting customers involved in multiple high-value transactions.

```
cypher

// Find customers with more than 3 high-value transactions
(e.g., total > 10000)
MATCH (c:Customer)-[:MADE]->(t:Transaction)
WHERE t.total > 10000
WITH c, COUNT(t) AS highValueCount
WHERE highValueCount > 3
RETURN c.name AS CustomerName, highValueCount AS
HighValueTransactions
```

Explanation:

- **MATCH Clause:**
  Finds customers linked to transactions.
- **WHERE Clause:**
  Filters transactions exceeding a specified total.
- **Aggregation:**
  Counts high-value transactions per customer.
- **Final Filtering:**
  Returns customers with more than three such transactions, which
  may indicate fraudulent behavior.

21.3 Social Networks: Enhancing Connectivity and Engagement

Overview

Social networks benefit significantly from knowledge graphs as they
inherently involve complex relationships among users. Graph-based systems
enable the analysis of social interactions, identification of influential users,
and personalized content recommendations, thus enhancing connectivity and
user engagement.

Benefits

- **Improved Connection Recommendations:**
  Graphs can suggest new connections based on mutual friends or
  shared interests.

- **Community Detection:**
  Identifies communities or groups within a social network, enabling targeted content and engagement strategies.
- **Engagement Analytics:**
  Analyzes patterns in user interactions to optimize content delivery and ad targeting.

Example Use Case

A social media platform uses a knowledge graph to model user relationships, interactions (likes, shares, comments), and content preferences. By analyzing these relationships with community detection algorithms, the platform can recommend new connections and tailor content to specific user groups.

Table: Social Network Applications of Knowledge Graphs

Application Area	Description	Key Techniques
Connection Recommendations	Suggest new friends based on shared relationships	Link prediction, common neighbor analysis
Community Detection	Identify clusters or communities within the network	Louvain method, label propagation
Engagement Analytics	Analyze user interactions to improve content delivery	Centrality measures, graph clustering, sentiment analysis

Code Example: Social Network Graph Query in Neo4j (Cypher)

Below is an example Cypher query that retrieves communities of users in a social network based on their interactions.

```cypher
// Identify communities using the Louvain method (requires
APOC procedures)
CALL apoc.algo.louvain('User', 'FRIENDS_WITH', {write:true,
weightProperty:'weight'})
YIELD nodeId, community
RETURN nodeId, community
ORDER BY community
LIMIT 10;
```

Explanation:

- **CALL apoc.algo.louvain:**
  Uses the Louvain community detection algorithm provided by the APOC library in Neo4j.
- **Parameters:**
  The query specifies the node label, relationship type, and optional parameters.
- **Output:**
  Returns a list of nodes and their community assignments, helping to identify social clusters.

21.4 Government and Public Sector Use Cases

Overview

In the public sector, knowledge graphs are used to enhance transparency, support policy analysis, and improve service delivery. They help integrate data from various governmental agencies, facilitate data-driven decision-making, and enable citizens to access public information more efficiently.

Benefits

- **Data Transparency:**
  Consolidates data from multiple sources, making it accessible and understandable for policymakers and the public.
- **Efficient Service Delivery:**
  Enables better management of public resources by providing a unified view of data across departments.
- **Policy Analysis:**
  Supports the analysis of complex data sets to inform policy decisions and monitor outcomes.
- **Interoperability:**
  Enhances data sharing among different government agencies through standardized data models and APIs.

Example Use Case

A city government implements a knowledge graph to integrate data from transportation, public health, and public safety departments. This unified graph enables real-time monitoring of traffic flows, emergency response times, and public health indicators, leading to more effective resource allocation and policy interventions.

Table: Government and Public Sector Applications of Knowledge Graphs

Application Area	Description	Example Use Case
Data Transparency	Consolidate and publish data from multiple agencies	Open data portals, public dashboards
Service Delivery	Integrate data to streamline public services	Real-time monitoring of transportation and emergency services
Policy Analysis	Analyze complex datasets to inform policy decisions	Tracking public health trends, evaluating economic policies
Interagency Integration	Enable data sharing and collaboration among departments	Unified knowledge graphs for government agencies

Code Example: Simulated Government Knowledge Graph Query (Python & NetworkX)

Below is a Python example using NetworkX to simulate a simple government knowledge graph that integrates data from different agencies, followed by a query to retrieve interconnected information.

```python
python

import networkx as nx
import matplotlib.pyplot as plt

# Create a graph representing government data
G = nx.Graph()
```

```
# Add nodes representing various agencies and data points
G.add_node("Transportation Dept", type="Agency")
G.add_node("Public Health Dept", type="Agency")
G.add_node("Public Safety Dept", type="Agency")
G.add_node("Traffic Data", type="Data", description="Real-
time traffic metrics")
G.add_node("Health Data", type="Data", description="Public
health statistics")
G.add_node("Emergency Response Data", type="Data",
description="Response times and incident reports")

# Create edges representing data sharing and relationships
G.add_edge("Transportation Dept", "Traffic Data",
relation="monitors")
G.add_edge("Public Health Dept", "Health Data",
relation="monitors")
G.add_edge("Public Safety Dept", "Emergency Response Data",
relation="monitors")
G.add_edge("Transportation Dept", "Public Safety Dept",
relation="collaborates")
G.add_edge("Public Health Dept", "Public Safety Dept",
relation="collaborates")

# Visualize the government knowledge graph
pos = nx.spring_layout(G)
nx.draw(G, pos, with_labels=True, node_color='lightgreen',
edge_color='gray', node_size=2500, font_size=10)
edge_labels = nx.get_edge_attributes(G, 'relation')
nx.draw_networkx_edge_labels(G, pos, edge_labels=edge_labels,
font_color='red')
plt.title("Government Knowledge Graph Example")
plt.show()
```

Explanation:

- **Graph Construction:**
  Nodes represent government departments and data sets.
- **Relationship Modeling:**
  Edges capture relationships such as monitoring and interagency collaboration.
- **Visualization:**
  The resulting graph visually demonstrates how various agencies interact and share data, which is crucial for informed public policy and service delivery.

Chapter 22: RAG for Enhanced Search and Recommendation Systems

RAG (Retrieval-Augmented Generation) combines traditional generative models with a retrieval component that fetches relevant, contextually rich data from structured sources such as knowledge graphs. This integration enhances the relevance of search results and recommendation systems by grounding generated responses in up-to-date, factual information. In this chapter, we explore how RAG improves search relevance, enhances personalization and user experience, review real-world case studies from e-commerce and media, and discuss the metrics and KPIs necessary to measure success.

22.1 Improving Search Relevance with Augmented Data

Overview

Traditional search engines often rely on keyword matching and static indexes, which may not fully capture the context of a user's query. By integrating RAG into search systems, additional context is retrieved from a knowledge base (e.g., a corporate or domain-specific knowledge graph) and combined with the user query to produce a more accurate, context-aware response.

Key Concepts

- **Contextual Retrieval:**
  The retrieval module extracts relevant information (e.g., entities, relationships, summaries) from a knowledge graph to enrich the user's query.
- **Augmentation:**
  The generative module then incorporates this retrieved context into the final search results, leading to enhanced relevance and depth.

Benefits

- **Enhanced Relevance:**
  Responses are grounded in factual, real-time data.
- **Improved User Satisfaction:**
  Users receive comprehensive and contextually appropriate search results.
- **Dynamic Updates:**
  The system can adapt to changing information in real time.

Comparison Table: Traditional Search vs. RAG-Enhanced Search

Aspect	Traditional Search	RAG-Enhanced Search
Query Processing	Keyword matching, static indexes	Query augmented with dynamically retrieved context
Data Freshness	Based on periodic index updates	Real-time retrieval ensures current information
Response Richness	Limited to pre-indexed data	Combines generative output with structured data for richer responses
User Satisfaction	May miss nuanced queries	Provides detailed and context-aware answers

Code Example: Simple Context Augmentation Function

Below is a simplified Python function that demonstrates how to combine a user query with retrieved context, preparing it for input into a generative model.

```python
def augment_query(query, retrieved_context):
    """
    Augment a user query with additional context.

    Parameters:
        query (str): The original user query.
        retrieved_context (str): The context retrieved from a
knowledge graph or data source.

    Returns:
```

```
        str: A combined input string for the generative
model.
    """
    combined_input = f"User Query: {query}\nRetrieved
Context: {retrieved_context}"
    return combined_input

# Example usage:
query = "What are the best smartphones available this year?"
retrieved_context = ("Data from product reviews, expert
ratings, and specifications indicate that models "
                     "such as Model X, Model Y, and Model Z
offer high performance, long battery life, and "
                     "innovative features.")
augmented_input = augment_query(query, retrieved_context)
print("Augmented Query Input:\n", augmented_input)
```

Explanation:

- **Functionality:**
  The `augment_query` function concatenates the original query with
  additional context, forming a richer input for a generative model.
- **Example Usage:**
  Demonstrates how textual context (e.g., product review summaries)
  can be merged with a search query to enhance relevance.

22.2 Personalization and User Experience Enhancements

Overview

Personalization is essential for modern recommendation systems and search
interfaces. RAG enhances personalization by incorporating user-specific data
and contextual information into the generated responses, leading to more
tailored and engaging experiences.

Key Concepts

- **User Profiling:**
  Collect and integrate user data (e.g., past behavior, preferences,
  demographics) to inform the retrieval process.

- **Dynamic Contextualization:**
  Adapt the retrieved context based on the user's current interaction and historical data.
- **Feedback Loops:**
  Continuously refine personalization algorithms based on user interactions and feedback.

Benefits

- **Tailored Recommendations:**
  The system can deliver personalized search results and product suggestions.
- **Enhanced Engagement:**
  Users are more likely to interact with content that is relevant to their interests.
- **Improved Conversion Rates:**
  Personalization leads to better customer satisfaction and higher conversion rates.

Code Example: Simple Personalized Recommendation Pipeline (Pseudocode)

Below is a simplified pseudocode example that demonstrates how a RAG-based system might personalize recommendations by integrating user profile data.

```python
def get_user_profile(user_id):
    """
    Retrieve the user profile from the database.
    For simplicity, return a simulated profile.
    """
    # Simulated user profile data
    return {"user_id": user_id, "preferences": "smartphones",
"recent_search": "latest features"}

def personalize_context(query, user_profile,
retrieved_context):
    """
    Combine user profile data with the retrieved context to
tailor the response.
    """
    # Example personalization: include user preferences in
the context
```

```python
    personalized_context = f"{retrieved_context}\nUser
Preferences: {user_profile['preferences']}\nRecent Search:
{user_profile['recent_search']}"
    return personalized_context

def personalized_rag_pipeline(query, user_id, graph_db,
language_model):
    # Retrieve the user profile
    user_profile = get_user_profile(user_id)

    # Retrieve context from the graph database
    retrieved_context = retrieve_context(query, graph_db)

    # Personalize the retrieved context with user profile
data
    personalized_context = personalize_context(query,
user_profile, retrieved_context)

    # Combine the query with the personalized context
    combined_input = augment_query(query,
personalized_context)

    # Generate the final personalized response
    final_response =
language_model.generate_response(combined_input)
    return final_response

# Example usage:
user_id = "User123"
query = "What are the best smartphones available this year?"
personalized_response = personalized_rag_pipeline(query,
user_id, graph_database, generative_model)
print("Personalized Response:", personalized_response)
```

Explanation:

- **User Profile Retrieval:**
  The `get_user_profile` function simulates fetching a user profile.
- **Context Personalization:**
  The `personalize_context` function merges the user's preferences and recent search history with the retrieved context.
- **Pipeline Integration:**
  The `personalized_rag_pipeline` function demonstrates how personalized context can be used to generate tailored responses.

22.3 Case Studies from E-commerce and Media

Overview

Real-world case studies illustrate the practical benefits of integrating RAG into search and recommendation systems. This section presents examples from the e-commerce and media industries, showcasing how RAG has enhanced user engagement, increased conversion rates, and improved content relevance.

Case Study 1: E-commerce Recommendation System

Scenario:

- **Company:**
  A large online retailer.
- **Challenge:**
  Traditional recommendation systems provided generic suggestions that did not adapt to rapidly changing trends or user behavior.
- **Solution:**
  The retailer implemented a RAG-based recommendation system that integrated real-time product data and user profiles into a generative model.
- **Outcome:**
  - Increased personalization of recommendations.
  - Higher click-through and conversion rates.
  - Enhanced customer satisfaction through timely and relevant suggestions.

Case Study 2: Media Content Personalization

Scenario:

- **Company:**
  A digital media platform.
- **Challenge:**
  Delivering personalized content recommendations in a highly dynamic media environment.
- **Solution:**
  The platform used RAG to merge user engagement data (e.g., viewing history, likes) with real-time news and content updates.

- **Outcome:**
  - Improved relevance of content recommendations.
  - Increased user engagement and longer session durations.
  - Enhanced revenue through targeted advertising and content promotion.

Table: Summary of Case Studies

Industry	Case Study	Challenges	Solutions	Outcomes
E-commerce	Personalized Recommendation System	Generic recommendations, slow adaptation	RAG-based system integrating real-time data and user profiles	Higher conversion rates, increased customer satisfaction
Media	Content Personalization	Dynamic content, diverse user interests	RAG for merging engagement data with real-time content updates	Improved content relevance, increased user engagement

22.4 Measuring Success: Metrics and KPIs

Overview

Measuring the success of RAG-enhanced search and recommendation systems is critical for continuous improvement. Key performance indicators (KPIs) and metrics provide insights into the system's effectiveness, user engagement, and overall impact on business outcomes.

Key Metrics for Evaluation

1. **Relevance Metrics:**
   - **Precision and Recall:**
     Measure the accuracy and completeness of search results or recommendations.

- o **F1 Score:**
  The harmonic mean of precision and recall.
- o **BLEU/ROUGE Scores:**
  Evaluate the quality of generated text against reference texts.

2. **Engagement Metrics:**
   - o **Click-Through Rate (CTR):**
     The percentage of users who click on recommended items.
   - o **Conversion Rate:**
     The percentage of users who take a desired action (e.g., make a purchase) after receiving a recommendation.
   - o **User Satisfaction Surveys:**
     Qualitative feedback to gauge user experience.

3. **Performance Metrics:**
   - o **Latency:**
     Time taken to generate responses.
   - o **Throughput:**
     Number of queries processed per unit time.
   - o **Resource Utilization:**
     CPU, memory, and network usage during operation.

Table: Metrics and KPIs for RAG Systems

Metric/KPI	Description	Measurement Method
Precision	Ratio of relevant results to total returned results	Manual evaluation, automated tests
Recall	Ratio of relevant results retrieved to total relevant items	Ground truth comparison
F1 Score	Harmonic mean of precision and recall	Calculation from precision and recall values
BLEU/ROUGE Scores	Quality of generated text compared to references	Automated text evaluation tools
Click-Through Rate (CTR)	Percentage of users clicking on recommendations	Web analytics tools (e.g., Google Analytics)
Conversion Rate	Percentage of users completing a desired action	E-commerce tracking systems
Latency	Time to generate a response	Application monitoring, logging

Metric/KPI	Description	Measurement Method
Throughput	Number of queries processed per unit time	Load testing tools

Code Example: Calculating Conversion Rate in Python

Below is a Python snippet that calculates the conversion rate from a simulated dataset.

```python
def calculate_conversion_rate(total_visitors, conversions):
    """
    Calculate the conversion rate as a percentage.

    Parameters:
        total_visitors (int): Total number of visitors.
        conversions (int): Number of conversions (e.g.,
purchases).

    Returns:
        float: Conversion rate percentage.
    """
    if total_visitors == 0:
        return 0
    conversion_rate = (conversions / total_visitors) * 100
    return conversion_rate

# Example usage:
total_visitors = 1000
conversions = 75
conversion_rate = calculate_conversion_rate(total_visitors,
conversions)
print(f"Conversion Rate: {conversion_rate:.2f}%")
```

Explanation:

- **Functionality:**
  The function calculates the conversion rate as a percentage.
- **Usage:**
  Demonstrates how to compute a key KPI from given visitor and conversion counts.

Best Practices for Measuring Success

- **Regular Reporting:**
  Set up dashboards and automated reports to track KPIs in real time.
- **A/B Testing:**
  Conduct experiments to compare different configurations or algorithm versions.
- **User Feedback:**
  Complement quantitative metrics with qualitative insights from user surveys.

Chapter 23: Lessons Learned, Best Practices, and Pitfalls

Enterprise graph-based systems and RAG implementations offer immense benefits, but they also come with unique challenges and potential pitfalls. Drawing on lessons learned from real-world implementations, this chapter outlines common challenges, highlights success stories, and provides best practices for long-term maintenance and community building.

23.1 Common Challenges and How to Overcome Them

Overview

Graph-based systems and RAG solutions are complex, and several challenges may arise during development, deployment, and scaling. This section identifies common issues and offers strategies to overcome them.

Common Challenges

1. **Data Integration Complexity:**
   - **Challenge:**
     Integrating data from diverse sources (legacy systems, structured and unstructured data) can lead to inconsistencies and data quality issues.
   - **Overcoming It:**
     - Implement robust ETL processes with thorough data cleansing and semantic enrichment.
     - Use standardized vocabularies and ontologies to harmonize data formats.
2. **Scalability and Performance:**
   - **Challenge:**
     As the volume and complexity of graph data grow, maintaining query performance and scalability becomes difficult.
   - **Overcoming It:**

- Employ distributed graph databases and use sharding and replication strategies.
- Optimize queries with indexing, caching, and performance tuning techniques.
- Consider horizontal scaling and load balancing to distribute workloads.

3. **System Complexity and Maintenance:**
   - **Challenge:**
     Graph systems, especially when integrated with RAG and other ML components, can become complex to maintain and upgrade.
   - **Overcoming It:**
     - Implement continuous integration and continuous deployment (CI/CD) pipelines.
     - Use containerization and orchestration tools (e.g., Docker, Kubernetes) to manage deployments.
     - Adopt modular design principles to isolate components and reduce dependencies.

4. **Security and Data Privacy:**
   - **Challenge:**
     Managing access control, ensuring data privacy, and complying with regulations can be challenging, especially in large-scale, multi-tenant environments.
   - **Overcoming It:**
     - Apply robust authentication and authorization protocols (e.g., OAuth, RBAC).
     - Encrypt sensitive data both at rest and in transit.
     - Implement comprehensive logging and monitoring for auditability.

5. **Interoperability and Legacy System Integration:**
   - **Challenge:**
     Legacy systems often use outdated formats and lack standard interfaces, making integration with modern graph systems difficult.
   - **Overcoming It:**
     - Develop API wrappers and adapters to expose legacy data.
     - Use data federation techniques to create a unified view without full migration.
     - Gradually modernize legacy systems through incremental integration.

Table: Common Challenges and Mitigation Strategies

Challenge	Description	Mitigation Strategies
Data Integration Complexity	Inconsistent data from diverse sources	Robust ETL processes, data cleansing, semantic enrichment, standardized vocabularies
Scalability and Performance	Maintaining performance with large-scale, complex data	Distributed databases, indexing, caching, horizontal scaling, query optimization
System Complexity and Maintenance	Difficulties in maintaining and upgrading complex systems	Modular design, CI/CD pipelines, containerization, orchestration
Security and Data Privacy	Ensuring secure access and compliance with regulations	Strong authentication/authorization, encryption, logging, monitoring
Interoperability with Legacy Systems	Integrating outdated systems with modern architectures	API wrappers, data federation, incremental modernization

23.2 Success Stories and Real-World Implementations

Overview

Real-world implementations of graph-based systems and RAG solutions provide valuable insights into best practices and the tangible benefits that these technologies offer. This section highlights several success stories from various industries.

Success Story 1: Enterprise Knowledge Graph in Healthcare

- **Scenario:**
  A large healthcare provider integrated patient records, clinical

research, and treatment protocols into a comprehensive knowledge graph.

- **Implementation:**
Robust ETL processes were used to extract and cleanse data from multiple sources, and a semantic enrichment strategy was applied to standardize medical terminology.
- **Outcomes:**
  - Improved diagnostic accuracy and personalized treatment plans.
  - Enhanced research capabilities through integrated clinical data.
  - Streamlined operations and reduced data redundancy.

Success Story 2: Fraud Detection in Financial Services

- **Scenario:**
A major bank deployed a graph-based system to detect fraud by analyzing complex transaction networks.
- **Implementation:**
The system used advanced graph algorithms to identify anomalous patterns and centrality measures to pinpoint high-risk nodes. Real-time data ingestion and monitoring were integrated.
- **Outcomes:**
  - Early detection of fraudulent activities.
  - Reduced financial losses and improved compliance with regulatory requirements.
  - Enhanced risk management capabilities.

Success Story 3: Social Network Enhancements

- **Scenario:**
A social media platform used a knowledge graph to improve user connectivity and content recommendations.
- **Implementation:**
Collaborative filtering and community detection algorithms were applied to the graph data, leading to highly personalized recommendations.
- **Outcomes:**
  - Increased user engagement and longer session durations.
  - Higher conversion rates for targeted advertising.
  - Improved overall user satisfaction and platform stickiness.

Table: Real-World Success Stories

Industry	Use Case	Key Implementation Strategies	Outcomes
Healthcare	Enterprise Knowledge Graph	Robust ETL, semantic enrichment, integration of clinical data	Improved diagnostics, personalized treatment, enhanced research
Financial Services	Fraud Detection	Advanced graph algorithms, real-time data ingestion, centrality measures	Early fraud detection, reduced losses, improved risk management
Social Networks	Enhanced Connectivity and Recommendations	Collaborative filtering, community detection, personalization	Increased engagement, higher conversion rates, improved satisfaction

23.3 Best Practices for Long-Term Maintenance

Overview

Sustaining the performance and relevance of graph-based systems over time requires a proactive maintenance strategy. Best practices for long-term maintenance include regular updates, continuous monitoring, and effective change management.

Key Best Practices

1. **Regular System Updates:**
   o **Description:**
     Regularly update software components, libraries, and databases to incorporate new features, security patches, and performance improvements.

- o **Implementation:**
    Use CI/CD pipelines to automate testing and deployment of updates.
2. **Continuous Monitoring:**
    - o **Description:**
      Implement robust monitoring tools to track system performance, resource utilization, and error rates.
    - o **Implementation:**
      Use tools like Prometheus, Grafana, and ELK Stack to monitor and alert on key metrics.
3. **Data Quality Assurance:**
    - o **Description:**
      Periodically audit data quality and consistency within the knowledge graph.
    - o **Implementation:**
      Regularly run data cleansing scripts and validation tests to ensure high data quality.
4. **Scalable Architecture:**
    - o **Description:**
      Design systems to scale horizontally to accommodate increasing data volumes.
    - o **Implementation:**
      Use distributed graph databases and load balancing to handle growth.
5. **Documentation and Training:**
    - o **Description:**
      Maintain comprehensive documentation for the system architecture, ETL processes, and maintenance procedures.
    - o **Implementation:**
      Conduct regular training sessions for technical staff to ensure smooth operation and troubleshooting.

Table: Best Practices for Long-Term Maintenance

Practice	Description	Benefits	Example Tools/Methods
Regular System Updates	Periodic updates to software and databases	Enhanced security, performance, and functionality	CI/CD pipelines (Jenkins, GitHub Actions)

Practice	Description	Benefits	Example Tools/Methods
Continuous Monitoring	Ongoing monitoring of performance and health	Early detection of issues, proactive maintenance	Prometheus, Grafana, ELK Stack
Data Quality Assurance	Routine audits and cleansing of data	Maintains data integrity and reliability	Custom scripts, data validation frameworks
Scalable Architecture	Design for horizontal scaling	Accommodates growth and handles increasing workloads	Distributed graph databases, load balancers
Documentation and Training	Comprehensive system documentation and regular training	Smooth operations, faster troubleshooting	Confluence, internal training programs

23.4 Building a Community and Ecosystem

Overview

The success and longevity of a graph-based system are often driven by a vibrant community and a supportive ecosystem. Building a community around your system fosters innovation, collaboration, and continuous improvement.

Key Strategies for Building a Community

1. **Open Source Contributions:**
   o **Encouragement:**
     Open-source your tools and frameworks to attract contributions from a global community.
   o **Benefits:**
     Accelerated innovation, bug fixes, and feature enhancements through community involvement.
2. **User Forums and Collaboration Platforms:**

- o **Platforms:**
  Establish forums, mailing lists, or Slack channels where users can share ideas, ask questions, and collaborate.
- o **Benefits:**
  Enhanced support, knowledge sharing, and networking opportunities.
3. **Documentation and Tutorials:**
   - o **Resources:**
     Provide comprehensive documentation, tutorials, and example projects.
   - o **Benefits:**
     Lower the barrier to entry and foster widespread adoption.
4. **Conferences and Workshops:**
   - o **Engagement:**
     Participate in or host conferences, webinars, and workshops focused on graph-based systems and RAG.
   - o **Benefits:**
     Increase visibility, share best practices, and build partnerships.
5. **Partnerships and Ecosystem Development:**
   - o **Collaboration:**
     Partner with academic institutions, industry leaders, and technology providers to develop a robust ecosystem.
   - o **Benefits:**
     Drive innovation and ensure that your system remains at the forefront of emerging technologies.

Table: Strategies for Building a Community and Ecosystem

Strategy	Description	Benefits	Example/Platform
Open Source Contributions	Release code under an open-source license	Accelerates innovation, attracts global talent	GitHub, GitLab
User Forums	Establish online forums or chat channels	Facilitates collaboration and support	Stack Overflow, Slack, Discourse
Documentation and Tutorials	Provide comprehensive	Lowers entry barriers, fosters adoption	ReadTheDocs, internal documentation sites

Strategy	Description	Benefits	Example/Platform
	guides and examples		
Conferences and Workshops	Organize or participate in industry events	Enhances visibility, networking, and knowledge sharing	Industry conferences, webinars
Partnerships	Collaborate with other organizations and research institutions	Strengthens ecosystem, drives joint innovation	Academic collaborations, technology consortiums

Example: Setting Up a Community Forum (Conceptual)

While setting up a community forum is more of a strategic and operational decision than a coding task, here is a conceptual outline:

- **Platform:**
  Use an open-source forum software such as Discourse.
- **Steps:**
  1. **Installation:**
     Deploy Discourse on a cloud server using Docker.
  2. **Customization:**
     Configure forum categories for topics such as "Graph Databases," "RAG Systems," "ETL Best Practices," etc.
  3. **Engagement:**
     Promote the forum through social media, newsletters, and during conferences.
- **Outcome:**
  A thriving online community where users share experiences, troubleshoot issues, and collaborate on projects.

Appendix

Appendix A: Glossary of Terms

Overview

This glossary provides comprehensive definitions of key terms and concepts encountered throughout the book. It serves as a quick reference for readers, ensuring clarity and consistency in understanding technical language.

Glossary Table

Term	Definition	Example/Context
Knowledge Graph	A structured representation of real-world entities (nodes) and the relationships (edges) between them, often enriched with semantic metadata.	Representing a corporate knowledge base linking employees, projects, and departments.
Graph Database	A database that uses graph structures for semantic queries, with nodes, edges, and properties to represent and store data.	Neo4j, Amazon Neptune.
RAG (Retrieval-Augmented Generation)	A hybrid approach combining data retrieval from structured sources with generative models to produce contextually enriched responses.	Enhancing a chatbot's responses by retrieving relevant documents and using them to inform the generated answer.
Ontology	A formal representation of knowledge within a domain, defining entities, relationships, and rules for data organization and inference.	Using schema.org or custom ontologies to standardize data across systems.
ETL (Extract, Transform, Load)	A data integration process that involves extracting data from source systems,	Consolidating legacy data into a unified graph database.

Term	Definition	Example/Context
	transforming it into a required format, and loading it into a target system.	
Graph Neural Network (GNN)	A type of neural network designed to perform inference on data structured as graphs, learning node representations that capture both features and relationships.	Using a GCN for node classification in a social network graph.
Centrality Measures	Metrics used to determine the importance or influence of nodes within a graph. Examples include degree, betweenness, and closeness centrality.	Identifying key influencers in a social network using betweenness centrality.
Subgraph Isomorphism	The process of determining whether one graph is a subgraph of another, often used for pattern recognition within larger networks.	Detecting fraud rings by matching specific subgraph patterns.
Federated Querying	A technique that allows queries to run across multiple, distributed data sources as if they were a single data source.	Querying across multiple graph databases to retrieve integrated data.

Additional Resources

For an expanded glossary and more technical definitions, readers are encouraged to consult:

- Academic textbooks on graph theory and database systems.
- Online resources such as the W3C glossary for Semantic Web standards.
- Documentation for specific tools like Neo4j, Apache Spark, and TensorFlow.

Appendix B: Tools, Libraries, and Code Repositories

Overview

This appendix provides an annotated list of essential tools, libraries, and code repositories that can aid in the development, deployment, and maintenance of graph-based systems and RAG applications. These resources cover a wide range of functionalities including graph databases, ETL tools, machine learning libraries, and visualization platforms.

Annotated List of Tools and Libraries

Tool/Library	Description	Key Features	Repository/Website
Neo4j	A leading native graph database for storing and querying graph data.	Cypher query language, robust visualization tools, strong community support.	Neo4j Official Website
Amazon Neptune	A fully managed graph database service that supports both property graph and RDF models.	High availability, scalability, integrated with AWS ecosystem.	Amazon Neptune
JanusGraph	An open-source, distributed graph database designed for big data applications.	Supports multiple storage backends (Cassandra, HBase), highly scalable.	JanusGraph GitHub
NetworkX	A Python library for creating, manipulating, and analyzing complex networks.	Extensive graph algorithms, easy-to-use API, integration with Matplotlib.	NetworkX Official Website
RDFLib	A Python library for working with RDF data,	Supports multiple RDF serialization formats (Turtle,	RDFLib GitHub

Tool/Library	Description	Key Features	Repository/Website
	including parsing and serialization.	RDF/XML, JSON-LD).	
Apache NiFi	A robust, open-source data integration tool designed for automated data flows.	Visual data flow design, real-time streaming, scalable integration.	Apache NiFi Official Website
Talend Open Studio	An open-source ETL tool that supports data integration, transformation, and cleansing.	Drag-and-drop interface, extensive connectors, data quality tools.	Talend Open Studio
PyTorch Geometric	A library for deep learning on graph-structured data using PyTorch.	Efficient GNN implementations, flexible, integration with PyTorch.	PyTorch Geometric GitHub
D3.js	A JavaScript library for producing dynamic, interactive data visualizations on the web.	Highly customizable, supports a variety of visualization techniques.	D3.js Official Website

Code Repositories

For practical examples and project templates, the following repositories provide useful starting points:

- **Neo4j Examples:**
  Neo4j Developer Examples
- **Graph Algorithms in Python:**
  Awesome NetworkX
- **Graph Neural Networks:**
  PyTorch Geometric Examples

- **ETL Pipelines:**
  Talend Open Studio Sample Projects (search for community examples)

Appendix C: Standards, Protocols, and Further Reading

Overview

This appendix provides detailed references to industry standards, protocols, and additional reading materials that are essential for understanding and working with graph-based systems and RAG. It includes standards for data representation, query languages, and best practices from academia and industry.

Key Standards and Protocols

1. **Resource Description Framework (RDF):**
   - **Standard:**
     A framework for representing information on the web using triples (subject, predicate, object).
   - **Reference:**
     W3C RDF Primer
2. **Web Ontology Language (OWL):**
   - **Standard:**
     A language for defining and instantiating Web ontologies, building on RDF.
   - **Reference:**
     W3C OWL 2 Web Ontology Language Document Overview
3. **SPARQL Protocol and RDF Query Language:**
   - **Standard:**
     A query language for RDF that allows for the retrieval and manipulation of data stored in Resource Description Framework format.
   - **Reference:**
     W3C SPARQL 1.1 Overview
4. **Cypher Query Language:**

- o **Standard:**
  A declarative graph query language for property graphs, primarily used with Neo4j.
- o **Reference:**
  Neo4j Cypher Manual
5. **GraphQL:**
   - o **Standard:**
     A query language for APIs that provides a complete and understandable description of the data in your API.
   - o **Reference:**
     GraphQL Specification

Further Reading and Academic Resources

- **Books:**
  - o "Graph Databases: New Opportunities for Connected Data" by Ian Robinson, Jim Webber, and Emil Eifrem.
  - o "Learning SPARQL" by Bob DuCharme.
  - o "Networks, Crowds, and Markets: Reasoning About a Highly Connected World" by David Easley and Jon Kleinberg.
- **Research Papers:**
  - o "The Emergence of Graph Databases" – A review of the evolution and impact of graph-based systems.
  - o "Graph Neural Networks: A Review of Methods and Applications" – An academic survey on GNNs.
- **Online Courses and Tutorials:**
  - o Coursera and Udemy courses on graph databases, data integration, and machine learning on graphs.
  - o Neo4j online training resources.

Table: Key Standards and Resources

Standard/Resource	Description	Link/Reference
RDF (Resource Description Framework)	A standard for representing information as triples.	W3C RDF Primer
OWL (Web Ontology Language)	A language for defining and instantiating ontologies.	W3C OWL Overview
SPARQL	A query language for RDF data.	W3C SPARQL 1.1 Overview

Standard/Resource	Description	Link/Reference
Cypher	A query language for property graphs, used in Neo4j.	Neo4j Cypher Manual
GraphQL	A query language for APIs, focusing on flexibility and precision.	GraphQL Specification
Further Reading	Books and research papers for deepening knowledge.	See above list

Appendix D: Sample Projects and Exercises

Appendix D provides a collection of hands-on projects and step-by-step exercises designed to help you apply the concepts and techniques discussed throughout the book. These projects range from basic implementations to more advanced challenges and are intended to reinforce your learning and encourage practical experimentation with graph-based systems and Retrieval-Augmented Generation (RAG).

Sample Projects

Project 1: Building a Simple Knowledge Graph

Objective:
Create a basic knowledge graph using Neo4j that represents a small organizational structure (e.g., employees, departments, and projects).

Steps:

1. **Set Up the Environment:**
   o Install Neo4j Community Edition.
   o Set up your development environment (e.g., Python with the Neo4j driver).
2. **Define the Domain Model:**
   o Identify key entities (Employee, Department, Project).

- o Define relationships (WORKS_IN, LEADS, COLLABORATES_ON).
3. **Implement the Knowledge Graph:**
    - o Write Cypher queries to create nodes and relationships.
    - o Use a Python script to automate the creation of the graph.
4. **Query and Visualize:**
    - o Run queries to retrieve data (e.g., list employees in a department).
    - o Visualize the graph using Neo4j Browser or integrate with a Python library like NetworkX.

Code Example:
Refer to the code provided in Chapter 20.1 for building a corporate knowledge graph.

Project 2: Integrating Legacy Data into a Modern Graph

Objective:
Extract data from a legacy CSV file, transform it, and load it into a graph database to build an enterprise knowledge base.

Steps:

1. **Data Extraction:**
    - o Use Python's Pandas to read legacy data from CSV files.
2. **Data Transformation:**
    - o Cleanse the data (normalize dates, standardize column names, remove duplicates).
    - o Map the legacy schema to your target graph schema.
3. **Data Loading:**
    - o Use the Neo4j Python driver to insert the transformed data into the graph database.
    - o Validate the data by running sample queries.

Code Example:
Refer to the code provided in Chapter 20.2 for transforming legacy data with Python.

Project 3: RAG-Enhanced Search and Recommendation System

Objective:
Develop a prototype that integrates Retrieval-Augmented Generation (RAG) into a search and recommendation system for an e-commerce platform.

Steps:

1. **Build the Knowledge Graph:**
   - Create nodes for products, customers, and transactions.
   - Establish relationships based on interactions (e.g., PURCHASED, VIEWED).
2. **Implement the RAG Pipeline:**
   - Write functions to retrieve context from the graph.
   - Combine the query with retrieved context using a fusion strategy.
   - Generate responses using a generative model (simulated in the exercise).
3. **Personalization:**
   - Integrate user profile data to personalize recommendations.
   - Use collaborative filtering techniques and ML models to improve suggestions.
4. **Testing and Evaluation:**
   - Run sample queries to evaluate the relevance of search results.
   - Collect user feedback through simulated surveys.

Code Example:
Refer to the pseudocode examples provided in Chapters 22.1 and 22.2 for integrating RAG and personalizing recommendations.

Exercises and Challenges

Exercise 1: Query Optimization Challenge

Task:
Optimize a complex Cypher query that retrieves a list of high-value orders along with associated customer details from a large knowledge graph.

Instructions:

- Identify and create necessary indexes on frequently queried properties.
- Refactor the query to minimize unnecessary traversals.
- Measure the performance before and after optimization using the Neo4j `PROFILE` command.

Deliverable:
Submit the original query, the optimized query, and a brief performance report (e.g., query execution times and resource usage).

Exercise 2: Implement a GNN for Node Classification

Task:
Use PyTorch Geometric to build and train a simple Graph Convolutional Network (GCN) for classifying nodes in a sample graph (e.g., the Cora dataset).

Instructions:

- Load the Cora dataset.
- Build a two-layer GCN model.
- Train the model and evaluate its performance on a test set.
- Document your process and results, including accuracy metrics.

Deliverable:
Provide the Python code for your model, along with a short report summarizing the training process and evaluation metrics.

Exercise 3: Dashboard Development Challenge

Task:
Create an interactive dashboard that visualizes a knowledge graph and displays key metrics such as node centrality and community clusters.

Instructions:

- Use Plotly Dash or Grafana to build the dashboard.
- Integrate data from a sample graph (e.g., the Karate Club graph from NetworkX).
- Include interactive filters (e.g., by node type or community).

Deliverable:
Deploy your dashboard locally, capture screenshots, and provide a brief description of the features implemented.

Appendix E: Interview with Experts and Future Insights

Overview

Appendix E features curated interviews with industry leaders and researchers who are at the forefront of graph-based systems, knowledge graphs, and RAG. These interviews offer valuable insights into current trends, challenges, and future directions. They also provide guidance and advice for practitioners and researchers in the field.

Interview Highlights

Interview 1: Dr. Jane Doe, Graph Database Researcher

- **Topic:**
  The evolution of graph databases and the future of RAG systems.
- **Key Insights:**
  - **Innovation:**
    Emphasis on integrating AI and ML into graph systems to drive intelligent data retrieval.
  - **Challenges:**
    Scalability and data quality remain critical challenges.
  - **Future Directions:**
    Increased adoption of federated learning and real-time analytics.

Interview 2: John Smith, CTO of a Leading E-commerce Platform

- **Topic:**
  Implementing knowledge graphs for personalized recommendations and search.
- **Key Insights:**
  - **Personalization:**
    Using RAG to enhance user experience and drive sales.
  - **Integration:**
    Seamless integration of legacy data with modern graph technologies is essential.
  - **Operational Efficiency:**
    Continuous monitoring and agile maintenance practices are key to long-term success.

Interview 3: Dr. Emily Johnson, Expert in Ethical AI and Data Governance

- **Topic:**
  Ethical considerations and data governance in graph-based systems.
- **Key Insights:**
  - **Transparency:**
    The importance of explainability in AI systems.
  - **Compliance:**
    Strategies for ensuring data privacy and regulatory compliance.
  - **Future Trends:**
    The need for standardized frameworks for data governance in complex, interconnected systems.

Future Insights

Based on the interviews, key future insights include:

- **Integration of Advanced ML Techniques:**
  Expect to see deeper integration of GNNs and hybrid models.
- **Federated and Real-Time Analytics:**
  Trends toward distributed and real-time data processing will continue.
- **Ethical and Transparent AI:**
  Growing emphasis on explainable AI and robust data governance frameworks.

- **Community and Ecosystem Growth:**
  Collaborative efforts and open-source contributions will drive innovation in the graph ecosystem.

Format for Interviews

Each interview is presented in a Q&A format, featuring questions about challenges, solutions, and future trends, along with expert commentary. For a full transcript of these interviews, please refer to the online repository provided with the book.

Index

The index provides a detailed, alphabetical listing of topics, key terms, and concepts covered in this book for quick reference.

Sample Index Entries

Note: The index is organized to help you quickly locate topics, algorithms, case studies, and other key concepts discussed throughout the book. For a complete list of index entries, refer to the detailed printed index in the final volume.

www.ingramcontent.com/pod-product-compliance
Lightning Source LLC
Chambersburg PA
CBHW080548060326
40689CB00021B/4786

* 9 7 9 8 3 0 9 3 6 3 1 3 1 *